The Flaws
That Bind

by
Rebecca Leo

ISBN: 978-0-9886191-2-8

Printed in the United States of America

This memoir-based novel was inspired by real people and events, but names have been changed to protect identities. It is not to be taken as 100% factual even though the experiences and many events are authentic.

Cover Artwork: *By the Sea*, Claire Hartmann
Cover Photo: Amanda L. Bicknell
Cover Design: Christopher Reilley

Big Table Publishing Company
Boston, MA
bigtablepublishing.com

TABLE OF CONTENTS

ACKNOWLEDGMENTS

Never ending thanks to my inspiring and talented writing partners, Robin Stratton and Thomas Bransten, whose guidance, encouragement, patience and friendship have not wavered through seventeen years as I filled shelf after shelf with revisions of this manuscript. Professor Jay Simmons at Boston University was the one who first helped me discover my writing voice and gave me the courage to persevere. My earliest memories are of Mother reading novels aloud to the family nearly every night which instilled in me the love of books, admiration for authors, and desire to write. Thanks to Susan Sayler who guided me with revising the manuscript and coached me in the use of social media. Without the encouragement, understanding and patience of my dear husband, William, I could never have completed this project. And finally, my deep gratitude to the many unnamed people around the world who have supported my family and contributed to our survival.

To my children who blessed me with the gift of motherhood, enriching and changing my life forever.

Every child is actually a little Buddha
that helps their parents mature and grow up.
~ Lu Jun, Father of Lu Lingzi,
Boston Marathon bombing victim (2013)

Strange is our situation here on Earth. Each of us comes for a short visit,
not knowing why, yet sometimes seeming to divine a purpose. From the
standpoint of daily life, however, there is one thing we do know: that man is here
for the sake of other men—above all for those upon whose smiles and well-being
our own happiness depends.
~Albert Einstein

Montreal, 1968

I

"Come on, Jacqueline, Alex says as he stuffs shirts and socks into his leather duffel bag. "You still have time to pack."

"I have to study." I gesture at the French books stacked on the table beside me. "I haven't even started the translation or–"

"We can study together on the train. Three hours to Toronto and three more coming back. We'll look up Cindy and Chuck, maybe go to a concert. Get our homework done and have fun too."

I shake my head, unable to remember the last time we had *fun* together. "I wouldn't be able to concentrate."

"But we've got the exact same assignments. It'll be easier doing it together… and faster." He takes my hand. "I want you with me."

A few months ago those eager brown eyes would have been irresistible. Now I steel myself to disguise how much his touch repels me. Withdrawing my hand, I move to the fridge.

"Are you mad at me?"

"No." I pretend to focus on pouring orange juice, but all I can think about is his adorable Cindy. He'll be hooking up with her, so why is he trying to drag me along? Getting stuck all night with her boyfriend is not going to happen. My hand shakes and I spill some juice. I wipe it up and then pass the glass to him. "I can't risk not getting a good grade. Some of us don't get all As without doing any work. Besides, you don't need me to renew our lease. Only one signature is required."

"Suit yourself," he sighs and glumly zips his well-worn bag. "But I'll miss you." He tucks a pipe into the waistband of his jeans, pats the pocket of his pinstripe shirt to ensure the tobacco pouch is there. "Better dash then. Maybe I can still catch a bus to the station."

When he turns, expecting a kiss, I offer my cheek. After closing the door, I listen to his footsteps racing down two flights of stairs. Then I hurry to the window and watch him turn the corner and disappear. Free at last!

I raise the pane and lean on the sill, gazing at the grubby street where shopkeepers are opening for Saturday business. The grocer sweeps up broken glass from smashed beer bottles, and then drags baskets of tired-looking apples, potatoes and onions out to display. Stacks of papers await customers in front of the newsstand. A thin tattooed woman approaches, holding an infant in one arm and dragging a crying toddler with the other. Near the curb a few stunted trees with grimy leaves struggle to survive. So unlike the view from my room back on the farm.

My upbringing in Iowa didn't prepare me for city life or existence outside the Bible belt. It wasn't designed to; Iowa's youth weren't supposed to leave. Success there came easily for me: cheerleader, captain of the girls' basketball team, a date for every occasion, valedictorian. Beyond decisions of whether to wear saddle shoes or white bucks, to read Jane Austen or Steinbeck in study hall, everything was packaged and served pre-cooked on a platter, no thinking required. Just follow the rules. Lacking the confidence to compete academically or socially in the big university arena of

Iowa City, I went along with my parents' wishes and enrolled in a small Christian college.

The first time I saw Alex he was speaking at a Young Democrats for Kennedy meeting, mesmerizing the crowd. *We have an opportunity that may never come again. The opportunity to support a President who will really make a difference. At this moment in history young people all over the world are looking to us for leadership, for making the right choices...* It wasn't what he said so much as his enthusiasm and conviction. A Kennedy in the making.

After his speech, students crowded around, firing questions. I waited on the fringes until everyone else moved away; then I introduced myself and told him I'd like to get involved. He shook my hand, smiling, suddenly less official. He was meeting some friends at the Rendezvous for a beer; would I like to come along? I wasn't of drinking age but went anyway. We squeezed into a booth with four others as Alex introduced me. I ordered coffee. Next thing I knew he was pouring beer into my cup from the pitcher, obviously not caring if the waitress noticed. It felt daring and sophisticated. I'd never been in a tavern before, but I liked the friendly atmosphere with students and community folks chatting together at the bar. As we walked to the dorm Alex suddenly stopped, put his arms around me and kissed me on the mouth. Only one kiss, but it sure left me wanting more. This wasn't just politics.

From then on we saw each other every day between classes or at night. During Christmas vacation I invited him to the farm to meet my parents. They were polite but surprised I would be going out with someone so, well, unmuscular. And he wore glasses, thick ones. Mother was pleased when she heard his father was a Lutheran minister, but became distraught upon discovering Alex no longer attended church. To me he was the epitome of an intellectual. Not only was he the most articulate person I'd ever known, he was also bilingual, fluent in German. When he proposed, I accepted immediately. Now, much as I hate to admit it, I realize my parents were right. But for all the wrong reasons.

Turning from the window, I glance around our crowded studio flat. Traces of Alex everywhere: the stand with a half dozen collector pipes, Dusseldorf beer mug, guitar leaning in the corner, stacks of magazines and spare eyeglasses on the bedside table, Picasso prints taped to the wall, portable typewriter, a full case of Heineken and cartons of empty bottles. The aroma of Amphora tobacco permeates everything.

I stack the breakfast dishes, carry them to the sink. As I run water waiting for it to get hot, I think back wistfully to how fun the first year or two had been. Joining the Peace Corps got us out of Iowa, but halfway through training Alex suddenly decided we should quit. He claimed the whole setup was a front for the CIA and rushed us away. At the time I didn't challenge his decision, just trusted his judgment and went along with his choices. But I hated being a quitter and never stopped wondering how our lives would be different if we had gone to Africa.

We'd ended up in Baltimore, him working as a reporter and me teaching junior high English and Spanish. Soon we became immersed in the desegregation and anti-war movements, joining marches on Washington almost every weekend. Many evenings our small apartment was noisy with radicals talking revolution, planning demonstrations. The gatherings always ended with Alex playing his guitar while everybody sang Pete Seeger, Woodie Guthrie and Joan Baez songs. Tone deaf and a terrible singer myself, I admired and envied his musical talent. I thought we were happy, working for something together.

Then, on one of those rare evenings when we were alone, he showed me an article in *Playboy*. "Open marriage," he said. "It makes a lot of sense."

I saw a photo of two bare-breasted women posing in a kitchen and two men with self-satisfied smiles in the background. Above it in large letters, the headline: *New Freedom*. My heart raced. "Group sex?"

"No. Swinging. Like changing partners for...for a game of tennis. Lots of couples are doing it; not just hippies."

"You want to be with another woman?"

"It doesn't mean we love each other less; it means we trust and respect each other enough that we can be intimate with others."

"But I don't *want* to be with anyone else!"

"Oh, come on! Don't be priggish. Marriage is evolving. Mark my word, there'll be a lot less divorce." He looked at me eagerly.

I held the magazine at arm's length and dropped it on the table. I should have refused right then, but knowing he loved my open-mindedness, I couldn't risk him thinking me a prude. "I'll read it later."

"Good. I've already thought of a couple I bet would like to swap with us."

Like a swap meet? If he really loves me, how can he want other women? And how can he bear the thought of me with other men? Holding back tears, I said, "But why do you–"

"It's our true nature, not what Christians would have us believe. In fact, equating love with sex is a distortion of Christianity. The essence of love is freedom!"

II

I carry a mug of iced tea to the small Formica table, armed for my assault on the French assignments. Mustn't let the morning slip away without accomplishing something. First, the translation for Ronsard's sonnet:

Vivez, si n'en croyez, n'attendez à demain:
Cueillez dès aujourd 'huy les roses de la vie

The telephone rings. I rise, glance at the clock, then the phone, and lift the receiver. "Hello?"

"Jackie?"

"Oh, hi, Dad." I sink onto the daybed, dreading to hear about the latest crisis. "Is everything all right?"

"Your mother's in the hospital."

"Oh no, what's wrong?"

"She got dizzy and was having trouble breathing. The doctor's doing tests. We'd sure like you to come out. I could use your help."

"What about Rick?"

"Your brother's very busy. And she's asking for you."

All aboard for the guilt trip! "Dad, Mom's heart flutters whenever she disapproves of what I'm doing." Like when I got in late on Saturday nights. *"I can't breathe!" she'd moan. And then Dad's accusations: "You're going to give her a heart attack! You want that? To kill your mother?"*

"This is different," he says. "It's been tough since you left."

"Don't you see? It's her way of controlling everyone. She worries herself sick to get me back to Iowa."

"But your being here would take the pressure off me. I really need you."

Alone in the house with him? I shudder, remembering the sweltering July night years before when Mother was in Milwaukee visiting her sister, and he came into my room... I push the image away. "I'm sorry; what did you say?"

"I'll pay for your ticket."

"Thanks, but this weekend I'm working on a tough assignment, and I can't afford to miss my classes. We paid a lot for them." Surely he can't argue with the economics.

"You can study on the plane."

I sigh. "I'll see what I can do. Tell Mother I hope she feels better soon."

I hang up, sit gazing into space, lacking the energy to stand. Of course Dad didn't even ask about Alex, much less invite him. Not that Alex would have gone, not after the debacle at our wedding with Mother wailing as if she were at a funeral. *"I just don't understand how you can marry someone who doesn't believe in God!" she reproached me at the reception. "He's an agnostic," I corrected her. "Just as bad!" she sobbed.* She wanted me to find a preacher's son bound for the Lutheran seminary, not the son of Christian Jews who had escaped the Nazis and then spent years as itinerant workers moving from one state to another. My parents never tried to make him feel comfortable, and are probably counting the days until our marriage is over. Since divorce is sin in their eyes, how do they know what to pray for? At this point, my not wanting to give them the satisfaction of saying *We told you so* might be all that's holding this marriage together.

I pour another mug of tea and sip it while staring unseeing out the window. If only I had stayed in Toronto and kept my job at the library until fall classes started, I could have dealt with the French later. But Alex had the same requirement and wanted to get it over with. So here I am, alone in this strange city, and when he returns, I'll have to hear, in the name of honesty, all the details about his great weekend with Cindy. Maybe I *should* fly to Iowa. Or be out Monday night when he gets back. But I can't avoid him forever. Why keep postponing the inevitable?

Wishing we had a fan, I get a damp cloth, wipe sweat from my face, and prop open the door to let in air from the hallway. Then I return to the table, listlessly take out the vocabulary list, sharpen a pencil, sip tea, flip through my French-English dictionary...

A sharp rap startles me. I get up, peer around the door, and look into the sparkling eyes of a slender man somewhat taller than my own five feet four.

"Hi," he says brightly. "Happen to know where Mary is?"

"No."

"We had plans to go out this afternoon, but she's not answering her door. I saw yours open, so thought I'd ask." He extends his hand. "I'm David."

"Jacqueline," I say reluctantly.

"Nice to meet you. Mary's hard to keep in touch with. Strange hours. She's a nurse, you know."

I shake my head. "I haven't met her."

"Figures. Nice girl, but busy. I live just a few blocks away. Makes it convenient to stop and see her, and sometimes I strike it lucky." He chuckles. "So, tell me, how long you been here? Don't believe I've seen you before." He leans against my doorjamb, smiling, looking relaxed in his khaki slacks and rust-colored t-shirt.

"I'm here for the summer, studying French."

"Well, you're sure in the right place. People don't mind speaking it with you, even if their English is better than your French. Like mine, for instance. Not very good, but I do my best in shops and whatever, just to get on with folks. Where're you from?"

"Toronto." I hold the knob, prepared to close the door, but manners prevent me.

"Nice place. I've been there a few times. You here alone?"

"No. My husband and I ..."

"He inside?" David gestures with his chin.

"No," I say, instantly regretting it. Quickly I add, "You work in Montreal?"

18

"Yeah, I'm a test engineer for Stone and Downing. Been here four years. I came to take a course at the Technical Institute. Like to fool around with electronics and invent things. That's why I signed up for the Royal Air Force when I was in England. But those prejudiced bastards made me sweep hangars after I finished basic instead of sending me to school like they promised. Pissed me off! I did great on the tests, too. Got the highest scores in my whole unit. I found out when I sneaked into the office and saw the reports. Those SOBs!"

"What a shame!" I shake my head, glance at my watch. "But if you'll excuse me—"

"My parents sent me to England when I was sixteen, fresh out of Jamaica. Took me over on a boat and left me to fend for myself."

"You're Jamaican?"

"Surprised, aren't you? Don't think I'm black enough?"

"Well..." My eyes sweep his chiseled features, tawny complexion, wavy dark hair.

"Most people don't realize Jamaicans come in all colors. We're a mixture—African, European, Chinese, Indian, a bit of Arawak. My father's English, and my mother is part African. At home, they call me a red man. Too light to be black, too dark to be white."

I shift my feet and am obvious about looking at my watch. "Well, sorry I don't know where Mary is. But I have to get back to work."

"I should too. Need to change the oil in my car. It was great meeting you." He smiles brightly, holding my eyes with his gaze. "Later then..."

I nod and close the door. The heat is stifling! Almost two hours since Alex left. My weekend of freedom slipping away. Should have completed at least half of the assignment by now. I pick up a pen and resume copying the new vocabulary words, pronouncing each as I write it: "*chambre, bain, cuisinette...*"

Almost immediately I get up again and look in the refrigerator. Nothing appeals to me. What I really want is a frosty root beer float. I wonder if they have them in Montreal, but I don't know how to ask. Maybe the shop across the street will have something refreshing. I sweep my hair up into a ponytail, grab my purse and head downstairs. Pushing open the front door, I see David peering at the engine of a car parked along the curb. As I dart down the steps, he hollers, "Hey! What's the rush?"

Liberated from the confines of the stuffy apartment, I'm in a more gracious mood. "Too hungry to study. Know where I can get some ice cream?"

He thinks for a moment and then slams down the hood. "I got a better idea. I'm headed out to a friend's house in Dorval. Since Mary isn't here, why don't you come? My friend's mom is a fantastic cook! On the weekends a lot of folks hang out there, play music, dominoes, ping pong..."

"Thanks, but I have to—"

"Call it a study break. You'll come back refreshed."

I'm tempted. A break might do me good. I've accomplished nothing all morning. And it is a three-day weekend.

As though reading my mind, he says, "Tell you what. I need to get some petrol for my car and clean up a little." He holds out his dirty hands. "I'll come back in twenty minutes. If you want to go, be ready. And if you don't, I'll leave you alone. But I guarantee, you won't be bored *and* you won't be hungry anymore."

"I'll think about it," I say and watch as he drives off. A few hours won't kill me.

III

Standing in front of the open closet I stare at my clothes, immobilized by indecision.

I could ignore his knock when he returns. Just be quiet and pretend I'm not in. But he's the friendliest person I've met here. And he speaks perfect English. Maybe it would be fun to go out and not be limited to my paltry French. Still, with Mother in the hospital, I should call Dad back, decide about going to Iowa.

I reach for one of my favorites, a black and white paisley silk shift. Then I put on shiny black flats and hematite earrings with pendant that Alex gave me on our third anniversary. I secure my long almond-colored hair with a headband and glance in the mirror. Softly draping my body, the dress reveals curves without looking cheap. The only problem is my pallid complexion. Need to find a place to lie in the sun.

A snappy tattoo on the door announces his return. I take a deep breath and open it.

He grins. "Haaay, lookin' good! I'm glad you decided to come."

I shrug, dismissing the comment, even though I like the admiration in his eyes. "If you don't feel comfortable at my friend's place, just let me know, and I'll bring you back, or we can go do something else."

"Okay." I lock the door, put on a smile and follow him out. The sun is bright, the breeze refreshing. Pansies line the sidewalk. A smiling mother passes, pushing a pram with one hand and leading a toddler by the other. A perfect June day. I have every right to enjoy it.

When we enter the house in Dorval, I feel like Dorothy dropped from a cyclone onto a Caribbean island. Calypso music fills the rooms. Jovial people, in accents I can hardly understand, offer food and drink. As we fill our plates David explains each dish and urges me to try all: souse, blood pudding, rice and peas, Pickapeppa sauce, chutney, plantain, yams, cho cho, scotch bonnet peppers, stout, Red Stripe beer. Relishing the pungent flavors, I hardly wince from the hot pepper. We find seats on the patio where several guys are slamming dominoes on the table so hard they crack like gun shots. The object of the game appears to be who can make the loudest noise.

"That's how we play it in the islands," David says above the din of the music. When we finish eating he takes my hand. "Come on, I want to show you something." He leads me to the basement where his friends are tuning instruments. "We're practicing for an audition at the Jamaican pavilion of the World Expo Center," he explains. "Want to hear a preview?"

"Sure." I sit and sip my second Red Stripe. David alternately shakes maracas and jiggles a tambourine while dancing around the room singing his own version of "The Banana Boat Song." Like Elvis Presley set to calypso, he never stops grinning and gyrating as lyrics flow from his lips. Obviously he's a natural performer, enjoying every minute. I picture him singing on a beach beneath coconut palms, framed by the sparkling sea, radiating passion and joy. Impressed by his confidence, I clap enthusiastically as they segue into "Yellow Bird" and then a poignant rendition of "Sunny." *Yesterday my life was filled with pain. Sunny... You smiled at me and washed away the rain...*

It's dark when we finally head back to the city. Though David didn't drink much, his driving alarms me. "What's the speed limit here?" I ask.

"Don't worry. I'm keeping my eyes open for cops. I owe a lot for tickets so I have to be really careful. But I'm an excellent driver. Started practicing before I could reach the pedals. Used to sneak my dad's car out of the garage at night. I'd prop myself up on the seat with pillows and drive around the mountains for hours as fast as it could go. The old man never figured out why he was using up so much petrol!"

"Well, no need to rush now. I don't have a curfew." I grip the armrest.

"Relax! It's slow drivers who cause collisions. If you go fast enough, no one else can hit you!"

Eyes glued to the road, I do not join his hearty laugh. When he asks if I'd like to drive through downtown Montreal, I say yes, knowing he can't speed there. He slows down as we enter the nightlife district along Boulevard St. Laurent. Brightly-clad people crowd the walkways and outdoor cafés.

"Looks like everybody in the city is out," I say.

"Yeah. Summer's short. Have to enjoy it while we can. How about a drink?"

"Well..."

"Just one." He's already pulling into a parking space.

The dark club, crowded with sweaty bodies, thunders with music and voices. I try to read David's lips but can't, so I just nod without being sure what he's saying and sip the rum and ginger the bartender puts in front of me. Then we're on the dance floor, jostled from every side. David glides confidently with the music, pressing me against his limber body. I watch other couples, trying to figure out what to do with my feet.

"Loosen up," he says, lips against my ear.

"I'm trying," I shout back, "but I'm tone deaf and have no rhythm. That's what Mother says."

"Just relax and let me guide you."

Still I stumble against his feet. At the end of the set, he orders refills.

"After this," I say, "I really have to go."

"Okay. Too crowded here anyway."

We finish our drinks and return to the car. As he merges with traffic, he talks about his band, but my mind is too foggy to respond. Belatedly I realize he has passed the turn-off to my place. Next thing I know, he's parking again.

"I just moved here." He points to a two-story building on the corner. "When my wife and I split up a few months back, she took the children. Sent them to Jamaica to stay with my parents so she could go to school in Toronto. It's hell not having my kids. I gotta get down to see them soon."

Wife? Kids? "Oh," I say, "how many do you have?"

"A girl and a boy."

"It ... it must be tough... I mean, being away from them."

"Yeah, but they're better off with my parents than with her. I just have to make sure I get to Jamaica before she goes and takes them away. Doesn't know the first thing about raising kids. She's an idiot. French Canadian. Couldn't speak a word of English when I met her. I taught her practically everything she knows. She can't look after herself, so I got her into a school. She's taking a course in data entry to get a job. Hey," he brushes the back of my neck, rests his hand on my shoulder. "I haven't finished unpacking yet, but I'd like to show you the place. Want to come in?"

"I don't think so. I'm pretty tired, and it's late." Too late, I suddenly remember, to call Dad.

"Whatsa matter? Don't you trust me?"

"It's not that. It's just... I'm so..." I sigh. He's been a perfect gentleman all evening. "Okay. But just for a few minutes."

IV

We get out, and he guides me around blinking amber lights on the sidewalk illuminating a striped barricade with the words *Attention: Danger.*

"No need to translate that," I laugh. "Even I can understand it!"

"These lazy French," he scoffs. "They've been working in this hole ever since I moved here, and they're still not done." He pauses under a light in front of the building to locate his key, then opens the door and enters ahead of me, switching on lights.

Vinyl floors combined with bare windows and walls produce a cold atmosphere. Stacks of unpacked carton boxes and two gigantic speakers connected to a stereo system furnish the living room. "What kind of music you like?"

"Folk mostly, and some rock. Dylan, Elvis, Baez ..."

"Well, I just put together this long-play tape that's a collection of my favorite calypso and jazz. If you don't like it, let me know and I'll play something else." He adjusts the volume and mix. "What can I get you to drink? Wine? Beer? Juice?"

"Nothing, thanks."

"Well, I'm having a beer. Can I bring you some water?"

"Fine."

He returns in a moment and hands me a glass of ice water. "Sorry there's no place to sit." He glances at the boxes. "Hey, want to see some pictures of Jamaica and my kids?"

"Sure."

"Photography's one of my hobbies. I was always taking their pictures. Come in here." He motions me to follow and switches on a light as we enter a room containing a bed with bookcase headboard and a blue metal footlocker. Taking out an album, he sits and pats the mattress beside him.

With the album open across our laps he shows me photos of two children laughing in a wagon, splashing in a kiddie pool, stroking a puppy. "They're adorable! What are their names?"

"This is Wendy." He points to the curly blonde. "And this is William...Willie. He was just learning to walk when I took this."

I study more snapshots on the next page. "I can see why you miss them so much."

"Yeah. They'd be a lot bigger now. Kids grow so fast." He stares as though trying to imagine what they would look like and shakes his head despondently. "I need to get down there soon."

"You're worried?"

He shrugs, pulls out another album. "Here's my parents' place." The gleaming white house with red tile roof is surrounded by lush shrubs and trees.

"It's charming!" I exclaim as he presents pictures of it from every angle. "Doesn't look like a bad place for your children to be."

"Jamaica's beautiful all right. I miss it."

While he replaces the album, I get up to examine the single adornment on the walls, a framed diploma. "You're a hypnotist?"

"Yup."

"I saw it done once in high school."

"That's stage hypnosis. I do therapeutic. You know, for treating problems."

"Like what?"

"Addictions mostly, and pain. Stuff like smoking, nail-biting, over-eating. Hypnosis is a level of relaxation where the subconscious is receptive to suggestions. It's a normal phase we all go through when falling asleep and waking up."

"It really works?"

"Absolutely. Both of my children were born while my wife was hypnotized. She was awake the whole time —no anesthesia and no pain. You've never done it?"

I shake my head. "When a hypnotist came to our school I volunteered but wasn't picked."

"Well, here's your chance." He grins.

I laugh. "No, thanks."

"Why not? I don't use pendulums or candles or any weird stuff. Just my voice. And remember, it's not possible to get someone to do anything against their will under hypnosis."

"What kind of suggestions would you give me?"

"Nothing specific. Just feel-good things like you're relaxed and happy."

"Well, I've always been curious, but right now I'd probably just fall asleep." I suspect I can't really be hypnotized, but still I wonder how it feels.

"So, I'll wake you up. It's simple." He gestures at the bed. "Just lie back and relax."

Still skeptical, I kick off my shoes and lean against the pillows.

His voice is low, smooth, confident. "Close your eyes and listen to the sound of my voice. You are very relaxed ... You are sinking into the bed ... Take a deep breath and hold it. Now start to let it out slowly as I count. One ... two ... three ... let it out slowly ... four ... You are more and more relaxed ... five ... All you hear is my voice. You are going into a deep sleep ... You will remember nothing I say after you wake up ..."

The next thing I remember is his soothing voice saying, "You are waking up... five ... four. You are happy, relaxed...two ... one. You are totally awake. Open your eyes."

With great effort I raise my lids, but they drop again as if weights are attached.

"Open your eyes," he repeats.

Groggily, I obey. How long have I been out?

He's smiling at me. "How do you feel?"

"Relaxed," I murmur with enormous effort.

He chuckles. "You went out like a light! A natural."

Natural for what? Just what went on while I was under his spell? All that rum... I swing my legs off the bed and grope for my shoes.

David touches my chin, turns my face toward him. Holding my eyes with his, he leans forward, and his lips touch mine, lightly, tentatively. Then lingering, more insistent. I stiffen, but while I debate whether I should pull away, his arms go around me. His touch, firmness, scent of strangeness, ignite a spark. Gently he pulls me closer, strokes my hair. Goose bumps prance across my skin. The next kiss is more urgent, the embrace stronger. His tongue presses into my mouth, dispelling any resistance I have.

V

The aroma of coffee wakes me. I open my eyes a crack. Strange blinds on a strange window half block the sunlight. Then David appears carrying two steaming mugs. "Good morning, sleeping beauty. Here's some Blue Mountain brew, fresh from Jamaica. Hope you like it with milk and sugar."

"Good morning." I raise myself on an elbow. "Yes, that's fine." I sit up, arrange pillows behind me, pull the sheet to my throat. He opens the blinds, and sunrays stream into the chilly room. I cautiously test the hot coffee as images of the night before take shape in my mind. Coming out of hypnosis, wondering if it had worked, the feeling of him lowering the zipper of my dress, my inability to resist... What a push-over!

David kisses my cheek and settles beside me. "Been to the World Expo yet?"

"No."

"Then let's go today. You'll love the international pavilions."

So it wasn't just a one-night stand. Relieved I say, "Sounds interesting."

"It is. You gotta see it."

"Can we stop by my flat first? I need to make a long-distance call."

"Sure. And you should put on some comfortable shoes. We'll be walking a lot."

He buys a newspaper and waits in the car while I rush up to the flat. Grabbing my birth control pills, I pop one in my mouth and slip the pack into my bag.

I dial my parents' number, but no one answers. Probably Dad has gone to church. I shower and dress leisurely. Then I try the number again; still nothing. Maybe he went to the hospital after church. Hopefully to bring her home. But I can't keep David waiting forever, so after one more try I rejoin him.

At the Expo Center, we eat lunch at the Jamaican pavilion, and then set off on a virtual trip around the world, stopping in China, Thailand, Australia, Ethiopia, Mexico, Trinidad... Exotic aromas, flavors, music, and languages saturate my senses. While I inhale sage and curry and swing to a tango beat, I read posted information as David talks with a man at the Trinidadian booth. When I ask if the man he's been laughing with is a friend, he shakes his head. "Never saw him before, but he asked me to look him up the next time I get to Port-of-Spain." He flashes the man's card. I'm amazed how he's able to strike up a conversation with anyone. Have never seen anybody so glib.

David offers to cook dinner at his flat. Boneless pork roll, rice, corn and applesauce are not exactly Epicurean fare, but they go well together. Uncorking a bottle of Chablis, he pours two glasses and clinks his against mine. "Here's to us."

I smile and drink. "So, I'm curious, how did you get into the Royal Air Force?"

"That's a long story. Starts back in Jamaica. My parents sent my brother and me to boarding schools from we were about ten. Rough places. Caning in the morning, caning in the evening. Got so tough, my ass was like leather. But when I couldn't take it anymore, I'd do something so bad they had to send me home. My old man went crazy! Eventually I was thrown out of so many schools, my parents didn't know what to do with me. That's when they took me to England and left me. Out of sight, out of mind."

"That must have been worse than boarding school!"

"Yeah. So when things got really desperate, I joined the Air Force, mainly for the food, but also because of the training they promised. Wanted to be a pilot. Doesn't everybody?" he laughs ruefully.

"Not me. Can't stand heights, and planes make me really nervous."

"What else? Tell me about yourself."

"Well, my life's pretty dull compared to yours. I spent most of my childhood on a farm in Iowa. My parents and brother still live there, and my nieces and nephew are growing up in the very house my grandparents built."

"Hmmm. What kind of farm?"

"They grow corn mostly and raise livestock like cattle and pigs and chickens."

"How big is the place?"

"Around 400 acres."

"Wow! Must use tons of heavy equipment on a property that size."

"Yeah. When I was little we farmed with mules, but not anymore."

"So why did you leave?"

"Borrring. I mean, everything the same. Everybody white, Christian; all think the same, sound the same. I knew there had to be more to life; didn't think that everything different was necessarily the work of the devil. My ticket out was college." I tell him about Alex, our aborted attempt to join the Peace Corps, and our anti-war activities. "Strange how much we hated the war, but how many good memories hating it created. You know, doing something that felt important."

"What brought you to Canada?"

I don't object as he refills my glass. "The war. If it weren't for Vietnam, we would still be in the U.S. But we got burned out after all the protests didn't seem to do any good. We wanted to work *for* something rather than always being anti-this and anti-that. After Alex applied to grad school and got accepted at Toronto, we headed north with the flood of draft resisters."

"He's a draft dodger?"

"No. He has a medical deferment. Bad eyes. But even in Toronto we couldn't escape the war. Got involved in a support group for dodgers, and our place became a haven for people crossing the border. Alex went back there this weekend to take care of some business, but he's probably staying with his girlfriend. She's subletting our flat."

David's eyebrows shoot up. "His girlfriend?"

"Sort of."

"That doesn't bother you?"

Why did I bring this up? I lift my glass and empty it. What the hell. "Actually, I wish he'd never come back. But not much chance of that."

"Why?"

"It's complicated." I briefly sketch Alex's notions about freedom and love. "The worst part is when he tells me about the women he's seduced."

"Why does he tell you?"

"Honesty is *very* important to him." I can't keep the sarcasm out of my voice.

"Seems cruel, to tell you." David looks troubled as he fills my glass a third time.

"It goes with being left-wingers. You know—free speech, free elections, free love. I've tried to be consistent, but it's not working for me."

"This honesty thing... does it mean you'll tell him about us?"

"That's our agreement."

"So you go out with other guys, too?"

"Not much."

"Doesn't it bother him?"

"No. Guess he doesn't really care." My nose stings as I fight back tears. I pat my lips with the napkin, swallow resolutely and force a smile. *"Merci, pour un bon souper.* I could say it better in Spanish but need to practice French. Correct me if I'm really bad, *si'l vous plaît."* I rise and begin clearing the table.

"Leave them," David says. "Let's go listen to music."

The soft jazz mellows us as we stretch on the bed, his arm cradling my head. Weariness sweeps over me. His breathing slows and I wonder if he is dozing off. Then he nudges me and says, "How about spending the night here? I don't work tomorrow, so we could do something if you're free."

Am I ever. Absolutely nobody to know or care whether I come home or not. "Well, I have homework, but no class because of the holiday—"

"Good. If the weather's nice, we can have lunch at a sidewalk café. I'd like to take you to a little place that serves the best bread you'll ever taste in your whole life. Let's shower now and get comfortable."

"Okay." Too late to call Dad. I'll try again in the morning.

My head is clearer that night, so I'm acutely aware of his efforts to please me. With arms supporting his torso, he watches my face and keeps asking what I like as he eases inside, retreats, enters again, and withdraws, each time making me want him more. Like an orchestra conductor, he builds one mini crescendo after another. And then to my astonishment, I actually have an orgasm. Finally he breaks into a frenzy that ends with an agonizing bellow of primal triumph. Collapsing at my side, he flops one arm across my tummy. When his breathing returns to normal, he nuzzles my cheek. "Has anyone else ever made love to you like that?"

"Not exactly." Despite my aversion to comparisons, I like him using the word "love."

"Thought so." He reaches to switch off the lamp.

VI

We languish in bed and don't leave the flat until midday. Downtown we walk along sunny sidewalks lined with umbrella tables in front of cafés and bistros. Our tiny table is cramped, but the *pain, poisson,* and *fromage* are, as he had promised, delicious.

In the afternoon we are strolling hand-in-hand through a grassy park under towering pines when David announces without warning, "I want to go back to Jamaica. And I want you to come with me."

Startled, I chuckle derisively. "Why are you tempting me?"

"I'm not. I really want you to come. Say yes!"

"Don't be silly. I..."

"This is no joke. I'm serious."

"But it's so sudden." I look away, trying to get my bearings. Alex *did* go on vacation with someone else. Maybe... Finally I say, "How long do you plan to stay?"

"I want to get a job and live there."

"You mean *move* to Jamaica?"

"It'll be fun. I can tell you're an adventurous person."

"But we just met. You can't expect me to–"

"Why stay with a husband who doesn't appreciate you? Come to Jamaica with me."

"But grad school? I can't possibly–"

"It's sunny all year. You'll never have to shovel snow again!" His eyes fairly dance, entrancing me with his enthusiasm and sheer audacity.

I picture Alex's return. The prison gates clanging shut, every moment a pretense. I must admit the last two days have been really special. Maybe I should consider his offer. But move to Jamaica? Endless summer, sandy beaches, fruit trees everywhere. And no Alex! No more details of his other women. A whole new life, free of hypocrisy. "This is too sudden. I, I need time to think about it."

"Then you'll discuss it with your husband, and he'll say you can't do it!"

"You have to admit this is awfully quick."

"I'm for real, Babe." His eyes feel like probes into my soul. Then he draws me to him, urgently, and murmurs into my ear, "You didn't seem to doubt that last night."

His kiss makes me tingle all over; I don't want it to end. Finally I say, "I'd like to go with you. I really would. But I can't give you an answer yet. I'm sure you wouldn't want me to make such a big decision lightly."

"You're right. Let's get together Wednesday night. You can tell me then."

VII

When he brings me back to the flat, we kiss goodnight, and I creep inside the building. Dawdling up the stairs, I indulge in a fantasy about Alex saying he's in love with Cindy and wants a divorce. If only! Belafonte's "Jamaica Farewell" lyrics run through my head: *Down the way, where the nights are gay, and the sun shines daily on the mountain top, I took a trip in a sailing ship, and when I reached Jamaica I made a stop...*

As I enter, Alex cries, "There you are!" He puts down his pipe and opens his arms.

I hug him perfunctorily and then busy myself with putting away my shoes and earrings while he reports on the meeting with our landlord. "And in the evening," he says, "I went to a concert with Cindy and Chuck at City Hall. Tom Paxton was fantastic. Wish you could have been there."

"I'm glad you had a good time."

"How was your weekend?" He takes out a pouch and proceeds to roll a joint.

"Well, I didn't get as much studying done as I'd hoped. My dad called. He wanted me to come out because Mother was in the hospital. But you know how it is–if I took all her emergencies seriously, I'd be flying to Iowa every month."

"What did you tell him?"

"Said I'd let him know, but every time I called no one answered. I'll try again tomorrow to see how she is."

"Hmmph."

"And I went to a gathering on Saturday, some friends of one of our neighbors. Met a few folks from the West Indies. But, I'm sorry to say, I didn't quite finish the translation, and I'm not ready for the vocabulary test. How about you? Want to review?"

"No. I just want to be with you. Come on, relax with me." He inhales deeply, holds the joint out to me. "Good stuff," he coughs. "Got it from Chuck."

I take a mini puff and hold the smoke briefly in my mouth before blowing it out.

"You didn't get anything. Try again."

He watches as I inhale. Instantly the room is swirling. I choke, releasing the smoke. My lungs are expanding, too big for my chest. Coughing, I gasp, "I need ... fresh air."

"Strong, eh?" He grins, inhales again, offers it to me.

"No!" I rise. "I'm going out."

"Aw, come on. Don't be so uptight." He stubs the joint in an ashtray, stands, puts his arm around me, and nibbles my ear. "I want to make love to you."

I stiffen, dreading the thought of his hand touching my breast. The room is becoming darker, smaller. I wrench away. "If I don't get outside, I'm going to puke!"

"But it's raining."

"I don't care." I grab my umbrella.

"Okay then. I'll go with you." He reaches for his keys.

So much for escaping. We walk without touching. I fiddle with the umbrella while he elaborates about his night with Cindy. When he says being with her only makes him appreciate me more, my heart sinks. I block him out and focus on The Platters' lyrics pounding in my head: *Please release me, let me go, for I don't love you anymore...*

Back at the flat, I rush into bed, turn my face to the wall, pull the sheet over my head and tune into my vision of Jamaica: the glistening Caribbean, promise of freedom.

VIII

On Wednesday I get through to Dad and find out Mother has calmed down and is having her afternoon rest. Relieved not to have to deal with more guilt, I send her a card.

That night I fib to Alex, say I'm going to the Expo with a guy I met on the weekend. "Capitalist bullshit!" he sneers.

"I think it'll be fun." I arch my eyebrows ever so slightly and go downstairs to wait in front of the building.

On the way to his place David stops to get a pizza. While we eat he tells me that for years he has been doing research and experiments, trying to figure out how to extract energy from water.

"Why?"

"I got the idea from a dream. There was this machine—looked like a flying saucer—that used water as fuel. It was so clear, like a vision. I haven't been able to get it out of my mind. I'm convinced there's some way to extract free energy from water. The device in my dream might not involve actual perpetual motion, but it comes close, because it seemed to produce energy without using up matter. If I can prove that's possible, it'll make Einstein obsolete."

"How so?"

Propping his foot on a chair, he rests one elbow on his knee and leans forward earnestly. "It'll disprove his theory of relativity. That's what they're afraid of. They don't want to see a little guy from Jamaica come along and prove Einstein wrong."

"Huh."

"The difficult part is measuring all the variables. Working with fluids in motion is almost impossible."

"I can imagine."

"Sorry, didn't mean to bore you," he smiles apologetically. "Tell me what you're interested in." He leads me into the living room and turns on the stereo. "What've you been studying?"

"Well, I majored in history. Now I'm working on my masters."

"To do what?"

"Understand the world. Figure out where we've gone wrong. Try to find a way to make it better. I don't believe in religion anymore and I don't trust politics. But I want something to give my life purpose. I'm so angry at what's happening in the States—all the racism and militarism—and I don't trust capitalism. So much evil comes from the profit motive."

"Canada's capitalist, too."

"I know, but I feel better living here because at least my tax money isn't used for war. I want to do something positive, make a difference in a good way, but I'm not sure how. Back in the States I belonged to SDS, but I never felt the protests accomplished much. Learning more about history might help me to figure things out."

"You believe what you read in history books?"

"Not everything. I mean, take the assassination of Kennedy. The Warren Commission has made sure that nobody alive when it happened will ever know the truth. I can't get over it! I mean truth is the essence of *everything*. How can a society progress without access to truth? How can we learn from mistakes?"

"You don't think Oswald killed him?"

"He may have been involved, but only as a patsy. The real murderers are in the corridors of power, people who felt threatened by what Kennedy represented. He gave hope to the young. Made us believe we could make a difference. But some people didn't want the changes he was unleashing, so they killed him and Warren hushed it up, protected them."

"Why?"

"Who knows? Maybe afraid for his own life. Or maybe he actually thought it was best for the country. Some day historians will recognize that in Dallas we actually had a bloody coup."

"That's pretty strong language," he says as though expecting me to recant.

"It's what I believe. And they didn't stop with just the President. No, they had to go after Dr. King and Robert Kennedy, too. So now the anti-democracy forces are in control. The name for it is oligarchy."

"America's going through hard times, all right. Guess you know more about it than me. Jamaicans like American money, but we know they don't give a damn about us."

"It's frustrating; makes me feel so powerless. I hate hypocrisy and injustice."

David rests his hands on my shoulders, his forest-colored eyes gazing into my blue. "Have you made up your mind? Are you coming with me?"

"Well, I told Alex a little about you, but I didn't say anything about us going away."

"What's holding you to him? Money?"

"Nothing, really. It's just that I haven't told him everything. But I do want to go."

"So?" he smiles expectantly.

"So," I smile back, "I will. I will go with you."

"Hooray!" He sweeps me up and swings me in a circle. "I knew I could count on you, just felt it. Trust me, I won't let you down!"

Seeing his joy, I can do nothing but kiss him. When he returns me to the floor, we continue kissing until I feel weak. But instead of moving toward the bedroom, he looks at his watch and says, "It's late. I better drive you back."

"Oh, all right." I agree quickly to hide my disappointment, and remind myself he is acting responsibly.

As we head out, he says, "Now, the next thing we gotta do is get your stuff moved over to my place. You should stay with me so we can get to know each other better while we prepare for the trip. How about moving your things on Saturday?"

"Let's talk about it on the phone."

"Not backing out, are you?"

"No," I try to assure him with another kiss. "But I haven't told Alex yet."

IX

All next day I agonize about how to tell him, dreading the ordeal of a drawn-out discussion about feelings and what went wrong. When we get home from class, he pulls a chunk of Muenster cheese and a jar of pickled herring out of the refrigerator. I pour us each a glass of iced tea and sit at the table. "Alex, remember the man I told you I met last weekend?"

"Uh huh. Mr. Expo." He opens the cupboard. "Any pumpernickel left?"

"Alex, I need to tell you something."

"Oh, here it is. Go ahead. I'm listening." He cuts a slab of cheese and offers it to me.

I shake my head. "His name's David. I like him a lot."

Alex's hand pauses in midair, his eyebrows raised questioningly.

"I've decided to move in with him. He's coming by Saturday to get my things."

"Your things?"

"Yes. I'm moving out."

"What are you talking about? Has this guy doped you?"

"No! I'm sorry, Alex. I don't want to hurt you—"

"I don't get it. Go ahead and have a fling if you want to. You know I won't stop you. But why move your stuff?"

"I don't want to live with you anymore."

"This is ridiculous!" He looks skyward, shaking his fists. "Lord! What's come over this woman? What did I do wrong? Tell me!" Without waiting for an answer, he turns back to me. "You owe me an explanation."

"You're not happy with me either. Admit it."

"Don't use that excuse. Have I been complaining?"

"I'm not looking for excuses or anyone to blame. It's just over between us. Let's finally be honest about it."

"Bullshit!" He turns his back, stands staring out the window. I wait. Finally he turns around and says in a voice I can barely hear, "Have you stopped loving me?"

Precisely what I didn't want to talk about. I shrug.

"I wonder if you ever loved me."

"I did! But then..." It seems mean to tell him how something happens to my spirit in his presence. That it dies a little more each day. Like strangulation.

"You haven't really thought about what you're doing. Leaving me is one thing, but moving in with a complete stranger, that's crazy!"

"I don't know what the future holds. But I do know we broke our marriage vows, and now our marriage is broken."

"So that's it! You're jealous of Cindy! Hey, she's just a friend. She means nothing to me, really. She's Chuck's woman, and we're all friends." He takes my hands. "I didn't know it bothered you so much. I won't see her anymore if that's what you want."

How can he be so dense! I'll never beg him to be faithful. It has to come from his heart. "Believe me," I withdraw my hands, "it's not about Cindy."

X

Somehow we make it through the rest of the week, and finally it's Saturday. Alex rises early and leaves without a word. I write down a phone number where he can reach me but don't leave an address. By the time David arrives, I have everything packed, and he helps carry my bags to his car.

Two days later Alex calls, wanting to talk. I take a bus and meet him at a park where children play on monkey bars and build castles in sandboxes. Awkwardly we walk, our feet and minds locked like train wheels on separate tracks. "This is too fast," he says. "Why not stay with me and just go on seeing him until you get over it?"

"That won't work. We ... we're moving to Jamaica."

"What!"

"He's from there. It's his home."

"You can't! You can't leave the country with him! You don't know a thing about this character."

"My mind's made up. I want to get some belongings from Toronto. David says he'll drive me. Do you mind if I go in and take a few of my things?"

"I can't believe this is happening."

"I won't disturb your stuff."

"I don't give a damn about the stuff. It's the betrayal. I thought I could trust you with my heart..." His voice breaks.

For the first time, I reconsider. Maybe it is crazy to rush off to another country with a stranger. But David is counting on me. His wishes have priority now. Mother's words flash through my head: *You have to get married. A woman's life isn't anything without a man.* The big question is *which* man. The answer will write the history of my future. One thing is certain: I do *not* want it to be Alex.

"I'm sorry. I never wanted to hurt you. I tried, I really did, to do things your way, but it hasn't worked. I can't be the wife you want."

"Let's sit for a minute." He motions to an empty bench. We sit, backs to the wind, and stare into space. "I want you to go to a counselor with me. We need to figure out what's wrong."

I shake my head. "It's too late."

"It doesn't have to be. Let's work on this together."

"We made choices and this is where they've led. There's no turning back." Easier to let him think I'm in love with another man than to admit how much he's hurt me. My pride just won't let me. Even back when my second grade teacher made me stand in the corner as punishment, I pretended to like it and wouldn't sit down when she said I could.

"I've already found a shrink..."

"Good. You'll have someone to help you through this. It'll take time, but you'll get used to it." I rise. "I have to go."

We walk toward the street. At the gate I stop, unsure of how to say goodbye. The habitual kiss won't do, neither will a hug. I reach out to shake his hand, but it feels absurd. To soften the gesture, I peck his cheek. So phony. There doesn't seem to be a graceful way to end it. I turn and hurry toward the bus stop. It suddenly hits: I might never see him again. My vision blurs. I dare not look back. For one thing I am grateful: he never mentioned "love," the word that could have made me fall to pieces.

Staring blindly out the bus window on the way back to David's flat, I wonder if any marriage can survive cheating, even if it's honest, fully-disclosed infidelity? If we had children, it might be worth trying to patch things together. At least there's not the problem of dividing up a family and all the pain that entails. Best to call it quits now—no more pretending it's cool for my husband to have girlfriends.

XI

David loses no time in tying up his affairs and making arrangements for our trip. He trades his Nash for a large station wagon with a roof rack and installs heavy-duty springs. The plan is to pack everything in it and drive to Florida. From Miami we will fly to Kingston, shipping what we can't carry on the plane.

To celebrate my twenty-fifth birthday he takes me to a West Indian restaurant and then to the club where we first danced. It's less crowded, but my dancing is no better. After a couple of drinks, we leave and walk hand-in-hand along the street, inhaling aromas of sweet william and evening primrose that border the sidewalks. Without cards or gifts from family, it hardly feels like a birthday. If any have been sent, Alex doesn't know where to forward them. For now, David is my family, my world.

"Hold on a minute." He stops, pulls me to him, kisses me firmly on the mouth. "I love you. And I hope you'll always be happy with me. I need to make sure you know that. I've wanted to go back to Jamaica ever since my kids went, but not alone. Jamaican women don't understand me. I need an American woman with me, and I know you're the right one." He seals his declaration with another kiss, taking away the last shred of doubt about my decision. His love makes everything right. I must not, will not, disappoint him.

Jamaica, 1968

I

We leave Montreal in the station wagon. The load towering above the roof rack makes it looks like an elephant packed for safari.

"Don't you think you're driving a little too fast?" I say, white knuckled and bracing for impact.

"I told you, I'm a good driver. And I fixed this car to take it." He focuses like a race driver on gauges and dials and the road ahead.

Being tense makes me tired and sore, so after awhile I force myself to keep my eyes off the speedometer. I take deep breaths and try to relax, enjoy the scenery.

When David gets tired, I drive, but then he complains, "You're going too slow. At this rate it'll take a month to reach Miami!" I refuse to be bullied and stay within speed limits until he insists on taking over and drives even faster "to make up for lost time."

Our first real stop is at a campground in Virginia Beach. We pitch the tent and inflate air mattresses, but spend an uneasy night as David worries about all the things he has to check on the car in the morning.

We cook breakfast on a campfire, and while I clean up, he gets out his tools and goes to work under the hood. Then he jacks up the wheels one at a time to examine shocks, bearings and brakes, apparently knowing how every piece should work. I help by pressing on pedals and handing him tools. Between jobs I sit nearby in the sun, ready to jump if he needs help.

Noticing his dirty hands, I get a towel to wipe the sweat dripping from his face and hold a bottle of water for him to drink. "Thanks, Baby," he says. "I was hoping to be done before it got this hot. Can you pull this shirt off me?" He raises his arms and bends forward while I tug it over his head.

As he resumes jacking up another wheel, I admire his muscular back with sweat glistening on it and his biceps bulging as he strains to loosen a stubborn nut. So different from Alex who keeps his muscles inside his cranium and calls AAA for car problems.

When I get out the paperback I've been carrying in my handbag, David notices and asks, "What're you reading?"

"The Bridge of San Luis Rey."

"What's it about?"

"A monk in Peru investigating the lives of people who died in an accident. The story takes place a long time ago, but the themes are universal."

"Like cars? Lots of brands, but basically all have the same parts and problems. Can you take the rocks away from the front tire and move them to the back wheel for me?"

"Sure." I get up. "That's a good analogy. The premise of the story is there's a reason for everything. I guess that's how engineers look at life, too. But when it comes to suffering and the things called accidents, the cause can be hard to figure out. This writer looks beyond the obvious to understand a higher order—"

"Dammit!" he yelps, dropping the wrench. "Bring a rag. Quick!"

I run to the tent. "And water, and a bandage!" he shouts. I rush back with the first-aid kit to clean and dress the bleeding welt on his knuckle.

It's late when he's satisfied that the car is road safe, so we cook over the campfire again and settle down for another night in the tent. We make love tenderly and are nestling in the sleeping bag when he says, "I'm glad you're here. You really trust me, don't you?"

"Mm hmm. Watching you today reminded me of my dad. Farming is his main thing, but he's always building and fixing stuff, too, and trying out new things. When he was young he was a boxer, and during the Depression he became a hobo. He's a great carpenter, but horses are his passion. He trains and races them, makes saddles and harnesses, shoes them. Loves everything about horses. Even paints pictures of them."

"Hope I get to meet him sometime."

"I don't think you'd like Iowa. Not a very exciting place."

"Well, maybe he'll come to Jamaica. To see his grandchildren."

"What grandchildren?"

"If you stick with me, we'll soon have some for him." He caresses my stomach. "You need a baby."

"I do?" I'm shocked. Pregnancy has never been in my plans. The one time my period was late, Alex and I were terrified. Waiting for the test results was like awaiting the verdict for a capital crime. When it came back negative and my flow resumed, we went on with our lives without discussing when or if we'd ever start a family.

"I understand women." David kisses my cheek. "Hello? Anybody home?"

"I... I don't know. It... it just takes a lot of courage to have children, especially in these times with the threat of nuclear war...plus over population–"

"You worry too much. You can't fix the whole world. But no rush. Take your time getting used to the idea. And get some sleep now." He kisses me again and rolls over.

But I can't sleep, can't stop thinking. A baby with David. Can he really want more children after so much difficulty with the two he already has? Me, a mother? Shocking as the idea is, I don't feel panicked like with Alex. More surprised and excited than afraid. It'll definitely take time getting used to.

The next morning we repack our gear and cross Chesapeake Bay on what seems to be the longest bridge in existence. Judging by his speed, David's confidence in the car has been restored. I make no comment when he gets a ticket in Georgia.

We drive straight through Florida to Key Largo and camp at the State Park. David says staying there a few days will get me acclimated to the tropics. When I swim in ocean water for the first time, its heat amazes me as sweat actually streams down my face. Mosquitoes are merciless at night, so we zip up the tent, listen to his transistor radio, and make endless sweet love.

One night he complains about my name, thinks "Jacqueline" is too formal, but I won't let him call me "Jackie." I tried to discard that when I went to college even though my parents won't stop using it.

"So how about 'Jac'?" he asks.

"Hmm, that's different, but I like it." His own name just for me makes me feel special. I hold him close, nuzzle his head and whisper "I love you" for the first time.

While David delivers boxes to the shipping company, I do laundry to get ready for our flight the next day. At the Laundromat, I struggle with a letter to my parents. Keeping Mother out of the hospital is my number one priority. Tiptoeing through the minefield of what can't be said, I discard one draft after another. Finally I walk across the street to a gift shop and buy a postcard with beautiful palm trees lining a shimmering beach. On it I write:

Dear Mother and Dad,

You'll never guess where I am—Florida! Beautiful weather, and finally I got to swim in the ocean! From here a friend and I are flying to Jamaica. I'll write from there.

Love, Jacqueline

II

Boarding the Air Jamaica flight in Miami, I feel as if I have already arrived on the island. Surrounded by melodious accents, I can't take my eyes off the flight attendants. Unlike American cabin crews, each wears a different colored mini-dress—lime, magenta, turquoise, tangerine—all accentuated with silk scarves painted in tropical flower motifs. Their flawless makeup convinces me the airline must recruit at Miss Jamaica pageants.

All the passengers—who, David tells me, are probably mostly homeward bound, since tourists don't go down during the heat of August—are drinking Red Stripe beer or rum and ginger. Unlike domestic flights where travelers isolate themselves behind magazines, laughter ricochets around the cabin. Making our way down the aisle amidst drinking and lively chatter feels like mingling at a cocktail party.

When we get to our row, David indicates I should take the window seat. "Maybe you'll get a look at Cuba," he says, "and I want you to see Kingston on our approach."

Passengers behind us create a commotion as they struggle to stash bundles under seats and in overhead compartments. Seeing them buckle gigantic stuffed animals into a vacant seat, I nudge David. "Wonder if they bought an extra ticket for those."

He glances over and calls out, "Looks like you're bringing Miami's zoo to Jamaica!"

"Oh, just a few things we picked up for the pickney," says the tall, curvaceous blonde with a smile. "Gotta cheer them up after we've been away all weekend." She wears a scanty white halter dress with a hemline that extends nearly to mid-thigh, revealing fulsome expanses of satiny copper-tone skin. Her equally tall, bronze-tanned companion has on a stylish bush jacket and white twill slacks. Both glitter with gold jewelry.

"So you came all the way to Miami to shop?" David asks.

"We always do," the man answers. "Everything's cheaper so it more than makes up for the cost of flying."

"But what about the hotel?"

"We're lucky. You know, relatives here."

David just nods; then he asks if I'd like another drink and orders refills for our neighbors, too. Twisting in his seat, he keeps chatting, exchanging names of schools, relatives, parishes of origin, and possible mutual acquaintances. Before long they manage to discover common ground—David's parents know hers. What's more, David's brother Philip was in the same class at boarding school with her brother.

The conversation reminds me of Iowa where people have similar obsessions with bloodlines, property, and religious affinities. I can think of nothing to contribute beyond an inane question about their children, and no one asks me anything. Then I remember David's earlier comment about Jamaicans liking the money Americans spend, and it hits me how insignificant I am to them. Suddenly my cutoff jeans, cotton pullover, and sandals feel more crude than hip. To hide my embarrassment, I open the airline's complimentary magazine and pretend to read.

When David finally turns back to me he reaches over to squeeze my hand. "How're you doin', Hon?" His peck on my cheek feels patronizing, like an attempt to make up for the attention he's been lavishing on the blonde. "It's good to get to know people," he whispers. "Very important in Jamaica to have the right contacts. You'll see."

It's dusk when the captain announces our approach to Palisadoes International Airport. Stretching across me, David points out Kingston, the Red Hills where his parents live, and a long narrow peninsula we will drive along to reach the city.

In the chaotic terminal, relatives, eager to greet arriving loved ones, invade the baggage claim and customs area, along with taxi drivers hawking fares. Skittish as a cat in a strange house, I cling to David as he makes way for us through the maze while keeping up non-stop banter with officials, porters, and fellow travelers.

A calypso band vies to be heard above the cacophony of people carrying bouquets, banners, and balloons. Welcomers, like travelers, are dressed up, perhaps in their finest. How wrong I was to assume island dress would be casual!

By the time we get past customs, David has managed, through a shouting exchange with taxi men, to bargain for an acceptable fare to Red Hills. As we bounce along over potholes riddling the road into the city, I note the absence of fare meter, shock absorbers and air-conditioning. Sweat starts trickling down my neck and I ask David if we can open the window.

"Only a little," he says. "This road hasn't been paved yet, so we don't want to let in dust." Seeking a compromise between breeze and dirt, we roll the windows up and down, but even with them up, I keep coughing.

In a different dialect from the one he used on the plane, David pumps the driver for information on politics and changes since his last trip home and explains pieces of the conversation to me. The Prime Minister, though still popular, is under fire from the opposition for not delivering fast enough on campaign promises. In the few years since independence, foreign money has poured in to build roads, factories, banks, shopping centers, hotels, schools, and housing. It generates jobs for people who support the ruling party but not everyone is sharing the benefits.

"See those new houses!" David points. "Not there last time I was home. Pre-fabs, but they look good." The development is painted in bright rainbow colors. To the driver he says, "Dat's great! Houses for da people dem ta live ina."

After passing through what David identifies as "the heart of Kingston," we begin a steep ascent on a curvy road which goes in, out and around hairpin turns up a serrated hillside. Finally we can open the windows and breathe clean air that feels at least ten degrees cooler than at the airport. "This is it, Red Hills," he says. "Mum and Dad won't believe their eyes when they see us. And I wonder if my kids will know me. It's been almost six months. Willie's only two. You think he'll remember me?"

"Your parents aren't expecting us?"

"No."

So that's why no one greeted us at the airport. "Are you sure this is all right, arriving unannounced? What if nobody's home?"

"Don't worry. There's always somebody around, and they have plenty of room."

"I hate to impose..."

"Believe me, they wouldn't have it any other way. You have a lot to learn about Jamaican hospitality. Just relax. Everything will be okay. I should warn you though, about my brother. His house is next door. We don't get on. He's always been jealous of me, so don't be upset if he seems strange. That's just the way things are."

"Oh."

"My parents think he's perfect. But that has nothing to do with us. I'm here to see my kids."

He leans forward and commands the driver, "Here we be. Turn dere on de right before de big poinciana dat."

III

We enter a driveway shrouded in vines and halt in front of a rambling house. "Wait here while I go see who's home," David says.

Dogs bark. Outside lights go on. Faces appear at barred windows. A door opens and a tall handsome man in his thirties walks onto the verandah. "David?"

"Yes. Can you make these dogs stop barking and let me pass?"

"Okay now, quiet down, boys," Philip orders the dogs. "Quiet!" When the barking stops, he says in a British-sounding accent, "What brings you here?"

"I'm home. And I've brought a friend."

"Oh. I'll call Mumsy." Philip turns, goes inside.

When David's mother appears, they embrace briefly and speak in low tones. Soon they are joined by a tall, slightly stooped man resembling Philip but larger in the midsection and with receding hair.

David returns to the car and asks the driver to help him unload. I get out and wait while they deposit our bags on the steps and David pays the man. Then leading me to the verandah, he says, "Mumsy, Dad, I want you to meet Jac," and extends his arm toward them. "My parents, Precious and Jimmy."

We shake hands, exchange greetings. I'm impressed by how cordial they are considering David's failure to notify them. I'm also surprised at how well they're dressed in freshly pressed, casual clothes, as though they were expecting guests. Not the soiled housedress and dirty overalls my folks would have on this time of the evening. David bears a marked resemblance to his petite mother with her cappuccino complexion and curly black hair.

Precious, radiating a pleasing scent of lavender, says to David, "We weren't expecting you so soon, but now you're here, so come on in and see the children. I suppose they'll remember you."

Doors open, and in the distance a small girl with cascading blonde curls stands hugging a doorpost. David steps forward into the light. The child hesitates, then dashes toward him, arms outstretched, shrieking, "Daddy! Daddy!" He drops to his knees and hugs her as they bubble over with laughter and prattle. Then he stands, clasps her small body and raises her toward the ceiling as she screams, "Daddy! Don't drop me, Daddy!" It looks and sounds like a much-rehearsed and much-loved routine.

Finally relenting, he puts her down saying, "Let's find Willie." Hand-in-hand, they disappear.

Precious leads me to the verandah on the other side of the house where Jimmy sits in a recliner. "We've finished dinner," she says, "but there's plenty left. Will you have some?"

"Oh, thanks, but don't go to any trouble. They served food on the plane."

Well, Jimmy has a gin and tonic after dinner. Can I get you one too?"

"Sounds good. Thank you." She leaves, and I move to the railing of the verandah jutting over a cliff. Below lights of the Kingston metropolis twinkle across a wide plain and teeter unevenly up surrounding foothills. Dark mountains to the left are sprinkled with faint lights spread randomly along their slopes. The moonless ebony sky is emblazoned with more stars than I've ever seen. Fronds of towering palms brush pillars supporting the roof. A breeze teases my skin, sending shivers across my back and along my arms. The air is so pungent with fragrances I can almost taste it.

"Excuse me," a man's voice breaks the spell. I turn and see Philip approaching, hand outstretched. "Philip Wellington here. Delighted to meet you."

"Hi. I'm Jacqueline. Uh, you can call me Jac." We shake hands and then I open my arms, indicating the panorama. "This view! It's absolutely fabulous. What a place to live!"

"Yes, we're fortunate to have this spot on the ridge." With only a glance at the scene, he continues, "I hope you'll enjoy your stay." Nodding in a sort of half bow, he adds, "Now, if you will excuse me, do have a good night," and exits.

I turn toward Jimmy who gestures to a wicker rocker. "Have a seat."

"Thanks. Your home is beautiful. Everything's so different; I've never been in the tropics before. I don't know what any of these plants are, except for coconuts. And even those, I'm not sure about. Is that one?" I point to a tall gracefully swaying tree.

"No. That's a royal palm. Just ornamental. Doesn't bear nuts."

Prompted by my questions about the sights, smells and sounds bombarding my senses, Jimmy patiently explains, "The humming you hear is tree frogs. They get even louder after a fresh rain." He identifies nearby plants–jasmine, oleander, frangipani, elephant's ear–and mentions others that I'll have to wait for daylight to see.

A four-legged creature scampers across the floor, pausing to cock its head and stare at me. I stiffen, and Jimmy chuckles. "Just a lizard. In the States they call it a chameleon. Quite harmless. Useful actually. They eat flies and mosquitoes."

"That's nice to know." I watch warily lest it will scurry toward my leg.

Asking how long I have known David, where I'm from, and what my father does, he seems impressed by my parents' property, apparently enormous by Jamaican standards. My schoolteacher credentials appear to earn modest respect, yet I detect a note of skepticism about anyone associated with his younger son.

As we talk I am aware of subdued conferences going on in other rooms. Eventually David reappears and reports, "Mumsy has a room downstairs made up for us. Let's move our stuff down so you can get settled for the night."

The room has a table, chair, twin beds with mosquito netting, and boxes stacked in a corner. David shows me the bathroom. "Make yourself comfortable and get some rest. I'll say goodnight to the children and spend some time with Mumsy and Dad." His kiss is more sound than fury. Exhausted, I fall right to sleep and don't notice when he returns.

IV

When we get up in the morning, the others have eaten, so we breakfast alone in the dining room. David carries everything in from the kitchen where a cook is evidently preparing it. The first course is fruit which resembles a half of muskmelon but it has a deep tangerine color and apple-thin skin. "Papaya. Ever have it?" David asks. I shake my head. "Let me fix it for you." I watch as he sprinkles coarse brown sugar and squeezes a wedge of lime on it; then he adds a few slices of banana. "There you go," he says. "Just scoop it up with your spoon."

I taste a small wedge cautiously. In texture it resembles a peach, but the delicate, juicy flesh virtually melts in my mouth, almost like sherbet. "Ummm, this is delicious!" I eagerly refill my spoon. The fruit, gone all too soon, is followed by poached eggs, lightly-toasted bread that David calls "hard-dough" spread with marmalade, and Blue Mountain coffee even better than he served in Montreal.

I eat leisurely, enjoying every morsel while my eyes feast on the voluptuous scarlet flowers overflowing a basket on the table. "These must be—let me guess—tropical roses?"

David laughs and shakes his head. "Hibiscus. They grow everywhere."

"Why aren't they in water?"

"Don't need it. The blossoms last a day, whether they stay on the bush, are picked and put in water, or just left dry. Makes no difference."

"Incredible."

"They come in lots of colors, even black. When we go out to the garden I'll show you some hybrid varieties, but right now we've got to make plans. Come." He gets up and beckons me toward the verandah. "We have to find another place to stay." Mug in hand, he proceeds to pace, oblivious to the incredible view competing for my attention. "Dad got all uptight last night about us being here. I want to spend time with my kids, but it looks like that has to wait while we look for a flat." His voice grows strident, and his eyes glare nervously like a racehorse about to charge from the starting gate. "Since Dad has to go into town today, he has *generously* offered us a ride down. Guess we better go and see what we can find."

"Okay," I say blandly, trying to hide my shock at the reality rearing its head all around: the polite but cold reception of the night before; the animosity between David and his brother; the tension as his mother bustled about trying to maintain decorum; his father's suspicious questioning. Now this. David must feel so embarrassed.

I squint at the scene revealed by the dazzling sunlight: on the left, green mountains dotted with blistering white houses; below, a sprawling city with one small cluster of tall buildings; to the right, cobalt sea stretching to the horizon; before me a jungle of flowers, trees, fruits and vines leaping and cartwheeling down the precipice.

V

"How long were you at your last job?" Jimmy demands as he skillfully guides the Vauxhall sedan around a switchback curve.

David, sitting in front beside his father, replies, "Almost a year."

57

"Still jumping around. A rolling stone gathering no moss." Jimmy winds the car around steep, blind bends with the confidence of years of practice.

"I'm sure not like you," David returns. "Always acquiring things. That's all you think is important."

"And what do you consider important? Have you started a life insurance policy?"

"No."

"You have two children now. Time to take responsibility. Breeding kids doesn't make a man, as you seem to think. When you plan ahead, purchase insurance, that shows your manhood."

"I'm a lot more of a man than my brother who's never had any kids. And isn't going to either, it appears."

"Watch your tongue in my car and as long as you're staying in my house! Your brother's a fine hard-working lawyer. Owns his home, invests his money. Making something of himself."

"His own home, *right*! On the land you bought with the inheritance from my grandfather. The inheritance you all connived to cheat me out of!"

"Don't get started," Jimmy retorts. "You have one week to find a place to stay. And get a job. Don't expect any more from your mother and me. It's all we can manage—"

"One week! How am I supposed to—"

"Maybe you should have thought about that before leaving your job in Canada and rushing down here."

"My children are here! What did you expect? That I would forget about them? Is that what you were hoping for?"

"There you go again, thinking the whole world's against you."

"Not the world. Just *you* people. I give you two beautiful grandchildren—more than Phillip will ever do—and this is the thanks I get!"

"How about if I drop you off here?" says Jimmy.

"Fine." David turns to reach over the seat and squeeze my hand. "Ready to go, Jac?"

Jimmy pulls over and we hastily alight. "Thank you!" I call as he drives off.

David steers me along a path beside the road crowded with honking cars, donkey carts, smoking buses with bundles stashed on the roofs, bicycles, push-carts filled with coconuts, open trucks carrying men atop cargo, small vans jammed with passengers shouting out the windows. Music thunders and screeches from passing vehicles. In the center of the intersection stands a policeman in a crisp red, white and black uniform calmly directing traffic converging from five directions. It takes a moment before I realize why he's there: no traffic lights.

In front of the Halfway Tree post office beggars and hagglers vie for attention. David buys two ripe mangoes from a man with a bucketful. To a ragged, barefoot mendicant he says, "You should be ashamed of yourself, begging like this. Don't you have any pride? You're as good as anyone else and just as capable of working. Here's a shilling. Get something to eat, but don't let me see you begging again!"

The toothless man clasps the coin in his fingers and wags his head up and down. "Tank yuh, Massa, tank yuh. God bless yuh."

Handing me a mango, David mumbles in my ear, "I can't stand to see beggars. Before Independence we never had any on the street. It's a national disgrace! All because of slave wages. People who work all day cutting cane don't earn as much as these beggars get, so what's the point of busting ass? It's demoralizing for the whole country."

We turn into a narrow street lined with tall trees covered in red-orange blossoms. "Poinciana," says David, "and those hedges with the crimson and magenta-colored flowers are bougainvillea. Got terrible thorns, good for keeping out intruders."

"Certainly prettier than barbed wire," I observe as we move along.

"You remember the people who sat behind us on the plane? I think her mother, Mrs. Edmondson, lives near Poinciana Drive. I should recognize the name of the street if I see it."

He asks directions from a couple of people, and before long we arrive at a gatepost with a sign saying *Edmondson*. "What was her name? Nancy, I think. Said her mother has a few bungalows she rents. Let's check her out."

I wait by the gate while he strolls boldly into the yard and stops to pat two yelping dogs. At the door, he calls, "Alo there! Anybody inside?" When a servant appears, David says, "Good morning. Is Mrs. Edmondson home?"

The young woman nods. "Yes sir."

"Just tell her Mr. Wellington is here for her." He beckons me to join him at the entrance.

Within minutes of Mrs. Edmondson's appearance, David has provided enough credentials, including his acquaintance with her daughter and his own pedigree, to get us invited inside. We sit down, and the servant brings tall frosty glasses of limeade. "Delicious!" I exclaim and take another swallow, surprised how thirsty I am.

"Our lime tree is loaded. We get dozens every day," Mrs. Edmondson says proudly.

In the exchange of pleasantries, David soon discovers our hostess has a vacant rental unit undergoing repairs. He explains our interest, and convinces her to show it to us even though it isn't ready yet. The two-bedroom flat is roomy, albeit sparsely furnished, and definitely in need of maintenance.

Back on the road David translates the rental: forty pounds roughly equals a hundred dollars. I think it risky to spend so much on lodging when we have no income, so we keep looking.

Our day's search yields two other furnished units, both smaller than the first, and costing even more. At nightfall, we return to Mrs. Edmondson's and leave a deposit that she agrees to hold for a week.

As we bounce in a crowded van up the steep road to Red Hills, David says, "Looks like I'll have to find a job right away. But before I start looking, I've got to spend some time with my kids. I'll talk to Mumsy tonight. She'll understand."

She does, and we have a day of respite. While David plays with Wendy and Willie, I retreat to the privacy of our room and putter around washing clothes and reorganizing my suitcases. I abandon my attempt to compose a letter when I realize I don't even have an address or phone number to give my parents. They wouldn't understand. How could they, when I don't? Never have I felt so out of control, nor so exhilarated. My only anchor is David; he has followed through on everything. The more I experience of his world, the more confident I become that he's not putting me on.

Problems that have surfaced don't seem insurmountable. Obviously he's eager to get custody of his kids, though he never asked how I feel about it. Maybe he just takes it for granted that I'll assume a stepmother role. What to say if he asks? The kids are cute, but I don't feel motherly toward them. If his wife comes down and takes them away, will he be inconsolable? Want to follow her? No point in worrying, I finally conclude. His parents have made it clear they're the guardians. Nothing I can do except stick by David.

In the morning we ride into the city with Philip. While David sits in back reading *The Gleaner,* Philip points out landmarks—television station, new shopping center, headquarters of Jamaica's Defense Force, a teachers' college. Again we get out at Halfway Tree. David leads me along the line of buses searching for one to take us to the new industrial park where several companies are advertising for help. We have to change buses twice before we reach Marcus Garvey Drive, the dusty unpaved main street of the development. As we bump along David explains how the park's construction required the razing of Shantytown. To make way for the "march of progress" thousands of squatters lost their homes. The progress benefits investors, but scarcely provides a menial job for uprooted people. He points. "See those streams of smoke over there?"

"What's burning?"

"The city dump. That's where Shantytown refugees live now. Mangroves hide a lot of it, but those people actually live in old shipping crates, wrecked cars, and worn-out refrigerators on top mounds of garbage. That's the result of a government that sells its own people out to foreign capitalists. Development is important, but not at this price." He shouts to the driver, "Oiye, Mon, stop here for us, nuh."

Picking our way along a dirt path, we pass Gerber, Hess Oil, Grace Foods, Colgate Palmolive, Red Stripe, Allied Chemical and other companies. Each compound is surrounded by tall concrete and barbed wire fences with armed guards at gates.

David manages to gain entrance to several personnel offices. He fills out applications while I wait outside the barricades, standing in the shade of spindly coconut palms struggling to survive in their transplanted locations on the dusty roadside. He stays inside the Colgate plant so long that the heat becomes nearly unbearable. All I can think about is water.

When David finally appears, he's smiling. "The receptionist said they need a plant engineer, so I grabbed the opportunity and spoke to an assistant manager. It looks hopeful. I'm supposed to call back in two days, after they check my references."

The next day is more of the same—dust, noise, heat, stench, armed guards, application forms. At least I wear more sensible shoes and bring a bottle of water.

On the third morning David calls Colgate and makes an appointment for another interview. "No need for you to come," he tells me. "I'll catch a bus. You stay here and take it easy. Be ready to celebrate when I come back."

He pulls me close and kisses me long, intensely. On the verge of lowering me onto the bed, he abruptly stops and whispers, "Gotta go now, but hold that thought."

Much as I miss him, I do need a break from the streets. So much has happened and we've been here only five days! I try to read the newspaper but am quickly overwhelmed by reports of people, places and issues all meaningless to me. So I take a dusty Brontë novel from a shelf and recline on the bed, hoping to lose myself in romantic tribulations of the heroine, but, unable to concentrate long enough to get through a paragraph, I soon doze off.

Responding to a tap on my shoulder, I roll over, my mind's eye filled with kaleidoscopic images of ragged barefoot boys on bicycles, gigantic palm trees swaying overhead, policemen in candy-striped uniforms, a huge truck bellowing along a dusty road bearing down on me as I try to run, then drop my handbag, choke on the dust... I open my eyes and look at David. Struggling to get a grasp on where I am, I lean on my elbows, staring blankly. "Oh, it's you. Hi."

"I got it, Baby!" he pulls me up. "I'm now Plant Engineer for Colgate Palmolive!"

VI

Jimmy, obviously relieved we are meeting his deadline, offers to drive us to Mrs. Edmondson's. No sooner are we on the road than he says to David, "I assume that once you start collecting a paycheck, you'll contribute something to your children's expenses."

"Money! Is it all you *ever* think about?" David shoots back.

"Someone has to."

"Money is for spending. When I have it, I spend it. When I don't have it, I don't spend. At least I haven't got a pile of debts."

"Same old David. Never wanting to face up to responsibility."

"Same old Dad. Responsibility begins and ends with money. You can't see past it."

"You're lucky you found this Colgate job. Don't blow your chance for a fresh start."

"You would look at it like that. It never occurs to you Colgate might be lucky to get me! You never want to admit I'm a competent engineer. Just can't acknowledge that other people recognize my talents and are willing to pay for them."

"Wrong, David. I know you're very good when it comes to figuring out how stuff works and fixing things. I've always recognized that."

"You do a good job of hiding it."

"Let me put it this way. I'm glad you got this job. It's an opportunity to make something of yourself. Just don't forget your responsibilities to Wendy and Willie."

"You don't have to lecture me about responsibility. They never went hungry with me, not one day. The important thing is to keep them away from their idiot mother. But if I start giving you money, I'll never save up enough to take care of them myself. Don't you realize I'll need a car and a bigger house? Or do you just want to make it impossible for me to ever get my kids? Bet you've already been on the phone, probably telling Renae I'm here and she should rush down to get them away from their awful father."

"At it again, always suspecting people are out to hurt you."

At the Edmondson yard David unloads our bags. Jimmy gets out and assumes a stance of authority. Hands on hips to contain his shaking, he says, "I'm sure we'll be hearing from you, but I don't want you upsetting your mother. Understand, we've given our word to Renae to take care of the children until she comes for them. That means we won't allow them to stay with you, no matter how many rooms you have. If you've got any harebrained scheme to take the children, just forget it."

He turns to me. "Now, I want you to know I don't blame you for any of this. You seem a respectable person and probably have no idea of what's going on here. It's not my place to get involved in your life, but I'll just offer one piece of advice—"

"She doesn't need your advice," David breaks in. "She can think for herself."

I watch Jimmy drive off, wishing I could think of a way to breech the chasm, but it's too wide, too deep, too old, too none of my business.

VII

I unpack while David goes out for cleaning supplies. He returns carrying broom, bucket, mop, and rags. He holds up a bottle. "Dettol. Got it from Mrs. Edmondson. It's a great disinfectant; everybody uses it here."

"Just what I need. Thanks." Armed with cleaning apparatus, I head upstairs.

"I'm gonna check out the neighbors. It's good to know who's living around us. See you later," he calls, and the door slams behind him.

Unwilling to put our things where I can't vouch for the cleanliness, I scrub everything, upstairs and down. It feels like hours later when David returns. "Wow! You got this place lookin' sharp! See what I got–Mrs. Edmondson says we can use these pots for cooking until our boxes arrive."

"Cooking?" I sink onto a chrome and vinyl chair, my legs aching.

"Let's get some groceries."

"Okay."

I wash my face and put on a clean blouse. We walk to the main road and are waiting at the bus stop when a passing car screeches to a halt and rapidly reverses. Other vehicles honk and swerve around it as the driver jumps out waving his arms and shouting, "Hey! Wellington!"

David bolts toward him. "Dougie Cass! I can't believe it!" The two embrace and exchange a series of punches and exclamations. David motions me over and introduces us. When Dougie asks what he's doing on the island, David says, "Long story, Mon."

"I want to hear it. Let's get something to eat and catch up on things." Dougie opens the car door. "Jump in."

"Dougie's a friend from boarding school," David says as we get in. "We haven't seen each other in years."

At an air-conditioned Cantonese restaurant I have my first Jamaican-style Chinese food. I've never tasted anything so hot as the scotch-bonnet peppers swimming in soy sauce that Dougie and David pour over their pork-fried rice and use as a dip for each piece of sweet-and-sour ribs and butterfly shrimp. To their surprise, I match their consumption of hot sauce, but lag behind in cooling my torched membranes with bottles of Red Stripe.

I listen while they exchange memories of school days. Dougie, a scholarship boy, graduated at the top of their class, whereas David was expelled on the eve of graduation.

"Bastards!" he says. "My old man was bullshit, but he couldn't take the disgrace, so he bribed the headmaster at Cornwall to take me for another term and give me a certificate. That's when I learned anybody can be bought. They're all a set of hypocrites!"

"Now, let's see, the last time I saw you," says Dougie, "you were traveling around the island working for the company running gambling machines."

"Yeah, I installed and fixed them. I'd been on the job a few months when all of a sudden they up and send me to Trinidad. I thought it was a promotion, but on the flight over I got a tip-off that the company was actually Mafia. I had this feeling when we landed that my life was in danger. So instead of going to the hotel, I rode around in a cab for a while and then went back to the airport. Got on the next plane to Canada, and I've been there ever since."

"So that explains it," Dougie says. "I heard you were in Canada, but had no idea why. You won't see any gambling machines here now; government cleaned them out."

As we eat, he tells us his wife is the daughter of a prosperous banana grower. They have two children and own a house. He's a sales rep for Grace Foods and exudes confidence in their firm position on the rungs of a ladder to success and prosperity. The optimism of *nouveau riche* in an expanding economy.

After picking up the check, Dougie scrawls his home address and phone number on the back of a business card and hands it to David. "We live in a new development not far from King's House. I want you folks to come over and meet my family. Call and let me know when you can make it. I'll swing by and pick you up. Okay?"

"Sounds great," David says.

I add, "I'd love to."

Over the last round of drinks, Dougie continues reporting developments in the lives and careers of their school chums and he gives David an address where the guys often gather after work. "But call first. Sometimes we go other places."

Emerging from the restaurant's cool darkness into the twilight, Dougie drops us at a supermarket. Carefully we select basics to stock our kitchen and load them into a taxicab. Though weary, we feel satisfied with the accomplishments of our busy day. We shower and with the ardor of newlyweds christen our rented bed.

VIII

After David starts work, I concentrate on finding a job. Eventually I get an interview at The Academy, a private school not far from our flat that needs an English teacher. The Headmaster reviews my documents and shows me the campus, essentially a garden school. The separate buildings for each classroom have one side completely open. Connecting walkways are lined with palm trees and flowering shrubs. "This is all so beautiful," I enthuse as we return to the main building. "It should be named The Oasis."

To my delight, he offers me a contract pending confirmation of the references I supplied and government approval of a work-permit. We shake hands and I head home, excited to tell David.

But first he has a surprise for me: a blue Triumph coupe bought with his first paycheck. It appears to be in good condition; at least no visible rust and the upholstery isn't shabby.

"I really need this," he assures me. "You have no idea how much I hate riding on buses. Now I can get to work in half the time. Besides, the boss says I'm going to be on call at night to go in when there are problems the regular crew can't handle. And now we can go exploring on weekends. There are so many places I want to take you—the north coast, my old home in Mandeville—and we can take the kids to the beach."

"Sounds like fun," I say. "Now I have a surprise for you, too. I got a job!"

"What! That's fantastic! Where?"

When I tell him it's at the Academy, he says, "Perfect! With the car I can even drop you off at school in the mornings."

"But David, they don't pay much. Less than half of what I made my first year in Maryland."

"Take it anyway. With the shortage of teachers, you're sure to get a work permit."

I nod. "Okay, I just wanted to talk to you about it first. He said I could come by and sign the contract tomorrow."

"So tonight let's celebrate! No cooking. Dougie told me about a place on the waterfront where we can get some old time Jamaican food: bammy, escovitched fish, roasted breadfruit. The works!"

I like being reconnected with academic life. The student body is comprised of the children of British expatriates, foreign diplomats, American business people, and wealthy Jamaicans. Teachers are similarly diverse. During mid-morning tea break everybody gathers in the staff room for refreshments, impromptu meetings, and lively banter. Classes finish by 1:00 p.m., before the hottest part of the day.

I work hard to keep abreast of the British-based curriculum designed around the venerated Cambridge exam. Worried that students will find my classes irrelevant or boring, I put a lot of energy into designing worksheets and inventing strategies as I struggle to stay a step ahead. Most of my improvised lessons work, but not all. To reduce chaos when they don't, I sometimes send pupils to the Headmaster. But I hate doing it, knowing it reflects on my ability to command respect. Other teachers act so confident, as though behavior is no issue, but I'm ashamed to ask about their classroom management secrets for such questions will reveal my own inadequacies.

Before I can be paid, I have to get my work permit from a Jamaican consulate outside the country. Miami is closest, so I decide to take a Friday off to fly there. I mention this in a letter to my parents, as it seems a good way to let them know my trip to Jamaica has become a long-term thing. I also tell them I'm living with David. Straightaway they call to tell me about their forthcoming visit to my uncle and aunt in Tampa, insisting I meet them there. They even offer to buy the ticket. Despite the morality play that is sure to ensue, I decide to go, hoping it will make up for the worry I caused by running off to Jamaica.

IX

In Miami I obtain the permit with no problems and continue to Tampa. Though the sprawling home of my uncle and aunt is surrounded by tropical palms, yucca, and several varieties of hibiscus, it feels like a galaxy removed from Jamaica. I try to play the dutiful daughter role everyone expects as they exchange sentimental stories about my childhood, but I note a conspicuous absence of interest in what I'm doing now. Not one question about David or my job or even Alex.

The next morning I'm sitting in the den catching up on events in my journal when Mother appears. She plants herself squarely in front of my chair and with eyes glaring says, "We don't know anything about this man you've run off with, but I've been praying for you, and I'll keep praying until you come to your senses. Jesus was clear about the fact that adultery is sin. This is a millstone on my heart. My blood pressure's higher than ever. The doctor has loaded me up with pills, but I don't know how much longer I can bear it." Her hands are trembling. "It all started with the highfalutin' ideas you picked up in college. We *never* should have sent you. I've been hearing so many stories about those professors at Luther!" She shakes her head despairingly.

I sigh, wait it out.

"So I know you're not the only one this has happened to. We hoped you would find a nice minister to marry, but instead..." Her voice falters. She clenches the edge of a table to steady herself.

Just then Dad enters. "Don't go upsetting your mother again!" he glares at me. Then he puts his arm around her and purrs, "Just relax, Dear. Come and sit on the porch with the rest of us." He draws her away. Her hero—wonder what she'd do if she knew about the nude photos hidden in his workshop?

The three-day weekend drags like a wagon on flat tires. I can't wait to get back to David, but I play along with their tiresome rehashing of good old days and shopping for trinkets at malls. Auntie isn't much of a cook, so they take us to different early bird specials at 4:30 each afternoon. Her favorite place reminds me of a meat market. We have to take a number and stand around waiting until it's called. Early bird or not, the cost of the meal could feed a family in Jamaica for a month.

When my uncle takes us sightseeing in his air-conditioned Lincoln, I sit in back between my parents. Gazing out the window, Dad observes, "The houses don't look great along here, but those niggers sure have nice cars."

"Dad!"

"What?"

"Please don't use that word."

"It's just a way of talking. You know it don't mean nothin'."

"It offends me. And it's not what I expect from you."

71

"Well, you know what?" He rolls down the window. "Your smoking offends *me*. So let's make a deal. I won't say 'nigger' if you won't smoke. How about it?"

"But those are very different things. Smoking isn't racist."

"It's a nasty addiction."

"I'm not *addicted*. It's just a habit."

"Yeah, a habit that'll kill you."

"I don't smoke that much!" A lie. I've smoked on and off since college; now I'm up to a pack a week.

"I bet you smoke fifty cigarettes for every time I say 'nigger.'"

He's right and he knows it. "Okay, Dad. You stop using that word, and I'll stop smoking." I'll think about the how later.

Later starts that night: denying myself the ritual cigarette while reading before going to sleep. Still, my resolve carries me through the weekend. On the plane back to Jamaica, the struggle gets worse. Three times I reach into my purse to pull out a pack. Finally I give in, but after a couple of unsatisfying puffs, guilt gets the upper hand. I go to the lavatory and pitch the half-empty pack down the chute.

David's kiss at the airport confirms for me where home is. On the drive into town, I tell him about Dad's challenge. "Aside from the health issue, if I don't keep my word, I'll be the hypocrite, just paying lip service to equality but not walking the walk…"

"Nonsense!" he scoffs. "The two things are utterly unconnected. His bigotry is unethical; it hurts others. If you want to quit, fine, but it's nobody else's business."

I sigh. "It's hard. The word haunts me. It's as though every time I smoke a cigarette, some child is going to be called 'nigger.'"

"And I suppose the opposite is also true. If you stop smoking, there'll be no more prejudice in the world?" I don't answer. "Just putting this thing into perspective." He squeezes my knee. "Let me tell you about my busy weekend. Saw my kids."

"Really! How are they?"

"Fine. When I suggested taking them to the beach, Dad got all weird, but Mumsy saved the day. She offered to go along, so he shut up. It's great having the car to take them places. My parents just keep them up there in the hills. They need to get out more."

"Where'd you go?"

"The yacht club. You know how conservative Mumsy is. The kids went crazy in the water! That's the problem with over-protection—no self restraint when they're set free."

"Did your mother go swimming?"

"God, no. She never left her umbrella. But I think it was good for her to get away from Dad. How do you feel about me bringing them over here?"

"Fine," I say brightly, wondering what will be expected of me. Games, toys, food? Guess I'll find out.

X

Two days after returning from Florida I find a note in my box asking me to come to the Headmaster's office during my free period. I imagine the worst. What will David say if I get fired?

But to my surprise he offers me extra work in the afternoons tutoring three new children from Iran who speak no English. Much better than being fired! I try to disguise my relief by asking, "When will the new children be starting?"

"Next week."

"Great! It'll give me a chance to use the TESL skills I learned in Peace Corps training."

"Splendid! I knew we could count on you. Your annual salary will be increased by fifty pounds. Maybe you and Mrs. Harris can get together tomorrow to discuss the details." He rises, extends his hand. "Thank you very much."

I smile with relief. "Thank you."

I can't wait to tell Karen, a science teacher from the States I've become friendly with. During morning tea we often confide on school matters and swap stories about adjusting to island life. Her unfailing ability to find humor in everyday annoyances makes her fun to be with even though her flippant remarks sometimes remind me of TV sit-coms. Still, she's the closest thing to a friend I have.

When she hears about my extra work, Karen hugs me. "I guess the Big Guy really likes you! Deserves a celebration! I've been wanting to invite you and David over to meet Tom. Now we have a perfect excuse to party. How about dinner on Friday?"

"That's so sweet of you! I'll check with David and let you know tomorrow. But there's one condition: you have to let me bring something."

"If you insist. We'll talk later."

I walk homeward, brimming with excitement about all the good news I have to share. If only David's not late for dinner again! I so hope he'll go along with Karen's invitation. We hardly ever go out together aside from a couple of visits to Dougie's house. His wife Marie is nice enough, but too busy with her own life to show any interest in mine.

To my relief, he likes the idea. So after school on Friday I make a salad and chill two bottles of wine to take. Over dinner David and Tom discover common interests: both have lived in London, have children from former marriages, and are passionate about music and stereo equipment. David is fascinated by Tom's research at the university with an electron microscope, and his custom-built sound system draws David's admiration, the wattage even exceeding his own.

While Karen and I clean up the kitchen, she tells me of plans for Tom's children to visit them at Christmas. "Their mother spoils them rotten, so they behave miserably when they're here… treat me like a servant."

"It's only for two weeks. You have him to yourself the rest of the year. Think how miserable he'd be if he never got to see them."

"You're right, but it's so hard not to lose my temper."

"Well, remember this year they're older than last. They're bound to be different, so try to forget the past and start fresh. You may be surprised." Instantly I regret handing out advice on something I have no experience with. I might soon be tested myself.

When we join the men in the living room, Tom is rolling a joint. Shocked, I blurt out, "How do you know we're not FBI agents?"

"Who cares!" he laughs and passes it around. Even David is taken aback, but quickly recovers and gingerly takes a few puffs. I go easy, remembering how depression hit me the last time I smoked with Alex in Montreal.

On our way home, David confides, "I didn't feel a thing from the weed. Did you?"

"I thought it was pretty strong. Just glad it's not me driving down this mountain."

"I suppose it's because I didn't suck on it like Tom was doing. I've never tried the stuff before and wanted to see how it affected the rest of you. Guess you've had some experience."

"A little. Alex and I experimented when we lived in Baltimore."

"In London I saw people ruin their lives, become prostitutes and pimps to support their addictions. It's terrible, like slavery. Never want to mess up my head like that."

75

"Well, we didn't use any hard stuff, and only smoked pot to relax. Music sounds fabulous when you're high. Can hear notes I don't even notice otherwise."

"Music. That's what we need. I wanta fix the speakers and get my stereo set up. And we should get some carpet to dampen the sound. Whatdaya think?"

"Sounds good to me."

XI

Knowing David wants to bring his kids over on Saturday, I have the clothes washed and on the line before he gets up. After breakfast he opens the hood of his car and gets busy changing the spark plugs and replacing wires. I hand him tools and parts.

Then he washes and waxes the outside while I concentrate on the interior. I remove floor mats, sponge the vinyl upholstery, and do the windows, drying them with newspaper, a trick he showed me to prevent streaks. In my cleaning fervor, I empty the storage pockets on the doors. From the driver's side, I pull out a bag and look inside. Condoms!

"Jac, I need paper towels!" he calls.

"Okay." Trembling, I jam the package back into the pocket before he notices. Why does he have condoms? We don't use them! I'm filled with the same panic–confusion, fear and guilt–as the small child who peeped through the crack of my parent's bedroom door and saw Dad rocking atop Mother. Mechanically I continue to clean while fighting back suspicions. If I confront him, he might get mad at me for snooping or for questioning his faithfulness. Probably the box was left in the car by the former owner. Any fuss will just make me look like a jealous fool.

When we finish working on the car I go inside to fix lunch, and David calls his parents to arrange for the children's visit. Initial greetings are followed by a long silence. Then he explodes. "That's ridiculous! What about *my* rights as a father? And what do you really know about this woman? Do you realize she has no education? Can't even cook? Who is she to decide what's best for *my* children?" Another pause and then, "Well, it's clear whose side you're on! Just wait. You won't get away with this!"

He bangs down the phone, spins around, eyes blazing. "The rotten bastard!"

"What's going on?"

"Jeez, I hate that sonovabitch!" His arms flail, fists clenched. "Takes her side against his own son! Can you believe it?"

"They won't let the kids come over?"

"I won't let them do this!"

"How can you stop them?"

"Get a lawyer and sue the bastards! They're all in cahoots. They're scheming with the bitch. But I'm the father. I have rights!" He stops by the window, props one foot on a chair. With arm leaning on bent knee, he stares out, lights a cigarette. Exhaling, he studies the perfect smoke rings floating to the ceiling. Then he snaps his fingers and whirls around. "I know what's going on. They must've called Renae and told her about you. She's the jealous type, so it set her off. Okay, I know how to handle this."

"How?"

"Let them stew for a while. I'll call Mumsy later. I can get around her.

"What will you do?"

"I'll figure something out. Let's pack a lunch and go to the beach."

After a vigorous swim in choppy water, we collapse on towels. Sunlight dries the droplets on our skin and warms our bodies as we sip from bottles of Red Stripe. When I can't stand it any longer I break the silence. "Are you going to seek joint custody?"

"And involve the courts? No way. They always favor mothers. Men don't have a chance. Not only would they give her custody, they'd also make me pay. I'll support my kids when they're with me, no problem, but if I can't have them, I'm not giving her a penny."

He rolls on his side to face me. "Back in Canada she ran to the court twice, trying to get a restraining order against me, but I got her to drop it. She's such an idiot. I'll never forget what she did once. Wendy was just a baby, and I was working two jobs trying to earn enough to pay rent and buy food. Renae did nothing except look after the kid. We didn't eat very fancy...mostly rice and canned stuff. One day I decided to splurge and bought a whole chicken, our first fresh meat in ages. Guess what she did with it?"

"What?"

"I got home from work the next night, raving hungry, couldn't wait to sink my teeth into a juicy piece of chicken. She opened the oven, and there it was: shriveled, dry, hardly anything left. I asked what happened and she said she cut the skin off like Maman always did. Probably true. Her mother's stupid, too. So she took a perfectly good chicken, and totally ruined it! I didn't know whether to cry or kill her. There I was, stuck with this dumb broad, the mother of my baby, and she can't even cook a fuckin' chicken. What's a man supposed to do?"

"What did you do?"

"Slapped her."

I wince, look away, realize I'm holding my breath.

"Not hard, but hard enough to make sure she learned her lesson and would never do anything like it again. Then what does she do? Sneaks off and calls the police. The nerve of that bitch!"

"Did they arrest you?"

"No. They just gave me a warning and told her she could file for a restraining order, but I didn't let her get away with it. Hate to have cops poking around my life. In a way, I'm glad she finally ran off and brought the kids here. They're better off without her. I just have to play my cards right now so she doesn't get them back."

The sky has turned cloudy, the temperature suddenly drops, and the sea is now dark and turbulent. David gets up. "Looks like a squall coming. We better head home."

As I shake sand from our towels and gather empty bottles, Alex's words replay in my head: *"You don't know a thing about this character."* But Renae sounds so dumb. Maybe the children are in a better situation now. And who am I to judge—her or him? Having a family so young must be terribly stressful. I feel triply glad Alex and I had no children to suffer from our break-up or for us to squabble over ever after.

XII

Disappointments of the weekend give me extra determination to make David's birthday special for him. Even though I realize he might not feel like celebrating, I persist with secret preparations: a call to Precious for his favorite lime pie recipe; a trip to the shopping center for groceries, gift and card; a visit to Mrs. Edmondson to borrow an eggbeater. Since David started being on call, I never know when to expect him, and he doesn't like me phoning his office, but I want this to be a surprise so I just hope for the best and get busy preparing the meal: sweet and sour meatballs, fried rice, egg rolls, bean sprouts sautéed with onions and peppers—an ambitious menu, considering our few utensils. I keep washing pans to reuse.

I've just started the pie, when his car pulls in. Relieved, I open the door and greet him with a kiss. He sits, pulls off his shoes, and looks at the *Gleaner* while I prepare rum and gingers. Clinking glasses, I say, "Happy birthday, Honey!" and hand him the gift.

He's surprised. "What! I wasn't planning to celebrate. You shouldn't fuss…"

"When people love you, they like to fuss a little. Get used to it!" I kiss him again.

He reads the funny but slightly sentimental card, chuckling at the cartoon. Then he unwraps the book and looks at the inscription, *To David, With Love from your Jac.* "That's really nice." He fans the pages. "I need a good dictionary. Thanks a lot."

"I'm so glad you like it. Now relax with your drink while I put the finishing touches on dinner. I'm fixing a surprise. I didn't know what time you'd be home, so it's not quite done. I'll tell you when everything's ready."

"Okay. I'm really beat after working so late last night on that damn filling machine. Was after three when I got in. Been dragging all day. Whatcha fixing?"

"I told you, a surprise."

I slide the pie crust into the oven, then squeeze lime juice and grate the rind. Not having a bowl the right size for meringue, I use an enamel pot. As I turn the beater, it scrapes the sides and bottom making a tinny sound. The whites are beginning to thicken when I hear a resounding *Wallop!*

"Stop that racket!" David's voice thunders. "You know I'm tired!"

I drop the beater and rush around the corner. The dictionary lies splayed on the floor. David sits, elbows on knees, head bent, hands over ears.

"I'm sorry, David," I murmur. "I'm almost done. Just a minute more and I'll be finished." I retreat to the kitchen and resume beating, trying my utmost to keep the blades from touching the pot.

Just as the meringue peaks stiffen, David grabs me from behind. "I want some respect around here!" He clenches my shoulders and shakes me. "When I say 'quiet,' I expect obedience. Get that straight!" He shoves me against the cabinet. I catch myself somehow and manage to keep from falling as he stomps upstairs.

Groping for a chair, I sit, stare at the festive candles, flowers, new saki cups while stifling sobs, afraid to make noise. Why oh why didn't I pay attention when he said he was tired! It's his birthday! I should have listened instead of being so intent on my plans. Maybe if I apologize... No. He's resting. Probably has a headache. Mustn't disturb him.

I tiptoe to the bathroom to blow my nose and wash my face. Careful not to make a sound, I finally get the pie in the oven. As the meringue browns, I cautiously wash the utensils. Then I sit to await his reappearance.

I pick up the newspaper and turn to the Horoscope section, hoping it will account for his overreaction. "SCORPIO: This is a day of accomplishment for you as your ingenuity wins praise. Tantrums and emotional outbursts *must* be kept in check. You draw love to you, but too much of a social life may come at a high expense." If only I could show this to him! But that's not an option, for he scorns astrology. I sigh and look at my LEO sign: "Trust that you are just where you need to be right now, for many good reasons. Sometimes you have to let the doubt go and just enjoy love."

Hearing him on the stairs, I jump up and cast aside the paper. "I'm so sorry, David. I really am. I hope you got some rest." He doesn't respond. "Are you ready to eat now?"

"Sure," he glances at his watch, "if it doesn't take long." He sits at the table while I reheat the food. We eat in silence. When he finishes dessert, he lights a cigarette and says, "Not too bad. Thanks for trying the pie. Keep practicing and it might get as good as Mumsy's."

He pushes back his chair and goes upstairs. When he comes down he's wearing a clean shirt and smelling of after-shave. Picking up his keys, he says, "Gotta go out. Don't wait up."

Choking back tears, I clean the kitchen. Then I go upstairs and crawl into the empty bed. Opening my current Thomas Hardy novel, I seek escape in the vicissitudes of Bathsheba's fortunes and misfortunes.

XIII

David rolls out of bed and rushes downstairs to answer the ringing phone. Annoyed, I look at the clock. Not even 8:00. Saturday, our one day to sleep in.

His steps are heavy as he climbs the stairs. "It was my dad. Renae wants to see me."

"She's here?" I study his face as he buttons his shirt. "Did you know she was coming?"

"No." He pulls on his trousers. "How do you feel about me bringing her over? If she sees where we're living and has a chance to meet you, she might agree to let the kids come. We wouldn't be here long. I don't want to spend any more time with her than necessary, but we've got to win her over."

"Okay. Any idea what time you'll get here?"

"No."

I spend an uneasy day, not especially wanting to meet Renae, but I don't like the idea of him being here alone with her, so I can't leave. Whatever they decide will affect me in ways I can't even imagine, yet I feel powerless, an onlooker awaiting the verdict.

After cleaning the flat and fixing a casserole for dinner, I settle myself outside to soak up some sunshine with a glass of limeade and my new astrology book which I hope will help me understand David better.

Right away I'm shocked by how much he matches the Scorpio qualities—a virtual prototype of Scorpion personal charm, strong will and creative power. An "electrifying magnetism that draws the opposite sex into their charmed circle." In fact Scorpios are considered the "sexy sign of the Zodiac." It also confirms that a Scorpio man is "intensely interested in his family," especially his children's development. I'm shocked at how perfectly all the descriptions fit David, right down to the tendency to "fearlessly reach for the stars." And dismayed when I discover that a Scorpio "never reveals his true nature to anyone," and that the best marriage partners for Scorpio men are with women of other water signs, not with fire signs like myself. At least we're both courageous and independent thinkers. Leos are considered gamblers when it comes to love and many have two marriages, for we have a tendency to take risks and sometimes make mistakes. I have to admit, the book has my number... and his.

The sun is casting long shadows across the yard when I go inside. At the sound of David's car, I rush toward the door, but he's already opening it. "Hi, Honey," he says. "Renae, this is Jac, and here's our place."

We say Hi to each other. I offer a drink; she declines. Right away I notice how attractive she is. Her curly frosted hair is cut in a short trendy style. Tall and slender, she wears a short, snug-fitting black and white checked dress with large white collar, patent belt, and matching stiletto shoes. Chic, professional, not at all what I expected, given David's derogatory remarks. I wonder if she's a water sign and if he is still physically attracted to her despite his avowed disgust and hurt. And where have they been all day?

I can hear the clicking of her heels and his boastful voice as he leads her around upstairs. When they come down, he announces they are headed out. He kisses my cheek and whispers, "Thanks, Baby. Everything's fine." Aloud he says, "I gotta drive Renae back to Red Hills. See you later."

I have the casserole heated when he returns. While we eat, he tells me he spent little time with the kids, focusing instead on charming their mother. "That bitch is as cold as winter in Ottawa, but I finally got through. You were perfect; didn't threaten her at all."

"I'm so glad to hear that."

He looks at me sharply, then grins. "She'll soon come around. Just needs a little more time. I'll call her tomorrow."

He makes the call soon after breakfast. After the usual greetings, he pauses momentarily and then explodes. "What! How can you let her do that?"

Growing agitated as he listens, he finally retorts, "You'll regret this. I promise, I'll never forgive you sonsabitches! The whole lot of you are gonna pay for this! Just wait 'til I get through! You won't know what hit you, but take my word, it's coming! If you think …" He stops in mid-sentence and extends his arm. Looking quizzically at the phone, he says, "The bastard hung up!"

He slams down the receiver and faces me. "That ras clot jackass says Renae has decided to take the children back to Canada! Musta had it planned all along! The sniveling coward put her up to it. Even paying for it, I bet." He strikes the table with his fist. "I hate him! Hate him! Hate him!"

I wait out his tirade, mumbling words of comfort that he doesn't hear. I expect he'll go to the airport for a last opportunity to bond with the children, or to begin revenge on Renae and his parents, but he never mentions it.

Pigeon Island

I

I work late the last day before Christmas holidays making sure I have correctly calculated marks and written comments on each student's report. When I get home, David meets me at the door, his face glowing. "It's about time! I've got something to show you!" He takes my books and bag and grabs my hand. Come on!"

"What is it?"

"Close your eyes and follow me." He leads me outside and behind the building. "Here's our Christmas present. Open your eyes!"

I look up and see a huge boat perched atop a trailer. "That?"

"Amazing, isn't it? We're gonna have so much fun!"

"Wow! That's quite a boat. But how can we afford it?"

"Don't worry. I got a great deal! Wasn't even looking for a boat, but when I came across this—the owner needed money and I had the cash—it seemed too good to pass up. You like it?"

"It's... it's such a surprise."

"Yeah, but I've always wanted a boat, so I thought *What the hell.* Come on. All aboard!" He hops on the trailer, swings into the hull, and reaches down. "Grab my hand, and put your foot on the tire."

With his help I scramble aboard. Proudly he shows me steering wheel, compass, seats, life preservers, storage compartments, anchor, outboard motor... "The engine needs some work, but I can do it in a day or so. Then she'll be ready to launch."

"I can't get over this." I shake my head. Owning a boat seems like such a responsibility.

"And here's the best part–the plant's closing down a whole week for the holidays. So we can spend Christmas on her!"

"Oh."

"We'll camp for a few days on one of the smaller islands. Whadaya think?"

I've been worrying about how he'll handle not being with his children for the holidays, but now here's a way to avoid it all. I picture the two of us on a deserted island, far from mangers, Santas, spending frenzies, family pressures. Free to do whatever we want. "Which island you thinking of?"

"I'd like to check out Lime Cay. But no one's allowed to spend the night there. So after we stop, we can head on to Pigeon Island. I hear it's a great place to snorkel."

"Oh, I'd love to try that! I can't get over how clear the water is around here. Shall we get some masks?"

"Definitely, and fins and snorkels. Think I'll buy a spear gun, too, so I can fish."

"You know how?"

"No, but it can't be hard. Let's make a list of things we need to take."

For two days and nights we work, getting all in order for our voyage. David overhauls the engine and makes sure it's seaworthy. I shop for lanterns, food and drinks and pack everything in boxes and bags. He procures extra fuel tanks, spear gun, snorkeling gear, ropes, batteries, and inflatable rafts that will double as mattresses.

Christmas morning we load the gear, hitch the trailer, and head for the Port Royal yacht club where David pays a small fee to launch the boat and park the car. While I direct he backs the trailer down the ramp. The heavy boat strains the tiny car, so he tells me to put rocks behind each tire while he turns the winch, easing the craft down. The car holds as the boat settles into the water. No sooner does he secure it to the dock with lines than a grizzled white-haired man standing nearby shouts, "Mon, I tink ya got a problem."

David jerks his head around. Several inches of water are already in the hull, and the level is rising rapidly. "Blood clot!" he yells. "Our boat's sinking! We gotta get it out!" He runs to the trailer and cranks the winch. "Quick! Untie the bow line from the dock and pull it around to line up with the trailer."

I spring into action. Within a minute the boat is tilted up on the trailer with water gushing from an opening beneath the engine.

The man on the dock observes, "Looks like ya fergot sumtin', Suh."

"What you talkin' about?"

"De hole in de bottom a yer boat. Where's de plug?"

"Oh. That hole. It's for letting water *out*, right? Let's see, where'd I put it?" David rummages around, mumbling, "The other night I saw a thing that looked like a bottle stopper. Let me think. Oh, I know… Here it is!" He holds up an expandable plug. "This is for jammin' the hole, right?"

The man nods.

"All fixed," David says as he secures the plug in the hole. "Now we're set. Let's try again. Get ready, Jac, to tie the lines to the dock as I ease her down. Got it?"

"Let her go…"

We work quickly stowing gear, attaching lines, arranging charts, locking the car. When all is shipshape, David starts the engine. I don a life vest, and we cast off. Waving vigorously, I shout to the elder on the dock, "Thank you!"

David stands at the controls, feet planted wide, steering wheel grasped in both hands, proud captain of his vessel. I sit in the stern, watching water rush by. Sand bars are visible on either side just beneath the aqua surface. David steers between markers, keeping to the channel until we round the Port Royal point and leave the harbor behind.

When we near Lime Cay, he beckons me to him and says, "I wanted to go ashore, but I think it's getting too late. If we want to reach Pigeon Island before dark, we better press on. Okay with you?" I nod and return to my seat.

He guides the boat south and west. Beyond a headland at the southernmost tip of Jamaica, burgeoning waves swell into rolling hills and valleys. Heeding buoys to avoid shoals, David keeps the boat far out where the cobalt sea has become midnight blue.

"See how dark the water is," he shouts. "That means it's deep out here. Real deep."

Wind beating into his eyes, David strains to peer over the windshield made nearly opaque by salt spray. We plow westward for two hours, past a few small uninhabited islands. Finally we clear a point of land on the right which opens into a broad bay.

David points to the right. "Must be Old Harbour. And over there, that's gotta be Pigeon Island." He waves to the left. "We'll shoot for it."

He circles halfway round the island before picking a spot of beach to land on. Racing with the setting sun, we secure the anchor and unload supplies. By nightfall, the tent is up and everything inside. Using a flashlight we find enough dry firewood to heat a can of beans and make grilled cheese sandwiches. David inflates the air mattresses.

As the fire becomes embers, we lie on blankets in front of the tent, tuning in to the rhythm of our surroundings. The moonless sky is chaotically festooned with millions of stars. Waves break on the nearby shore with infinite variations of gushing sounds as gentle splashes grow to crescendos climaxed by thunderous crashes followed by water seeping into the sand or rushing back to sea. Hearing intermittent rustlings in the tall grass behind our campsite, we speculate about what other creatures inhabit our new neighborhood.

"Could be lizards," David guesses. "Or maybe mongoose or crabs. But don't worry. There aren't any poisonous snakes or spiders, or any dangerous wildlife in Jamaica."

Next day we investigate our paradise from end to end. Dozens of tall palms sway gently, dangling bunches of coconuts above our reach. Broken stone foundations remain where buildings once stood, and poles in the water mark the dock of a bygone era. When we stumble upon cracked limestone beds, David explains they were used long ago for evaporating seawater to produce salt. We see cold ashes in old fire sites, but no sign of recent human habitation.

We take the boat out and anchor it on a coral reef. After donning masks, snorkels and fins, we enter the water cautiously and begin our exploration of the dazzling, pulsating reef. Groups of brightly colored fish swim in unison, darting in and out, under and over the kaleidoscopic coral as the moving water carries the whole scene back and forth like a swaying branch. I notice small fish clumping together, whereas larger ones tend to travel in pairs or alone. When David arms himself with the spear gun and aims at a turquoise-colored parrot fish, I lag behind to avoid his line of fire. Becoming chilled, I climb into the boat to warm myself in the sunshine. David doesn't come out until he has shot a small snapper and three parrots. Shivering but elated, we light the campfire and feast.

"I notice our petrol's getting low," David says. "We used more than half of it coming here, so we don't have enough to get back to Port Royal. We'll have to go to the fishing village in Old Harbour tomorrow and buy some."

"How far is it?"

"I can't tell by looking, but I think if we head for those lights over there toward the left," he points, "maybe about five miles. Better get an early start."

We awake to an overcast sky and dark waves pounding the shore. Rather than spend time starting a fire to make breakfast, we cast off immediately. I grab bread and jelly, and a jug half full of water. Despite a choppy sea, we reach the village within an hour. I wait in the boat while David goes in search of food and kerosene to augment our dwindling supplies. He fills our water bottles, but since he's not a registered fisherman, he can buy no more than ten gallons of petrol. He learns of the rationing too late to prepare a bribe, so has no recourse but to leave with one tank still empty.

Returning against the heavy wind is slow. Whitecaps explode on the rolling surface of the inky liquid, and powerful waves slam our hull. I clutch the gunwale and brace myself, knees flexed to cushion the impact as we drop off the edge of wave after wave and crash into rolling gorges. David keeps altering course to avoid hitting the breakers head-on, but as the boat lists sideways, waves leap over the side.

Soaked through, I can't stop my teeth from chattering, as much from cold as terror. If we drown out here, sharks will devour us, leaving no trace. My parents will never know what happened. What a waste of life! I'll leave nothing behind, not a child, a book, a building, a garden, not even a tree. Why did I ever let him talk me into this?

David stands erect but relaxed at the wheel, his knees absorbing the erratic plunging of the boat. He looks like a cowboy astride a bronco, man and steed riding out the fury raging beneath. He glances at me and shouts, "Isn't this great!"

I nod weakly.

When we're about halfway back, the deluge strikes. Bolts of lightning tear across the sky, slashing into the sea. Thunderclaps follow ever closer to the flashes as the storm engulfs us. "We're taking on too much water!" David shouts. "Doesn't look like the bilge pump is working. You'll have to bail."

"With what?"

"There's a bucket in the bow. I'll tie this line around your waist and you can crawl up and get it. Stay low and hold the edge. I'll keep the boat steady as I can."

I stumble over and he secures the line. Inching forward, I hear him call, "You're doin' great. Just get the bucket and bail! This boat's riding awfully low."

I lurch fore and aft, starboard and port, as the tumbling craft tosses me like a shell in the surf. I'll be covered with bruises… if I survive. With the bucket finally in my grasp, I clamber back to the stern, brace myself, and begin scooping water that has risen six inches above the floorboards. No matter how fast I toss, the water level hardly recedes, but at least it stops increasing. Numb with cold, I continue bailing as David steers the boat onward in the direction, I hope, of Pigeon Island.

The black cloud passes over, and before we reach shore, the rain ceases. Shivering with cold and tension, we secure the boat. Then we start a fire under the tent awning, igniting the wet wood with kerosene. Finally we change into dry clothes and heat a can of soup that we devour with hard dough bread and Vienna sausages.

"We did it, Mate." David squeezes my hand. "I like how you kept your head out there."

"Thanks, Captain," I salute, suddenly warm. "You did a good job yourself."

"I learned a lot about the boat. Now I feel like I can handle anything old man sea wants to give me."

He pulls me close and kisses me in a way that makes me feel like Eve in the garden. Surely he's never shared an experience like this with anyone else. Out here he's mine alone. His hand slides under my shirt, seeking my taut nipples, and I melt in his embrace as a wave of passion engulfs us. When spent, we collapse like beached whales by the flickering campfire.

II

At dawn I get up and walk naked along the broad, low-tide beach, joyfully absorbing the sun's warmth as it rises in the cloudless sky. My eyes seek treasures the sea has left in my path–shells, bits of coral, polished green, blue and white glass. Back at the campsite, David rekindles the fire and brews coffee.

After breakfast I take an air mattress to the beach and lie down to read *Marjorie Morningstar* while he tinkers with the outboard motor. When I start sweating, I close my book, remove sunglasses, and walk slowly into the sea, enjoying the coolness teasing my skin as water creeps up my body. At rib level, I pause, steel for the shock of total immersion. Plunging in, I relax into a sidestroke and glide parallel with the shore. When I turn around and head back, I see David standing at the water's edge, pointing. He shouts, "Look! Over there!"

My air mattress is bobbing away from shore. "Oh, no!" I groan, realizing I left it too near the water and the rising tide snatched it. Rolling onto my stomach, I swim steadily toward the mattress. For several minutes I seem to be gaining on it, but then it emerges from the lee of the island and reaches choppy water. Catching wind, it increases speed, skimming along the surface like a plane hurtling down a runway about to become airborne. "Damn!" I grit my teeth, realizing I'll never reach it. I turn onto my back to catch my breath, lungs burning. When I look toward shore, David is but a speck on the beach.

I panic, suddenly realizing how deep the water must be. What kind of creatures are under me? Stop it! I tell myself. Calm down. Think this through. Remember lifesaving training. Don't go against the current. Swim diagonally toward shore. I take a few deep breaths and set out with intentional strokes heading inward at an angle. David is motioning me toward him. Then he runs to the boat, starts the engine, and speeds off in the direction where the mattress disappeared.

I alternate strokes, interspersing them with intervals of floating until I reach land and collapse panting on the sand. When I hear the engine, I open my eyes. David throws out the anchor, holds up the mattress and climbs from the boat. As he approaches, I sit up, trying to gauge his anger. "I'm so glad you got it! I'm sorry it got away. It was so stupid of me. I didn't know how fast the tide rises—"

"Don't worry. You didn't do it on purpose. I'm just glad I caught it. A helluva race. But now I'm worried about our fuel supply again. The trip to Old Harbour yesterday took nearly as much as we bought. So we might not have enough to get back to Port Royal, especially now."

Relieved he's not mad, I ask when he thinks we should go.

"I don't know, but the wind's already picking up, so it's too late for today." He peers at me. "You better get some clothes on. You're shaking like a leaf and your lips are blue."

By mid afternoon I'm sufficiently recovered to go with David in search of coconuts. After several attempts, he manages to climb far enough up a tree to break several loose. He opens the tops with his machete and we sit on the sand drinking the delicious water in the young jelly nuts. "See those holes under the bushes?" He points. "Probably crabs. They come out at night. We should try to catch some after dark. You ever eat crab?"

"Once when I was in Washington. Had to drink a lot of beer because they were so spicy. All I remember was the hot pepper and huge claws."

"Sea crabs. These land crabs don't have such big claws, but the meat in them is sweet, sweet. A lot of work getting it out of the shells, but we might have to survive out here on fish, coconuts and crabs."

I love his spirit. This is playing house at its best.

We gather wood on our way back to camp. Near dusk we build a large fire and set a pot of sea water on it to heat. Then armed with flashlight and canvas bag, we look for crabs. I aim light into the crabs' eyes to immobilize them while David grabs and stuffs them into the bag until we have enough for a meal. He drops them one by one into the boiling water. While they cook we pick bird peppers from a bush and crush them. With stones we crack the crab shells and pick out meat by firelight. What a feast! The crab is sweeter and the peppers hotter than anything I've ever tasted. Exhausted and satiated, we crawl into the tent.

Next morning we awake to the sound of rain pelting the canvas. It continues all day, through the night and all next day until our clothes, towels and bedding are dirty and sodden. As night falls David says, "I've had a belly full of this. We should make a run for it tomorrow morning if there's any break in the weather."

"I guess we could try if the rain stops."

"We'll have to leave early, because once we go, there's no turning back. No place between here and Port Royal to buy petrol, but we can't waste more fuel going back to Old Harbour. If what we have doesn't get us all the way, I don't know what we'll do. But I don't see any other choice."

"Okay, Captain."

By morning the rain has ceased and the sky is partially clear, while gusty wind chops the sea. David peers out of the tent. "Not raining, but still cloudy. Definitely a mixed bag."

"Do you think it's safe to go?"

He shrugs. "Still risky, but the thing is, I have to be back at work soon, and there's no sign of any major weather change. It could go on like this for days, even weeks. It's called Christmas winds. I say we make a run for it. You with me?"

"All the way." I try to sound cheerful.

We load the boat and cast off into a moderate breeze. Eastward we travel, plowing through swells of increasing height. After a couple of hours, David sights exposed rocks ahead and turns the boat farther out into high waves with whitecaps. He heads the boat directly into them, roller-coasting up and down. Suddenly he shouts, "Oh, my God! Hold on, Jac! Here's the big one. Don't know if we can make it!"

The bow climbs to the crest until the boat is vertical; then it shoots off the other side, airborne. The landing jolt dazes me, but I hear David yelling, "Rastafari! If the bow was down when we hit, we'd be swamped!"

Fingers locked to the gunwale, my body trembles. I can't speak.

"We can't take another wave like that," he calls hoarsely. "Gotta get to shore." He turns the wheel, and the raging sea hurls us toward the coast. Nearer to land, jagged rocks appear, obviously capable of making our craft flotsam in a second. Guiding the boat parallel with the coast just outside the shoals, he searches for a place to beach. Finally he points toward land and shouts, "A lagoon!"

Then the engine sputters. Chokes. Dies. "Damn it! We must be out of fuel!"

Terror-stricken, I simply look at him.

"Get the anchor," he shouts, still glued to the steering wheel. "Throw it out as far as you can." I lurch forward, clutching the gunwale with one hand. With the other I heave the anchor over.

"Come here!" he yells.

Pointing shore-ward, he speaks into my ear, "I'm gonna swim for that lagoon. I'll put on snorkel and fins and carry some rope. You stay here. When I get there, I'll pull the boat into the lagoon."

I watch as he ties one end of the longest rope to the boat, then coils the remaining length and hoists it over his shoulder. "I don't know how long the anchor will hold, so I gotta make haste," are his last words as he drops into the churning water.

The boat rises, falls, jerks around like a tilt-a-whirl with each onslaught from the sea. At any moment it could break free and hurtle toward the impervious rocks. My eyes don't leave David as he bobs through the waves uncoiling the heavy pack on his back. At long last, he stands in knee-high water. He struggles clumsily toward the lagoon, stepping high in his fins, the coral bottom apparently too sharp for bare feet. He stops and beckons, shouting something I can't make out.

I gesture back, trying to let him know I don't understand. "I can't hear you!" I shout, thinking sound might travel better land-ward than out toward me.

He keeps motioning and shouting something that sounds like, "Throw rope," but it doesn't make any sense.

So I yell back, "Which rope?"

Apparently annoyed by my inability to comprehend his instructions, he shouts again while beckoning, but the wind blows the words back in his face.

Knowing I must do something, I undo the rope he had tied to the boat. Then I hold the end up for him to see and call, "This? Throw this?"

His gesture looks affirmative, but I can't understand why he wants me to throw it. As his motions became more agitated, I finally heave the rope toward him. The end has hardly left my hand when his body convulses in paroxysm, and his shouts become audible: "Blood clot! You stupid moron! What the fuck are you doing? Wait'll I get my hands on you, you ras clot idiot!" His shrieking continues as he stumbles to and fro on the reef. "What am I supposed to do with this?" he screeches, waving the limp rope end.

I don't attempt to answer above the noise of the waves and wind. I haven't a clue of what to do next, but his anger frightens me more than the raging storm. The wide stretch of treacherous sea separating us is now my only protection. Then to my dismay, he climbs off the reef and begins to swim toward me. Bracing myself in a corner of the threshing vessel, I wait for disaster to strike....from the sea or from David.

III

When he reaches the boat, I lean over, despite my terror, and help him aboard. Fortunately, the grueling swim has exhausted him, so he just collapses on the seat and pants, head hanging as though he's about to retch. I cover him with a towel and hand him a dry pullover. When his breathing returns to normal and his shivering subsides, I offer a jug of water. "I'm sorry; I didn't understand what you wanted me to do."

He eyes me with contempt, shaking his head in disbelief. "God, I can't believe how stupid you are!" The boat lurches, nearly throwing him to the floor as he grabs the edge. "Now, I've got to go through it all over again. This time leave the rope tied to the boat. All you have to do when I signal is hoist up the anchor so I can try to pull the boat into the lagoon. Can you manage that?"

"Sure... now that I know what you want."

"You also have to watch for the boat getting swept toward the rocks. Keep an oar in your hands to heave away if it gets too close. Understand?"

I nod. He coils the rope and climbs into the roiling water.

This time we get the boat into the lagoon and secure the anchor in a pile of rocks. Looking around, we spot a wisp of smoke rising above nearby trees. "Come on," David says. "Let's see who's over there."

At the edge of a clearing we find a hut with a small flag whipping in the wind. On it is a lion's face. David calls, "Hoy. Good morning. Can we pass?" He waits a moment, then adds, "Hail Selassie I! Anybody inside deh?"

"Who's he?" I ask.

"Haile Selassie is the spiritual leader of the Rastafarians. Also Emperor of Ethiopia. He's a descendent of King David. Lots of credentials. Probably more powerful here than in Africa. The lion of Judah there," he gestures toward the flag, "is their symbol."

A tall young man with smooth light brown skin emerges. He has long dreadlocks and wears only khaki-colored jeans with a woven belt of red, green and gold strings. Behind him comes a short white-haired black man with deeply creased face and sharp piercing eyes. The two silently observe us. Then the younger speaks, "Hail, Selassie I."

"Hail," David returns. He explains our predicament and answers their questions. Then the two strangers withdraw a short distance and confer in low tones. I sense our fate is in their hands, but it doesn't frighten me.

The old man invites us into the hut and offers tin cups of rich herbal tea. While we sip his brew, the men continue discussing our dilemma.

Eventually they reach agreement, and David explains, "The channel to Port Royal is just around the point. Hezekiah here is gonna lend us some petrol and he'll cross the channel with me while you stay with his father. We'll refill his fuel can at the yacht club, then load the boat and haul it home. We'll come back for you on the land route. Hezekiah says the road ends about a mile from here. We can park there and walk in. You'll be safe. Just stay put until I return. Okay?"

"Okay," I agree reluctantly, "but I'll worry about you out there." I touch his face.

He takes my hand and kisses it. "I'll be all right. I can tell Hezekiah's a good seaman. He wouldn't agree to come if it wasn't okay. Our boat's bigger than their canoes and can take heavier seas. You go ahead and catch some sleep. It'll be a few hours before we're back."

I sit on a stump outside the hut and watch them launch the boat. Then the father invites me inside and refills my cup. He indicates a mattress on the floor where I can rest and gives me a sheet. Then he leaves. With tea warming my insides, I begin to relax for the first time all day. The sun sets, the hut grows dark and I fall into a deep slumber.

David's voice, first faint, then clearer, reaches me as though he is hauling me up from the ocean's floor. I open my eyes, see his face in dim lantern light. He leads me outside. The night is so dark, I can see nothing but stars. We follow Hezekiah along a steep path until the sliver of a young moon peeps out from a cloud, revealing a long ridge. David says, "Hellshire Hills. We have to drive over them to get into town."

Too drowsy to reply, I blindly follow up the rocky slope until we reach a fence.

"Okay, here's the car. Bend down and slip under this wire."

I do as instructed, mumble "Thank you" to our guide and savior, and slide onto the seat. David praises Hezekiah all the way back to Kingston as I nod in and out of consciousness.

Kingston, 1969

I

We're lying on the sheet, bathed in perspiration and the afterglow of lovemaking when David asks, "Are you ready to have my baby?"

Baby? "I... Already?"

"Well, I said before, if you stick with me, I'll give you a baby. I'm ready. Are you?"

I prop myself up on one elbow to see his face in the dim candlelight.

"How about it?" he asks. "Love me enough?"

"Of course I love you." I kiss his forehead. "There's no question about that."

"Maybe I should ask if you trust me enough."

"I sure trusted you with my life on the Pigeon Island trip."

"Some test all right." He squeezes my leg. "Well, I want more children, and I want you to be their mother. But there's one thing you have to understand. I could never bear to lose my kids again. Even if something happens and we stop living together, I still have to be able to see them."

"Well, I wouldn't want to have children if we couldn't raise them together."

"Parenting is a big responsibility and it doesn't end even if our feelings for each other change. We have to be realistic."

I nod solemnly. "I understand." Talking about splitting up a family we don't yet have rather robs the moment of its romance, but given what he's been through...

"Can we agree then that neither of us will ever deprive the other of our children, no matter what?"

"Okay." I hug him, basking in his confirmation of love.

"Just remember," he murmurs between kisses, "this is forever."

"It better be!" I poke him playfully. He answers with an attack of tickling so intense that I run to the bathroom to escape. I lock the door and glance in the mirror at a face so radiant I hardly recognize it. How lucky to be having a baby with a man who really wants it! Much more serious than getting married—you can't divorce a child. This will be far different than with his wife. He only married her because she was pregnant. But ours will be a love child.

I stop the pill right away, but my period continues. After four months, I convince David to go with me to a reproductive specialist. We both have exams and tests and return a week later for the results.

Waiting in the doctor's office, David thumbs through a tattered boat magazine. I gaze at prints and diplomas adorning the white walls and keep telling myself to think positive, but my heart is racing and my mouth feels as if I've been chewing on a sponge. I glance at David, wondering what we'll do if something really is wrong, but he's engrossed in an article. I uncross my legs, shift in the chair, do a few neck rolls.

Finally the doctor enters peering intently at an open folder he carries. I reach for David's hand. The doctor clears his throat, fixes his gaze on me and says, "It appears, young lady, that your ovaries aren't releasing any eggs."

I catch my breath, stunned.

"And you," he looks at David, "have a low sperm count." David's jaw drops as the doctor continues. "With such deficiencies, the likelihood of conception is less than one in ten thousand. But there are several things we can do ..."

"Never mind." David turns to me. "Let's get out of here."

My thoughts are a blur as he leads me outside. Then he cuts loose. "How can anything be wrong with my sperm? I already have two kids. There's got to be a mistake. Don't believe a word of it! I'm not paying some fucking doctor to tell me I'm sterile!"

II

I buy two books on fertility and study ways to increase our probability of conception. Every morning I check my temperature and mark it on the calendar. For several nights before the target date, we refrain from sex in order to strengthen David's sperm. Though the procedure leaches spontaneity from our love life, we persist. The worry about what will happen if I fail to produce for him gnaws at me, but he doesn't seem worried.

When David suggests moving to a bigger place, I remind him we can't afford to spend much more on rent.

"You're thinking small," he says. "Let your mind expand. It's time for better things. Look at the furniture!" He gestures. "Is this how you always want to live?"

"I've been willing to make do..."

"Well, I want to live where I can feel comfortable inviting my friends. And I need space to work on my invention. I hate having neighbors watch me use the hose in the yard. Their prying eyes and all the questions are so annoying I can't concentrate. I need a place where I can set up my apparatus and work without disturbances."

I start looking but quickly discover there's an extremely limited supply of affordable places. Then one day David gets home early, all smiles. "Come on," he says, "I heard about a diplomat selling a bunch of stuff. They're leaving the country, so the house will be vacant. Let's take a look."

In his usual style, David charms the entire family, learning more about them in half an hour than I would know after living next door for years. He even finds out how much rent they pay and the name and phone number of their landlady. As we drive away, he says, "Think about it! We can get the whole house with four bedrooms, three baths, quarters for two servants, and huge yard for just a smidgen more than we're paying now. Even a garage for the boat. If the rent doesn't go up, it's too good a deal to let go."

"It's nice, but awfully big. I mean, what will we do with four bedrooms?"

"Have you forgotten we're planning to have a family? Trust me, we'll use the space."

"Okay," I say, relieved he still believes we can have children.

We go to see the owner next morning and David wins her over, actually gets her to accept a deposit for the first month. Then we return to the house and, as he predicted, get some excellent deals on the furniture. He even goes for the car, a sedan with radio, tape player, leather upholstery and bucket seats. I see no need for it, but he is adamant. "What fun is earning money if we just save it?"

We move at the end of the month. Late one afternoon as I sit on our new verandah, serenaded by canaries chirping in the branches of shady almond trees, I stitch cushion covers for our Danish modern sofas. As the needle goes in and out, I plan how to tell David. But the moment he enters the driveway, I forget everything I've planned and dash toward him.

"David," I blurt as he gets out of the car, "we're going to have a baby!"

"You sure?" he looks wary.

Grinning, I nod vigorously. "The obstetrician said so!"

"Hooray!" He picks me up, spins around until I'm laughing, giddy. "What'd I tell you? That other quack was a friggin' liar. I'm not sterile and there's nothing wrong with you!" His emphatic kiss makes me feel like the luckiest woman on earth.

Releasing me, he says, "We oughta sue the asshole. All the worry and suffering he's put us through!"

"I'm just glad he was wrong."

"Well, I might not bother. Come and sit. I got news for you, too." I take my sewing inside and continue basting a zipper while he opens a Red Stripe, lights a cigarette and exhales a few smoke rings. "You know there's been a lot of politicking going on at the plant, and my boss has been under pressure from those big guys up in the States."

I nod. He's been talking about it for weeks.

"Three big shots from headquarters came in today and fired him, right on the spot."

"No!"

"Made him clean out his desk while they watched. They escorted him out and told him never to come back. Then they called a meeting with the engineers and foremen and explained what they expect. When the others were leaving, they asked me to stay."

"Uh oh."

"I could smell a rotten fish. The bastards started shoving figures and charts in my face showing their production goals. Then they tell me I'm on one month's probation. If the plant doesn't reach their goals by then, I'm out!"

"Oh, no! Don't they realize the problems you're dealing with?"

"They don't care, and they're not really trying to solve anything. Just looking for somebody to blame. First my boss; now setting me up to be the next fall guy."

"Is there any way you can meet their quotas?"

"You gotta be kidding! We'd have to operate for the whole month without a single power cut."

105

"Which is impossible—we have blackouts every week."

"Exactly. And always a few workers who don't show up, others come in late, and the delivery of supplies is always unpredictable. That's not even counting equipment breakdowns all the time because the production lines are cast-offs from factories in the States. And they wonder why we can't meet quotas!"

"So what can you do?"

"Start my *own* business. I've been thinking about it anyway and this is the perfect opportunity. I'll play their game for a month while I make plans. They have to give severance pay, so it should tide us over until the new business picks up." He stubs out his cigarette, gets up and goes for another beer.

Stitching rapidly, my thoughts race. What a time to lose his job! What if his business doesn't do well? I'll have to stop working before the end of the year, but what if we can't pay bills? The needle pricks my finger and I jam it into my mouth to stop the bleeding.

David puts more energy into setting up his new company, Wellington's Industrial Service, Ltd., than into meeting production goals at Colgate and is let go. Still he's furious when the severance pay amounts to less than he expected. But he pursues his business plan with more urgency, seeking my opinions and help with setting up the office. My conservative approach to finances counterbalances his tendency to believe any idea he comes up with will work.

We open a business bank account and arrange a line of credit. Our extra rooms become office and work shop. We design letterhead and prepare an introductory brochure. He buys office machines and gets the oscilloscope he's been wanting for a long while. Not only is it essential for analyzing the electronic problems of customers, but he can also use it in experiments for his inventions.

In addition to doing various small jobs, David gets maintenance contracts with a record manufacturing company, the flourmill, and a cement company which meet our basic expenses. The first payment arrives just before we exceed our overdraft credit.

To celebrate, he brings home a bottle of champagne. Popping the cork, he pours two glasses and toasts, "Here's to the success of our business." We clink and drink.

"And here's to our baby," I say, raising the glass again while my left hand, eager to detect the first pulses of life, touches my abdomen.

III

Some days David stays at the house too much; he always seems to need something–a snack, an estimate typed, a phone number, or sex. Other days he disappears and stays out late without even calling to let me know he won't be home for dinner. Wanting to do something social, I suggest inviting Karen and Tom over, but he can't find the time.

After a shower one night, he flops down naked on the bed and opens the latest issue of *Scientific American* while I lie reading *Life Before Birth*. Absentmindedly he scratches his groin.

"Ras clot!" He springs from the bed and dashes to the bathroom. "Come look at this!"

I follow and see him leaning over, gazing at a tiny object on the edge of the sink.

"What is it?"

"Crabs!"

"Crabs?"

"Yeah. Crab lice. You never seen them?"

"No."

"I bet you got 'em, too. Lie down and let me see."

He parts my pubic hair and finds two. "My gosh! I cry. "Get them off me!"

He crushes them between his fingernails. "There's probably more. I'll have to get some powder from the pharmacy. We'll both use it for a few days."

"This is disgusting! Where do they come from?"

"I can't imagine. I haven't been with another woman. Tell the truth now, you been cheating on me?"

"Of course not!"

"Okay. I won't blame you. But we have to get rid of them. I just hope the pharmacy is still open." He's already getting dressed.

The next time I go to the pharmacy I surreptitiously peek into a pamphlet on sexually transmitted diseases. The description of crab lice cites genital contact as the *only* means of transmission. Hands trembling, I return the pamphlet to the rack and hurry out. So there's been someone else! Who? It doesn't matter. Face burning, I head homeward, dreading the thought of facing him. He already denied being with other women, so confronting him will amount to calling him a liar. First those condoms in the car, then the late nights at Colgate, now this... If I pretend not to know, he won't have a chance to explain. What I fear most is that he can't. I walk slowly, my mind flailing as I struggle to corral my stampeding feelings.

After dinner David surprises me by asking if I want to go along to Dougie and Marie's house where some of the crowd are gathering. My attempts to get into the conversation fall flat, so eventually I give up and resort to providing the cheering section during the men's lively stories and exchanges of insults. I notice an undercurrent of innuendoes about other women. Nothing definite, just allusions suggesting a certain amount of cheating is not only tolerated but expected. I want to ask Marie about it but can't find a way without sounding snoopy or embarrassing both of us. If

Dougie is cheating, she won't want to admit it any more than I want to divulge my suspicions.

On the way home David reproaches me for not trying harder to befriend Marie.

"I'm sorry, David. But she doesn't seem interested in anything I say."

"Maybe you should try harder to find out what interests her. Why not talk babies?"

"I'll try."

The next week, after several nights of sitting home alone, I call Marie and invite her to a movie. But she can't–something about one of the children being sick–so I decide to go alone. I change my clothes and call a taxi. Knowing David will be upset if he comes home and doesn't see me, I write a note to cover myself: "Hi, David. Dinner is on the stove. I've gone to a movie. See you later. Jac." I omit telling which theater or expected time of return. Let him stew!

When the taxi arrives, I hurry, heart racing, to the waiting car, intent on getting away before he comes home. So many nights I've fretted over where he is and what he's doing. Let him have a taste of the same poison.

Much as I've wanted to see *2001 The Space Odyssey,* it's hard to pay attention. My eyes keep watching other patrons coming and going. I can't rid myself of the thought that David has been looking forward to the film, too. What if he's here with someone else? What will I do? Confront him? Or be quiet and keep it secret that I've seen him? How will I be able to hold it inside and still act normal? My hands grow clammy. John Williams' deafening score demands my attention. I try to concentrate.

When I get home, David's car is in front of the garage. Except for the light on the verandah, the house is dark. I open and close the door cautiously and walk across the living room. Suddenly I stop. Someone is on the sofa!

"It's about time you got in."

I suck in my breath. "Oh! Hi. I was just—"

"Prowling around in the dark can be dangerous. You're lucky I don't have a gun. Get your ass in bed." He rises and opens the bedroom door. I follow, all systems on high alert.

At least he doesn't question me, but... I can't remember what I planned to say anyway. In the dark I remove my clothes. No sooner do I crawl into bed than he flings his arm across me and gropes my breast. Then he turns me onto my stomach and rolls on top, his erection pushing against my thighs. Spreading my legs, he jams into my crotch and enters so quickly it burns. Abruptly he withdraws, then presses between my buttocks. It hurts worse. I writhe, try to get away, rise to my knees. But he pins me down, forces against my anus. I scream, recoil in agony.

"Relax, and it won't hurt," he commands, pounding against my rigid flesh. I reach for the edge of the bed to pull myself away, but he grabs my arm, twists it behind my back. His knees force my legs apart and his groin pummels my backside. "Let me in!" demands the unrelenting voice of a stranger.

"Stop! Stop!" I wail as pain, unlike anything I've ever known, brings tears streaming from my eyes. My body can't possibly take in more, but he keeps pushing. The agony mounts beyond endurance until my muscles collapse amidst a paroxysm of shrieks.

"That's better," he rasps. Faster, harder he thrusts. Then he lets out a bellow that drowns my screams. Withdrawing, he kneels above me, his breath on my neck, panting. "How'd you like that?"

"It hurt," I sob, "a lot."

"If you'd relax, it wouldn't be so bad."

I curl up like a fetus, clutching the pillow, listening to his breathing until it sounds like he's asleep. Then I tiptoe to the bathroom. The rag I use to wash myself is bloody. I quiver, so sore I can barely move. How will I ever have another bowel movement? I only hope he hasn't hurt the baby.

IV

David never asks where I went that night, and I don't bring it up. He's had his revenge, and I don't owe him an explanation anyway, not after all his nights out. But by Friday, I'm weary of the tension between us. If we're going to have a family, we have to get past it. Maybe an extra-nice meal will show him I'm ready to make up. On the way to school I ask if he'll be home for dinner.

"I think so," he says, "as long as there aren't any problems at the flourmill. I'm testing new controls for the scale today."

In the afternoon as I walk home from the bus stop, I plan the menu: roasted leg of lamb with mint sauce, stuffed baked potatoes, steamed okra, Waldorf salad, and pineapple upside down cake. All his favorites.

By six-thirty everything is ready. I turn the oven low and take a shower. Then I dust my skin with jasmine-scented talcum and put on my new dashiki. David still isn't home, so I mix a light gin and tonic and turn on TV to catch the evening news. When it's over, he still hasn't come. Despite my hunger, I decide to watch one more show before eating. *MASH* gets me laughing while my ear stays tuned for the sound of his car. Just as the show finishes, the phone rings.

I pick it up, expecting David, but it's Dougie. "Sorry," I say, "I'm not sure when he'll be back. Can I take a message?"

"It's okay," Dougie replies. "Nothing important. Thanks."

I decide to wait no longer. Marching into the kitchen, I dish up my dinner. With *Time* opened beside me, I settle at the table to eat and read, trying to keep my mind off David. The food is delicious. His loss. But mine, too. No fun eating alone, especially after going to so much bother.

The phone again. I answer guardedly, not wanting to raise my hopes. The foreman at the flourmill is looking for David. An elevator isn't working. If David can't fix it tonight, he needs to be there first thing in the morning. I promise to tell him.

My hand trembles as I write down the messages and put them on the desk. I don't know whether to be angry or worried. Not with his friends, and not working. What then? Can he be in trouble? Or with someone? If only I didn't set myself up–I shouldn't have bothered to try to please him. Don't know if I'm more angry with myself or him.

As I put away the uneaten food and clean up the kitchen, I wonder what to say when he comes home. I'm too furious to trust what might come out. I don't even know who to be jealous of. That's the worst part–feeling something is going on, but not really knowing. His denials make me doubt my own self. Probably I should just focus on the dinner part. An awful queasy feeling hits when I remember what he did the night I stayed out late, but I push away the thought and go into the bedroom. Moments later he appears in the doorway. "Oh!" I gulp. "So you're *finally* home!"

"What do you mean, *finally?*" He comes toward me.

I smell liquor. "Dinner was ready hours ago, but you never even phoned. People kept calling, and I didn't know what to tell them. It's embarrassing not having a clue where you are or when you'll be back. You know how that makes *me* look?" As I move toward the bed the words leap out: "I hope you haven't picked up more crabs!"

His fist strikes the side of my face. I reel, fall onto the bed, too shocked even to cry out. When I try to raise myself on my elbows, he slugs me again. I taste blood. Arms protecting my head, I roll away.

"Don't ever speak to me like that again!" he roars. "I go and come whenever I please, and I don't need lip from you!" He storms out. The stereo in the living room comes on. Loud.

Bewildered, I huddle on the bed, afraid to move, my world spinning out of control. I cover my ears to block out the sound, but it does little good as his harmonica drowns out the lyrics of "A

112

Hard Days Night." The song takes on new meaning. I open my eyes, see the doors to the hallway and outside are both shut. But he didn't bolt the verandah door when he came in.

I get up, grab my shoes and handbag, creep outside, close the door softly.

Across the verandah I run, up the driveway, out the gate. Turning one corner after another, I zigzag, terrified he's following. Finally I pause beneath a tree to catch my breath, get my bearings. Chest heaving and throat burning, I cling to the trunk to hold myself up. Headlights appear. I crouch and move around the tree to stay concealed as the car passes.

Keeping close to hedges, I make my way to a corner where a dim streetlight barely illuminates the sign: King's Court. Dougie's neighborhood! At a loss for anywhere else to go, I continue, moving quickly to hide whenever I hear a car or see headlights. Aside from fearing David might be looking for me, I don't want a stranger stopping to offer a lift or to ask what a white woman is doing on the street in the middle of the night.

I hate to disturb Dougie and Marie so late, and I know approaching their place at this hour is sure to make the dogs cause a rumpus and rouse the whole neighborhood. Then I see a phone booth at a bus stop and drop in a coin. After the fourth ring, a female voice says, "Hello?"

"Marie? This is Jac. I'm sorry to call so late."

"No problem. What's up?"

"I'm in a little trouble and need your help. May I come over?"

"Sure, but what's going on?"

"I'm nearby. It won't take me long. I'll explain when I get there."

"Okay. I'll be at the front door to keep the dogs quiet."

Clutching a robe around her slim frame, Marie opens the door and leads me to the kitchen. She pulls out a chair, brushes back a tendril of brown hair, and motions me to sit. "Now, what's happening?" she says as she turns to fill a kettle.

I sink onto the chair and lay my head on the table. After catching my breath, I look up. "David hit me. Twice. And I ran out."

"The jerk! Are you okay?"

"I think so." I touch my face, wondering if there are marks. "I just ran."

"Has he ever hit you before?"

"No. He shoved me once, but this time he really slugged me. And I'm pregnant."

"I know. He told us last time he was here. He was on cloud nine. How do you feel about it?"

"I was glad, at first. We've been trying for quite a while, and I thought we were ready. Now this happens ... I don't know. I don't just want a baby; I want a family, a happy family."

"Don't we all," she says wryly while pouring hot water into the waiting teapot. "Does he know where you are?"

"No, he doesn't even know I left. He was listening to music in the living room."

She fills two cups and sits at the table. "Dougie hit me once. I'll never forget it...or let him forget. I walked out on him, too, and didn't go back for a week. Stayed with my sister. He came over to apologize and take me back, but I wouldn't go."

"Really?" I'm shocked. "When was that?"

"After Lisa was born, and before I got pregnant with Lexi. I took Lisa with me, so of course it hurt him a lot 'cause he was crazy about his baby girl."

"What happened? I mean, obviously you went back. Why?"

"Well, he kept apologizing and saying he'd never do it again. I held out for awhile, but he called every day and sounded so sincere. I didn't think I had the right to keep him away from his child forever, so after he suffered for a week, I agreed to return, on certain conditions: He had to tell my father what happened and promise him he'd never hit me again. That was hard, but he did it. I still held out until he also agreed to get me a new car, new bedroom set, and full-time nanny."

"Did he?"

"I wouldn't be here now if he hadn't." Her voice is cold, matter-of-fact. "You have to teach these men how to behave. Their mothers didn't." She rises. "Come now. I'll make up a cot for you in the children's room. We can talk more in the morning."

V

I stay in bed and pretend to sleep until the children are dressed. When I get up only Marie is home. Over coffee she asks about my plans, and while I struggle to put together an answer, the phone rings. She answers, listens for a moment, says "um hum" a couple of times, and then "Hold on a minute." Pressing her hand over the receiver, she whispers, "It's David. He wants to speak with you."

I sigh and nod as she hands me the phone. "Hello."

"What a relief to find you! I've been so worried! Look, I'm really sorry about last night. We've got to talk. I'll be right over." *Click.*

I put down the phone and look at Marie. "He's coming over. Says he's sorry and wants to talk. But even if he promises it won't happen again, how can I be sure? My father's not here to hold him to any agreements. Maybe I should report this to the police."

Her laugh is bitter. "You gotta be kidding! This is Jamaica, Sweetheart. You're living with the guy, so it's a domestic squabble. Police won't get involved. No law against a man hitting his wife."

"There's not?"

"No. Why not listen to what he has to say before you make up your mind?"

"Okay." I take a determined deep breath. "I'll try."

She brushes my hair back to examine my face. "Your cheek's swollen, and there's a cut on your lip."

115

I nod.

"And your eye. It'll be really black in a couple of days."

"Oh no! I've got to go to work."

"You'll have to make up a story and wear dark glasses. You can stay here as long as you want. If you need to get some of your stuff, I can drive you over later. Decide after you talk to him. Now I have to pick up the girls from their grandmother's and go to the store. That'll give you time to talk. I'll be back in an hour or so."

"Thanks for everything. Helps to know you've been through this and worked it out."

"More or less." She flashes a sardonic grin. "Good luck. You'll need it."

When David arrives, I open the door reluctantly.

"Let's go," he says.

"I thought you wanted to talk."

"I do, but not here."

"Here is fine. Marie's gone out, and I haven't seen Dougie." My hand grasps the doorknob.

He shrugs. "Have it your way." He flops down on the sofa and tosses his keys on the cushion beside him. "This is fine. No problem."

I close the door and sit on the chair opposite him.

"I'm sorry about the way I went off last night. When you brought up the crabs, I got mad. I mean, I thought it was all settled. But you threw it in my face like you never believed me. I told you months ago, before you got pregnant, it's absolutely essential that we trust each other."

"I've tried, David, but I never know where you are, and when you say one thing, then do another. I mean, like last night, you said you'd be home for dinner, but ..."

"Sometimes it's impossible for me to get to a phone. Do you really expect me to call you when I'm up on a ladder thirty feet in the air working with two hundred and forty volts of live electricity

116

and I'm hurrying like hell to try to get done because it's about to rain and I..."

"The flourmill called looking for you. You weren't there."

"That's a lie! I was there the whole time. Goddamned foreman... doesn't know his head from his ass! Like I said before, we have to trust each other. Trust means believing, even when appearances look otherwise. Sort of like religion. Might be asking a lot, but it's necessary in any relationship–business, marriage, parenting, even between teacher and student."

"David, will you promise never to hit me again?"

He nods. "I promise."

I don't move. I expected defiance and resistance, not a sincere apology.

"Now can we go home?"

Still, I hesitate, try to remember the details of Marie's advice. But he rises and holds out his hand. "Come on now. I won't hurt you. I love you."

I take his hand and stand.

"It was nice of Marie to take you in, but you can't go on being a nuisance here." He opens the door.

I pick up my purse and follow him to the car. He opens the door and I slide in. But as he's backing out he says, "You really embarrassed me! Running over to my friend's house in the middle of the night. I wonder how many lies you told them. How can I face anybody now? Everyone will be talking!"

"What?"

"You'll have to do some explaining to Marie, so they'll realize it was a misunderstanding ... just you getting hysterical. Make an excuse about how on edge you are 'cause you're pregnant or something."

"David, I–"

"You have to stop being such a dumb ass baby. You weren't in any danger."

"You hit me!"

"Shut up! Okay? Can you? My head's aching from all your whining."

We drive the rest of the way in silence. When we get home, he says, "Get me some aspirin. After what you've put me through, I need a handful."

My hand shakes as I open the medicine cabinet and reach for the bottle. I give it to him with a glass of water.

"You don't realize who I am," he says. "You don't understand me or pay attention to my needs. You stay in your protected little shell at school and here in the house, but don't have a clue what I go through out in the real world, busting my ass to make this business go. Worrying about bills. Working all hours of the day and night. And what do I get when I come home? Nagging! You don't appreciate my trying to get ahead so you won't have to work when the baby's born. All the responsibility on me, all the time. When will you grow up and act like an adult, instead of bitching about what time I get in? I can't believe how you carry on!"

"I understand how hard you work, and I'm amazed at how well the business is going. It's really great! But you are *not* to hit me again."

"I told you, I won't! Listen—" he steps closer. "This world's bigger and a lot more complex than you can imagine. I have a lot to offer the whole planet, much more than this little business. My inventions could be the answer to the coming energy crisis. But I have to work on them more. I *can't* let you upset me all the time. I wanted to build a new model today, but you're not letting me get anything done. Things can't go on like this." He finishes the water. "God, this headache!" He presses his temple and squeezes his eyes shut. After a moment he looks at me. "You used to believe in me, but now I'm not sure..."

"I do want you to succeed. I really do. That hasn't changed."

"In order to create, I need peace and freedom. And from you I need trust. Always have. Don't try to tie me up. Ever! You understand?"

I nod.

He takes my hand. "You've got to realize, I'm not doing this just for myself. It's for you, too. For our children. For the future. For the whole world. If only I can get this invention to work, it will change *everything*. You have no idea how big it is."

"Probably not, but I believe it's important." He's right. I have lost sight of the bigger picture, of why I love him so much–his caring about more than the mundane things that occupy other people day in and day out. I feel ashamed for being so petty. "I'm sorry, David."

He looks at me pensively. "Better call Marie; tell her it was a misunderstanding."

"All right."

Marie listens to my explanation about David being overworked and how my nagging set him off, and that he promises never to hit me again. Even before we finish talking, I hear him call my name. I thank her, hang up, and go to our room. He's lying on the bed. Naked.

"My head's better now," he says. "Come rest with me."

I leave space between us, but he moves nearer and kisses me, first tenderly, then more urgently, but still trying to please me. The sweet relief of forgiveness.

VI

When I look in the mirror Monday morning my eye has bloomed in shades of purple, green and wine, with a hint of mustard around the edges. Makeup is useless. I have to call in sick. I sit staring at my battered reflection. I'll miss a day of work, maybe more, because he hit me! I'll have to wear dark glasses, and lie! Make up a stupid story about walking into a lurking door or something.

David peeks into the room. "See you later, Honey. I'm off to the flour mill."

119

"Okay. Bye." I listen to his car pull out of the driveway. Is this to be my life–black eyes and lies? With Alex, all I had to worry about were his affairs. At least he hadn't kept me in the dark about them. And I was never afraid of him. Repulsed, yes, but not afraid. Maybe I should call him. By now the counseling should have helped. He might listen to me, give an honest response. I get up and make the bed while rehearsing a conversation, but no matter how I put it, my situation sounds appalling. I visualize a scenario in which Alex, glad to hear from me, expresses undying love and begs me to return. Finally I abandon all pride and dial his number. He answers straightaway.

"Alex." I hesitate before forging ahead. "It's Jacqueline. How are you?"

After a pause he says icily, "What do *you* want?"

"I... I'm in trouble and don't know what to do."

"What kind of trouble?"

"Well, I'm still with David and I'm teaching school. We moved into a nice house, so all that's fine. We decided to have a family, and I got pregnant. But a couple days ago, he... he hit me. I have a swollen lip and black eye, and can't go to work. And I, I can't stop worrying he might do it again. I never know what to expect or how he'll react."

"Oh, gee, poor Jackie!"

"Alex, please! I need your advice."

"A little late for that, isn't it? I told you not to go away with the creep in the first place! But you wouldn't listen."

"I know, but–"

"I can't believe it! You run off with another man. Get pregnant with his baby while we're still married, and now when he hits you, you come whining to me!"

He's so right. "I don't blame you for being mad."

"Mad? Me mad? You're the one who's mad! Must be absolutely insane!"

"Alex, I–"

"I'm sorry for you, but there's nothing I can do. You got yourself into this; you'll have to get yourself out. Don't call me again."

A click. Then silence.

"Okay, Alex, I won't," I whisper into the dead phone and replace the receiver. Such bitterness! Then the tears come. I cry until my throat aches. He can't help me. No one can. I'm alone. Should I leave? Get out of Jamaica before this goes any further? Once the baby is born, David will never let us go.

VII

After agonizing for hours, I call Karen and listen to her report on happenings at school. Finally I get to the point. "The reason I wasn't there today is David and I had a fight, pretty bad one. This whole thing about having a baby might be a mistake. Do you know anything about getting abortions here?"

"Oh, my God! What happened?"

"I can't go into details right now. Maybe I'm over-reacting, but I just need to know my options."

"Okay. No pressure. I'm sorry to hear you're having such a rough time, but I'm glad you called. Actually I know of a doctor who does them. Hold on a minute while I look for the number." In a moment she's back with it. "Give his office a call and make an appointment. If you want company, I'll go with you. Okay?"

"Thanks, Karen. Thanks so much."

I manage to schedule a visit before the end of the week. While Karen drives me over after school I get her promise not to tell anybody else.

"Don't worry. Your secret's safe with me."

"You're a good friend." I squeeze her hand.

As we approach the medical area, I say, "Just drop me off in front of the building. I can catch a bus home. And listen, I really appreciate your help. Thanks again."

The doctor says, "You appear to be at least four months along, maybe more. We don't do abortions after the first trimester. So it's too late to consider termination."

Stupefied, I stare at my clenched fists.

Then he's standing in front of me, hand outstretched. "I'm sorry we're not able to help, but you are perfectly healthy and should have no trouble carrying this pregnancy to full term. Don't hesitate to call if I can be of further service."

Tears welling, I rush from the office. In wilting heat I wander through a shrub-filled labyrinth amongst medical buildings. Hummingbirds and bees dart and buzz around me. Mockingbirds perch overhead taunting their foolishness. A red-headed John crow swoops low, scouting carrion.

As homeward-bound workers hurry past, I slump onto a bench and sit; have no idea for how long. Gradually a feeling of peace creeps over me, and thoughts of the future begin taking shape. I'll accept the consequences, whatever they might be, of getting pregnant and making that promise. No more wavering. Only our baby matters now. Not my selfish concerns. The baby is the most important thing in my life. The doctor says I'm perfectly capable of carrying it full term. I'll do whatever's necessary to bear it and to be the best mother in the world. So what if David isn't perfect? He's my baby's father. I'll make the best of it, like Marie and all the others. I'm a woman now. Time to give up romantic illusions.

I stand and head toward the bus stop. This is my life, for better or for worse.

Kingston, 1970

I

"You're puffing up like a porcupine fish," David observes as I come out of the shower.

"I know." I admire my bulging abdomen in the mirror. "I should switch to maternity clothes, but I don't have the time to make anything."

"Hmmm." He eyes me momentarily. "Oh, just so you know, I'll be getting home a little late tonight."

At least he warned me, so after school I go shopping instead of rushing home to cook. I find a pattern for a mini-length tent dress and buy cloth for two different versions: one piece of peach-colored airy chiffon, and another soft multi-colored paisley fabric. I'm cutting out pieces of the chiffon when David walks in.

"Oh!" I look up. "You're home already. I didn't fix any dinner."

"Don't worry about it. There's probably something leftover in the fridge." He hugs me from behind and kisses my neck. "You look busy."

"Mm hmm. Racing with mother nature."

"Can you take a break? I've got some stuff to unload from the car and it would help if you could hold the doors open."

"Okay, I'll be right there." Still tingling from his kiss, I put on my sandals and follow him outside.

He is untying a rope that holds his trunk lid down. When it pops open, I gasp. "A sewing machine!"

"Like it?"

"Yes! It's just like my mother's! Almost identical to the one I learned to sew on. That was a Singer, too!" I throw my arms around him. "It's the best gift you could give me!"

I make dresses, then curtains for the nursery and a matching cushion for the rocking chair. David paints the walls sunshine yellow, and I put a fresh coat of white paint on the used furniture. Whenever I need a break, I sit in the chair and dream of rocking our baby. Not knowing if it's a girl or a boy makes it all the more exciting. The larger I get, the more I fall in love with the person inside me.

I think Dr. Spock's *Baby and Child Care* offers good advice, but David has his own ideas about birthing and babies. When I read him a passage about weaning, he scoffs, "Follow everything Spock says, and you're going to have one spoiled kid." I can't imagine a cold-turkey approach, but don't pursue it. Time for that later.

"But," he says, "we should start practicing if you want me to hypnotize you for the delivery."

"Okay. When can we start?" Since reading about breathing exercises for different stages of labor in Kitzinger's *Experience of Childbirth* I've been thinking they'd go well with hypnotism, but I wanted him to offer.

"Too late tonight; maybe next week."

During the month we interview several obstetricians and choose Dr. Hall who welcomes the presence of fathers and is willing to try hypnosis instead of sedatives.

Determined as I am to put all my effort into building a family without any more game playing, I still hate it when David isn't home by midnight. I go to bed, filled with dread that he's with someone, and the night drags as I keep waking, looking at the clock, wondering. But when he finally comes in, I always pretend to be asleep.

At least he stays home more on weeknights. He works on his invention for long periods and sometimes asks for my help. I turn switches and faucets on and off, hold pieces of copper in a vise-grip while he solders them, and search through boxes for electronic parts. I even try to read a book about electricity but can't understand it. After struggling halfway through, I give up, figuring it's enough just to know the names of a few tools and parts.

My swollen ankles and legs become so uncomfortable that it's difficult to get around at school, so I quit in my sixth month and put all my energy into preparing for the baby. Marie gives me a slew of information, but I keep thinking about my mother. If only I could share my joy with her and Dad. However, not wanting to deal with her hysteria, I've decided to wait until after the delivery before telling them.

During a routine exam Dr. Hall discovers I've lost weight. He says the baby is overdue and labor will have to be induced immediately.

"But I want to have a natural birth!" What would Kitzinger think?

"It's not safe to wait any longer. The oxygen supply in the placenta shrinks rapidly after a baby reaches full term."

"Will you have to use drugs?"

"Usually one injection of Pitocin is all it takes. If labor doesn't start then, we can break your water, but I doubt that'll be necessary. Be in the maternity ward at four."

Once I'm in the labor ward, time stops. Every sound, smell, movement and feeling is magnified. David stays at my side feeding me lemon drops and reading aloud from *Myra Breckenridge*, the paperback I tucked into my bag. As my contractions become more frequent and intense, he sets the book aside.

Speaking softly, he puts me into a trance that lets me rest between the powerful rushes. With his reminders to keep my breathing light as a hummingbird's, I manage to rise above the pain most of the time. But when a gigantic onslaught crashes against my pelvis like a tsunami striking a beach, I know the baby has control. All I can do is surrender. Amidst the clamor of nurses and the smell of disinfectants, David holds my hand as I'm wheeled into the glaring light of the delivery room. Just before midnight the climax comes to the most thrilling experience of my life: our son's first cry.

II

It's all new: first time in a hospital, first child, first attempt to breastfeed. I have a private room and excellent nursing care, including instruction on bathing the baby, changing diapers, and tending to his navel. I don't get much rest and am exhausted when David arrives the next night carrying flowers and camera. He snaps pictures from every conceivable angle, then sits and holds his son, cooing and kissing him.

When the baby cries, David passes him to me. "Hey, guess what I got for you," he beams.

"What?"

"A washing machine."

"You did!"

"And I hired a maid. Betty's just a day worker. She'll come to clean, cook and do laundry during the week. But we'll be alone nights and weekends."

"You're pampering me."

"Believe me, it'll take all your energy just to look after the baby and do the company paperwork."

The second night David rushes into my room just before visiting hours end. "Sorry I'm late." He kisses my cheek and our son's head. "Had a breakdown at the record studio, but everything's up and running again."

Moments later the head nurse peeps through the door to inform him it's time to leave. "But I just got here," he protests. I'm not bothering anybody."

"I'm sorry, Sir. Rules are rules. After nine we dim the lights and keep it quiet."

"Okay, mum's the word," he crosses his lips with his finger. "I won't make any noise, and won't tell a soul if you just pretend you didn't see me here. Okay?"

"Not at all. We have sick women who need rest."

"We're not disturbing them. This is a private room."

"Same rules for everybody."

"Convenient for you, treating everybody the same. Then you don't have to bother to think!" His voice has risen.

I cringe, clutching the baby, fearing the noise will waken the whole ward. The stout nurse glares silently over her prodigious bosom.

"Okay. I'll leave," he relents, "but I'm not putting up with this another night. Tomorrow I'm taking my son home."

"Well, Sir, you'll have to see if the doctor's ready to release them."

"Like hell I will! I'll be here first thing in the morning, and there's nothing you can do about it!" He turns to me. "Be ready to leave early."

"Okay," I murmur, rocking the baby.

I'm still breastfeeding the next morning when David enters. "Why aren't you ready?"

"He's not sucking, and the nurses have been in and out of here constantly..."

"I can't wait all day. I've got work to do."

Hastily I wrap our son in a blanket, throw my belongings into bags, and follow David through the ward. As we pass the front desk, the nurse hollers, "Wait! I don't have release papers."

Without breaking stride, David calls over his shoulder, "We don't need them. Everybody is fine. You have our address to send the bill."

At home, David helps me out of the car and into the bedroom. He uses another roll of film getting shots of the baby lying on the bed and gazing around his new abode. When he starts crying, I try to feed him, but my nipple won't stay in his mouth. David watches apprehensively. "I can see this is going to take a while." He looks at his watch. "I better get going. Got work to do at the cement plant."

Betty arrives next morning and explains she will come five days a week. "Doan fret 'bout nuttin' 'cept lookin' after yuh pickney. When ya wants anyting, jes holla."

Aside from all the work she does, I like having Betty there, crooning soft melodies as she shuffles around the house in her broken-down loafers. Hopefully she will use her first paycheck to buy new shoes.

Marie comes to visit and answers my barrage of questions, assuring me the baby is perfect in every way. I start an exercise routine to get my body back into bikini shape and attack the backlog of company paperwork. Looking after the pickney, I discover, is indeed plenty. I try to nap while he sleeps, but never get enough rest. Perpetually tired, I'm not much company for David.

Everyone wants to know the baby's name, but it takes awhile for us to decide. Searching for something that fits, I pick a different one each day: Aquarius, Jude, Jason, Michael, Solomon, Emanuel, Julius, Anthony. Some names get reruns. When I try Jonathan, we both like it and decide to make it official: Jonathan David.

Jonathan is about three months old when David arrives home at midday and pokes his head into the nursery while I'm changing his diaper. "As soon as you finish, get Betty to look after him and come outside. Got a surprise."

A small blue Cortina is parked in the driveway. "All yours," David says. "It has a few scratches, but runs well and is economical. Perfect for shopping and errands."

"David! Are you sure we can afford it?"

"We can't afford *not* to. Take a test drive. If you don't like it, we won't keep it. Needs new tires pretty soon, but you should get a few thousand miles out of these."

It's perfect. Excited about my new freedom, I buy an infant seat so I can take Jonathan when I go out.

"Hello, my dear!" Precious bubbles when I answer the phone on a Saturday morning. "Sorry to trouble you, but we just heard we have another grandson. We're so pleased! Congratulations to you both! How are you doing?"

"Fine. We're fine. It's been so long... How've you been?"

"Very well, thank you. I bought something for the baby and wonder if we can drop it off. We're dying to see the dear little boy. I hope you don't mind."

"Not at all. I'd love to see you!" I regret having lost touch with them. Despite David's criticisms, I can't help liking his mother, but I haven't contacted her for fear of his disapproval. Maybe now I'll have a chance to get to know her better.

"How would it be if we stop by today?"

"Great! But hold on a minute while I check to see if David will be home."

I find him in his workshop. He seems indifferent to the call and says he has to go out. I explain to Precious, "David has to do some work today and isn't sure what time he'll get back. But I'll be here with Jonathan, so you can come anytime."

"Splendid! We'll drive down this morning. Now don't go to any fuss. We'll just stop by for a few minutes."

I'm rushing around to bathe and dress Jonathan and make limeade when David says, "So they found out. I was wondering how long it would take. My cousin Michael probably told them. I ran into him when I was having lunch in New Kingston the other day. Figured he'd pass the news. I don't mind them seeing their grandson, but I don't want any part of it. I'm going to the record company. You can handle them, I'm sure."

When they arrive, Jonathan is asleep in his pram. Precious insists he not be wakened. They just peep at him and marvel at how beautiful and chubby and healthy he looks. Then Precious draws a gaily-wrapped package from her bag. "Just a little something for our grandson. I hope he can get good use of it. Sorry it's such a small thing, but it was only yesterday we heard, and we didn't want to come empty-handed."

She has a way of talking without paragraphs, never leaving an opening between thoughts, but eventually I manage to get them to sit on the verandah where I serve drinks, and Jimmy asks about David's business. As soon as I open the box containing pajamas and shirts, they hurry off, as though they had agreed beforehand exactly how many minutes their visit would last.

III

After months of testing and adjusting, David feels his invention is ready for patenting. But first he has to search the U. S. Patent Office files to determine if such a device is already registered. Confident none is, he decides to go to Washington and do it himself.

During David's absence Jonathan becomes fussier, especially at his evening feeding. He keeps spitting up and screaming. I try everything I can think of to soothe him, but nothing makes any difference. One evening when he's howling with his back arched I notice lumps in his abdomen. Immediately I call Marie. "He's in such agony. I'm afraid he might have appendicitis. Or maybe he's allergic to my milk!"

"Sounds like gripe," she says. "Give him gripe water."

"What's that, and where do I get it?"

"Any pharmacy. Sorry I didn't tell you about it before, but I didn't know he was having problems. Some babies get it, and others don't. If you look in your Spock book, you'll find it's called colic."

"Oh, I've heard of that. I'll look it up. But right now I'm going to the pharmacy. Thanks!"

The gripe water seems to help. At least, it relieves my anxiety, and he doesn't spit up so much.

When David returns he sees the patting, burping, jiggling, rocking and gripe water routine that has become part of Jonathan's evening feeding. "You're spoiling him!" he explodes. "Good God, I go away for ten days and the kid takes control! Just put him in bed until he shuts up."

"I can't! He's in pain! All the gas—"

"Give him to me!"

"No!" I turn away, rush to the nursery, put Jonathan in the crib, and pat his back, trying to get him to relax. Then I leave, closing the door. As I dish up food for dinner, he's still wailing. But I sit down with David anyway and try to eat.

After a few bites, David slams his fork and knife on the table. "This is ridiculous! If he wants to cry, I'll give him something to cry about." He gets up, grabs a newspaper and rolls it into a rod. Opening the door he commands, "Quiet now. Hear me? Be quiet!" Jonathan keeps crying. "All right, tough guy, you asked for it." *Whack! Whack!*

"Stop!" I rush in.

"Get out!" He pushes me into the kitchen and closes the door behind us. "Let him think about that for awhile." He looks at me. "Whatsamatter? You got a problem?"

"He cries because he's in pain. It's how babies let us know what they need!"

"Nonsense! Your holding and patting is spoiling him. If he's been fed and changed, there's no reason to cry. It's your fault, but he's the one who has to suffer until I can teach him not to cry."

"But babies cry for other reasons besides hunger and wet pants. What if he—"

"It's all part of living. A father's job is to make his kid tough, teach him discipline. But it doesn't help when you treat him like a mama's boy. Listen. He's still at it." He grasps the newspaper and opens the door.

When I hear the first *whack!* I dash in. "Stop, David! Please!"

As Jonathan howls, I reach for him, but David punches my arm. When he hits Jonathan again I try to snatch the paper, but he whirls around and grabs my hair. "You better learn to have some respect!" he snarls and rams my head against the wall. Then he pushes me out of the room and slams the door.

The knob won't turn so I pound. "Open up!" Jonathan is still crying, but I don't hear any more whacks. The hitting seems to have stopped, so I retreat to the bathroom. One look in the mirror makes me gag. Blood is smeared around a cut above my left eye and my cheekbone is puffy. When I touch my head a handful of hair falls out. I sit on the commode, shaking as I press a wet cloth against my stinging eye. I think of calling the police, but Marie's warning comes back. Probably no law against spanking children either. My head throbs.

David bangs on the bathroom door. "Enough moping. Get out here and clean up the kitchen."

I wait until Jonathan is quiet before opening the door. Without looking at David, I proceed to clear the table.

"You see," David says, "he's starting to learn. It wouldn't take so long if you hadn't spoiled him when I was away. If you think I like hitting him, you're wrong. But it's my duty to teach him. Don't get in my way again. Just makes it harder for everybody."

"He's only four months old!"

"There's no such thing as too young for discipline. If children learn to behave the wrong way, eventually they have to unlearn it. Easier to do it right to start with. Just do as I say," he glares. Then he turns and heads for his workshop.

Much as I try to follow David's method, he accuses me of being inconsistent and blames me for confusing Jonathan. I'm constantly on edge, afraid he'll launch another discipline routine. I need to talk to somebody, but can't bring it up with Marie because David might find out. Then he says something so bizarre that I can't contain myself. I call Karen, and she agrees to meet after school the next day.

IV

I pick her up at the gate and we chat about my "new" car as I drive to a secluded *cul de sac*. After parking, I say, "I know so little about babies that I don't trust my own judgment with Jonathan. David thinks he knows it all because of his other children. It's hard to argue when I'm so unsure of myself."

"I know what you mean. That's why I don't say much about Tom's kids. After all, I'm not a *real* mother," Karen says ruefully.

"This is hard to talk about. I'm so mixed up. But I've got to tell someone."

"Take your time."

"David, he... he hits Jonathan to teach him not to cry."

"What! What's wrong with the man? You can't let him get away with that!"

"It gets worse," my voice breaks. I swallow hard and continue. "A couple days ago he said it's time to train Jonathan to stay home alone so we can go out at night."

"That's crazy!" Karen hands me a tissue. "He's not fit to be a father!"

I wipe my eyes and take a deep breath. "He says I spoil Jonathan, but I'm always afraid of David hitting him so my tension probably makes him even fussier."

"Jonathan's only six months old for God's sake! Babies need love."

"I agree. But David thinks discipline is more important than anything else. He gets in such a rage sometimes ... I don't know where all his anger comes from."

"Who cares. This has to stop! He's taking advantage of you being all alone in Jamaica. He could never get away with this if you had family here. Have you asked them for help?"

I shake my head. "We're not close. I write occasionally, but not about David hitting us. They already think I'm headed straight for hell because I don't go to church and we're not married. Having a baby must be the last straw as far as they're concerned. If I tell them about this, they'll probably say it's what I deserve."

"Maybe you should give them a chance; their grandson is involved now."

"But what can they do?"

"If he knows you're talking with them, he might be more careful."

"It's worth a try. Maybe I could say they're planning to visit us."

"Don't underestimate him," Karen cautions. "It sounds like he has a serious problem. I'm afraid you and Jonathan could be in real danger. Have you thought about leaving?"

"Sometimes. Especially when he hits Jonathan." I press my lips together to stop the trembling; then I continue barely above a whisper. "I hate him so much then. But before I got pregnant he said he couldn't stand to lose any more children, and made me promise I would never take his child away."

"Obviously he doesn't learn from his mistakes. Should Jonathan suffer because of your promise?"

I shake my head. "But I don't have the right to deprive him of knowing his father."

"You don't have the right to let your son be abused!"

My face burns with shame. I can't argue. "Thanks for listening. You've given me a lot to think about, but I have to go. Jonathan must be awake. I'll drive you home."

At Karen's yard her parting words are: "Call me if he ever hits you or Jonathan again. And don't leave your baby alone. Ever! If he wants to go out, I'll baby sit. Promise?"

"Okay." I try to look convincing. "Thanks for listening."

V

I feel guilty about washing our linen in public, as though I've betrayed David. Karen can never understand why I stay with him. She wouldn't think his generosity, the potential of his invention, or our shared passion to make the world a better place could justify the abuse of Jonathan, not for one minute. And of course, she's right. I follow her suggestion and write to my parents, trying to avoid the usual points of contention.

Dear Mother and Dad,

I hope this letter finds you healthy and happy and enjoying a good harvest. When it's over maybe you can get away from the farm for awhile and come to Jamaica to see your new grandson. I'm sending a few pictures. He can already roll over by himself so I have to watch him all the time. I'm so glad he's finally sleeping through the night now! Our business is doing great and David hired two new technicians. It keeps me busy with all the paperwork. David bought me a car, so I can take Jonathan along when I go shopping and do errands. The maid we had at first didn't work out, but now I'm training a new one. She has good references and we're hoping she'll do better. Time will tell. David always says, "A new broom sweeps clean, but an old one knows the corners." I guess we'll always have to be vigilant. Tell everybody "hello" for me. And remember, now you have a place to go when you want to escape the winter. Let me know when you can come. David wants to meet you, and I'm sure you can't wait to see Jonathan.

Love, Jacqueline

I enclose snapshots and seal the letter. They aren't likely to come, but I hope the invitation will encourage them to acknowledge Jonathan as their grandson. When I tell David they might be visiting us, he says, "Fine."

After he starts crawling, Jonathan is constantly on the verge of pulling things over or grabbing something breakable, but David insists we not childproof the house. I fear he'll hurt himself or break a lamp or vase, but David says to leave everything where it is because kids have to learn what they may and may not touch. He demonstrates when Jonathan reaches for a glass on the coffee table. "Watch this," he says and smacks his tiny hand. "He won't forget that!" But the resulting shrieks upset him, so he picks up Jonathan, throws him into his crib, and closes the door. When the crying doesn't cease within the minute, David goes back clutching his rolled newspaper. I pray for Jonathan to be quiet.

Teething makes him even fussier, but he'll have no part of the pacifier or teething ring. I try to orchestrate his schedule to have him fed, changed, and tired by dinnertime, all ready to plop into bed when David gets home or before. His late arrivals no longer bother me. The later the better.

As Christmas nears, David says, "We won't be getting many service calls during the holidays, so it's a good time for a vacation. Let's we go camping out at Negril."

"Camping? With Jonathan?"

"Yeah. Negril's the best beach on the island. We can take the tent and snorkeling gear. It'll be good to just get away and relax."

I picture it: watching Jonathan every moment to protect him from mosquitoes, flies, ants, water, sun ... all the outdoor perils. No refrigerator, no maid to help. "Okay," I say.

When David arrives home the next evening, Jonathan is sitting in his high chair while I coax the last spoonful of pureed vegetables into his mouth. I wipe his hands and face and settle him in his walker so he can wheel around the house on his own. Soon I have dinner on the table and we sit down. David is dishing up the curried goat and rice when Jonathan rolls over to me, arms outstretched, whining. I dare not pick him up, so instead I dash to the refrigerator, grab his chilled teething ring from the freezer and try to get him to bite on it as I guide his walker into the living room. "I hope that helps," I say as I return to the table. "His gums have really been hurting today, and I think he has a fever."

Not about to be mollified so easily, Jonathan flings the ring away and howls in outrage. I jump up, grab him and march resolutely toward his room, picking up a bottle of honey water on the way. I lay him in the crib, put the nipple in his mouth, and hurry out to rejoin David. Within moments his cries resume.

"Jesus Christ!" David pounds the table. "You can't even keep the kid quiet long enough for me to eat my dinner! You think I work all day to come home to this!"

"I'm sorry, David, but try to understand how painful teething is. He hurts, and he doesn't know why."

"Listen here. Get that ras clot baby to shut up *now*, or I'll go in and do it myself. If he goes on like this at Negril and tries to ruin my vacation, God help me, I'll kill him!"

I rush into the nursery, crush a baby aspirin in Jonathan's tiny spoon, and dissolve it with water. Sitting on the rocker, I cradle him and slip the spoon into his mouth. He swallows the aspirin and sucks on the bottle as I rock and wonder how I'll ever manage such a situation on the beach. Before it's empty, he drifts off. I put him in the crib and return to the dining room, but David has already gone to his workshop.

As I clear the table my mind keeps replaying the words, *If he tries to ruin my vacation ... I'll kill him!* I picture us at the beach: no one I know for miles around, no phones, no doctor. What if Jonathan runs a high fever from teething, or gets sick from mosquito bites? So much Dengue fever recently. What if it rains? Judging by his behavior at home, there's a hundred percent probability of Jonathan fussing. It'll be interpreted as *ruining* David's vacation. And then, I can't imagine...

While it's still early I tell David I'm tired, take a shower and get into bed. But I can't sleep with visions of Christmas tragedy crowding my head. It's only a week away. Jonathan's teething could be worse then. The trip feels like a disaster without brakes hurtling our way.

VI

After David leaves the next morning, I make three phone calls, go to the bank, and pack two suitcases. I put them in my car, buckle Jonathan into his seat, and tell the maid we're going out. Within a half hour, I have dropped off the luggage and parked in the long-term lot at the airport. On the seat I leave a hastily-written note.

David,
I can't stay and let you harm Jonathan any more. By the time you see this, I'll be a long way from Jamaica. I'm sorry I can't keep my promise, but when you threatened to

kill him at the beach, I had no choice. I have no idea what
the future holds, but at least Jonathan is safe.

Jacqueline

When the plane takes off Jonathan is already asleep in my
arms. I look out the window as the Palisadoes peninsula, Kingston
Harbor, and the Jamaican shoreline quickly shrink and disappear
beneath clouds. Then I close my eyes, breathe deeply, and for the
first time in months, begin to relax. Once I made the decision to
leave, it was unbelievably easy. Now I can use my own judgment
and take responsibility for my son's well-being. No more Big Daddy
looking over my shoulder, criticizing every move. No more
withholding affection, denying love.

Iowa, 1970

I

Wispy snowflakes fall on piles of ice and grimy slush lining the runways at O'Hare. Nothing to look at but unrelenting bleakness while I await our connecting flight. The thought of where we'll be by nightfall makes me shiver. Air so frigid we can see our breath, icy roads, snow blanketing the ground and heaped in mini mountains which won't thaw until spring... I nuzzle the warm chubby cheek of my cherub and wrap the blanket more tightly around him.

Images of the yard we left in the morning still fill my mind's eye: hedge of magenta-colored bougainvillea and blazing red poinsettias bordered by white Queen Anne's lace. There'll be no more walks with Jonathan in his pram, soaking up the sunshine. And we might never again see coconut trees or play in sand at the seaside. I dread what lies ahead: cooped up inside for days and months; bundling in heavy clothing for every venture outdoors; chapped skin cracked by dry furnace heat. But Jonathan will be safe.

Christmas in Iowa is not exactly at the top of my wish list, but I'm in no position to be choosey. I'm grateful that Mother has promised to bring blankets and winter clothing to the airport. And what else? Will she treat me as an adult? Respect my decisions on raising my son? She's sure to be loading up on nerve pills. Won't be easy for any of us. I sigh. Beyond the tall windows in front of me, the sun, obscured by gray haze, looks tiny, more distant than ever.

As other travelers move toward an exit, I heft Jonathan onto my shoulder and cover his face with a flannel receiving blanket. Not warm enough, but all I have. I pick up our bags and follow others down the ramp. Arctic air slaps my face, frosts my lungs as I hurry along a cleared path on the tarmac to the commuter plane.

It's already dark when we reach the eastern Iowa airport. Bags slung on both shoulders, I cradle Jonathan on one arm, clutch the hoary railing with the other hand, and make my way carefully down the steps. Inside the terminal my parents wait, arms laden with coats, blankets and scarves.

"Let me have those," Dad reaches for the bags.

Mother hands me a quilt. "Wrap this around the poor boy. And here's a coat for you." She looks at my sandals. "I brought boots, too. They might not fit perfectly, but at least they'll get you to the car."

"Thanks, Mom." I look around for a seat.

"I'll hold him while you put those on," Dad says, reaching out, but Jonathan recoils, clutching my shoulder and burying his face against me.

"He's in a shy stage," I say.

"We've been so worried since your call," Mother says. "What in the world is going on?"

"It's pretty complicated, and I'm too tired to explain right now." I sit and struggle into the boots while clumsily balancing Jonathan on my lap. "We can talk tomorrow."

Dad says, "We better get going. It's a long drive, and they're getting ready to close the airport."

I glance around; we're the only passengers left in the terminal. My parents fuss over their grandson while bundling him for the cold. Dad loads the luggage, and I settle in the back seat, wrapping Jonathan in the quilt on my lap.

As Dad drives, I stare out the window at towering piles of snow bordering a cleared track. Beams of cold light intensify as they come near, reminding me of descriptions about dying: journeys through long white tunnels with bright lights at the end. But this brightness holds no warmth. Still, a part of me *is* dying–the hunk of my heart that remains in Jamaica. The farther we get from the airport, the more I feel as if I'm breaking loose from orbit and hurtling into cold, numb space. Both the life left behind and the one I now face amongst frozen Iowa cornfields are creations of others. Will I ever be more than an exile, a visitor in other people's worlds? Overwhelmed by questions I cannot answer, I feel my eyelids getting heavier and give up all resistance.

When we arrive at the farm, Dad carries our bags upstairs to my old room. Mother has tried to make it comfortable with an electric blanket for me and an antique cradle heaped with quilts for Jonathan. The second floor, I remember too well, has no heat ducts. My exhaled breath forms clouds in the room, and the windows are opaque with frost. A picture of my high school graduating class hangs on one wall and another holds a framed print of some artist's conception of Jesus Christ, a detail added by Mother after I left. My childhood vanity set still rests on the lace dresser scarf, now yellowed. The double bed is covered by my white chenille spread of junior high vintage. These artifacts of youth witness the long-awaited homecoming as my spirit shrinks. Will I ever get out?

With stiff fingers I turn the electric blanket on high and change Jonathan's nappy. He sneezes twice before I can wrap the quilt around him again. I take him into the big bed to keep him warm beside me.

Next morning I carry Jonathan downstairs before changing him. Already he has sniffles, and I worry he might get a fever or sore throat. As the day passes I gradually disclose the story of why we came. I tell about the beatings and David's beliefs on discipline. "I finally left because I was afraid he'd *really* hurt Jonathan."

143

As I recount David's threat to kill him on the camping trip, Mother gasps, "Oh no!" clutching both hands to her chest. Dad pauses from bouncing Jonathan on his knee and looks at him closely as though searching for marks. They keep shaking their heads in consternation, asking "Why?" Finally Mother says, "What kind of family does he come from anyway?"

"I don't blame his family. They seem decent, but David doesn't get along with them. Maybe it's because of the boarding schools. His parents sent him and his brother away to school when they were pretty young. He must not have liked it, because he got into lots of trouble and received some terrible beatings."

"Jamaican boarding schools?"

"Yeah. When he finally got kicked out, his parents were so embarrassed that they took him over to England and dumped him there all alone at sixteen. He's still bitter about it. Being from a privileged West Indian family, he didn't know how to cope with all the prejudice and discrimination in England. He fell in with bad company and had quite a struggle to survive. I heard these things in bits and pieces, and I suspect there's a lot more I don't know. He mentioned being in reform schools, but I'm not sure why. He even joined the Royal Air Force but encountered prejudice there, too. Said he spent a month in solitary. It's hard to imagine what that did to him."

"How did his brother turn out?" Mother asks. "What is his name again?"

"Philip. I think he's a huge part of David's problems. David hates him. Always has, as far as I can tell. He says his mother favored Philip. Maybe she did, because this goes beyond normal sibling rivalry."

"I don't know why people do such things..." Her voice trails off with more head shaking.

Not wanting to talk about sex with Mother, I say nothing about David's infidelity. Nor do I mention the violence with his first wife. They don't need to know I had warning signs but ignored them.

Besides, I can't entirely call it a mistake. If I had left David back then, I wouldn't have Jonathan now. Inconceivable.

When my brother Rick brings his family over, I have difficulty relating. Ditto when other relatives and neighbors stop by. As they talk about machinery, crops, church, illness, recipes, linoleum, the price of corn, names of people only vaguely familiar, I feel disconnected from it all, as though I'm encased in a glass bubble.

On our third evening Mother beckons me to the phone whispering, "I think it's David."

How did he find me? What will I say? "Um, can you tell him to hold on? I'll take it upstairs." Heart pounding, I grab Jonathan and hurry up the steps. "I have to talk to Daddy," I murmur and kiss his cheek. Then I arrange blankets around him in the crib and rock it with my toe as I sit down and pick up the extension phone.

"Hello?"

"Jac! I'm so glad to hear your voice! How are you? How's Jonathan?"

I hear a click as Mother hangs up. "How did you find me?"

"I know you. Figured it out right away."

No rage or recriminations? His friendly tone confuses me even when he says, "Why didn't you tell me you were homesick?"

"That's not why I came."

"I can't believe I won't be with my son on his very first Christmas! How is he anyway? I miss my boy."

"Well, nobody here has threatened to kill him!"

"What?"

"You said if Jonathan cried and got on your nerves when we went camping, you'd kill him! Well, you're not getting the chance."

"Come on! You're just using that as an excuse. You know I love Jonathan."

"How dare you talk about love after the hateful things you said!"

145

"Whoa there! That was just a way of speaking to let you know how important it is to train the boy properly so he learns how to behave. Now you're twisting my words to make me sound bad. You must have been looking for an excuse to get away. I suppose you really missed your parents and all, but you could have gone up there any time. You didn't have to pull this runaway drama."

"You've got it all wrong. I love Jamaica. I had no desire to leave. I only came to protect Jonathan ... from you! No other reason."

"When will you be home?"

"Home?"

"Yeah. How long you gonna stay there?"

"I haven't made any—"

"I love you, Jac, and I miss both of you so much. But I want you to have a nice Christmas with your mom and dad. I'll manage all right here. No big deal. When the holidays are over though, you need to make plans to come home. We're a family and have to stick together."

"But I ... I'm not —"

"I understand. You need time to think. I'll let you go now. But I'll call back soon. I have to know how my little man is doing. And remember, I love you. Both of you."

I put the phone down carefully and look at it, wondering if anything he said is true.

II

The rituals of Christmas—candlelight service, caroling, eggnog, wrapping gifts, feasting—feel strange, empty, boring. It's hard to believe I lived this way for twenty years. Everybody asks the same question—am I home permanently, or just for the holidays? I can't answer.

The promise of another call from David haunts me. Impossible to anticipate what ploy he might use, so I can't prepare, but I keep reminding myself not to be fooled by his sweet talk. He's just being nice because I have Jonathan. Still, a part of me doesn't want to think that's the only reason. Doesn't want to give up believing the *I love you* which I've cherished for so long.

Dad answers the phone on the night before New Years and holds his hand over the mouthpiece, glowering. "He wants to talk to you again. I have a good mind to–"

"It's all right, Dad." I hurry over. "I'll take it."

He hesitates, shakes his head, reluctantly relinquishes the phone, and leaves the room.

I hold the receiver for a moment, gathering courage; then I say, "This is Jacqueline."

"Hi, Honey! How are you? And how's my boy?"

"He's still alive, no thanks to you."

"Oh, come on! Stop playing games. I really want to know how both of you are. I hear there's been a terrible snow storm up there."

"Yeah. Jonathan has a cold. A little fever, too, and his nose is a bit plugged. But I'm watching closely and giving him vitamin drops and keeping him inside."

"That blasted weather! You should never have taken him there. The sooner you come back, the sooner he'll get better. Have you made reservations?"

"No."

"Listen, Jac. You know how much I love Jonathan. You've no idea how it hurts me when I have to discipline him, but it's only for his own good. That's why I get so upset over your spoiling, because it's me who has to straighten him out again. If you keep forcing me to be the disciplinarian, he'll always be afraid of me. But I don't want him to think of me as the bad guy. I want some good times with my son, too. Don't I deserve that?"

"Don't try to blame me for what you did. If Jonathan is afraid of you, it's because you hit him, not because of me." The thousands of miles between us emboldens me. No matter what I say, he can't hurt me or Jonathan. "You did the same thing with your other children. You haven't learned a thing."

"I've learned we have to cooperate. If you'd take more responsibility for disciplining him, I wouldn't have to do it all. I'd like to be gentle, too, but you haven't given me a chance. I really want to work with you, but we can't do it over the phone."

His regret sounds genuine. Of course. This is his worst fear come true. But I'm infuriated by how he's still trying to control me, even two thousand miles away. As I toy with the idea of hanging up, he says, "We're a great team, Jac. I need you with me. The world is waiting for my invention. I need you to help me get it patented. This is the answer not just to Jamaica's problems, but the whole world's. Think of it—free energy. Can you imagine what a difference it'll make?"

"A big one," I oblige, though annoyed by his transparent attempt to reel me in.

"Right! This is the most important thing you could be doing. I know you love me, even if it's hard for you to admit right now. You and Jonathan will be safe here. I promise."

"Why should I believe you?"

"Have I ever lied to you?"

"Yes."

"I've said hurtful things, but never lied."

"You're lying right now. Just like you lied about the crab lice."

"I was trying to protect you. I knew you'd be hurt, and I felt so bad. It was a stupid mistake, and I couldn't bear the thought of you being disappointed in me. But you're right, it was a lie. I own it. And I'm sorry. But it has nothing to do with Jonathan."

My heart sinks. So it hadn't been my paranoid imagination. But the victory gives little satisfaction. "You're only admitting it now because I have Jonathan, and you'll say anything to get him back."

"Of course, I want him back! He's my son. I love him. I love you, too. And I need you. Need you like I've never needed anyone else. Before you got pregnant I told you I couldn't stand to..." His voice breaks; I think he's crying.

"I'm sorry it's turned out like this," I say softly. "But coming back is not the answer. I've got to get off the phone now."

"I don't know what I'm going to do after you hang up. This house is so empty without you and Jonathan. I'll call again ... soon."

This is not what I expected. At worst, I feared he might follow and try to kill me. At best, I hoped he would simply give up on us as he had on his first family. Maybe he really does love me...

I look around. My parents have disappeared. Zipped in his terrycloth sleeper, Jonathan has nodded off on the carpet. I carry him upstairs and tuck him into the cradle. Then I climb between flannel sheets and lie there wide awake.

How can I find work, set up a home, care for Jonathan all on my own? I have little money, no car, have never lived alone. After all my efforts to create a better life, I could end up right back here, landlocked in the Corn and Bible Belt. Not the life I envisioned for myself or my son. Hard to tell if I'm more scared, disappointed, or just plain sad. But I mustn't give up!

Maybe I should go back to Jamaica but not live with David. That way I'll still be keeping my promise. And, for better or worse, Jonathan can grow up knowing his father. But after all the things I've told my parents about David, I'll never convince them of such a plan. Still I have to do something. I'll talk to Dad first. Finally, I sleep.

The next evening I find him alone in the living room. Sitting tensely on the edge of the sofa, I say, "I need your advice, Dad."

"What about?"

"Well, you see, before Jonathan was even conceived I promised David that regardless of what happened between us, I'd never take his child away. I'd like to keep my promise as long as Jonathan can be safe, but I need your help."

"What're you getting at?"

149

"I think I might go back to Jamaica but not live with David."

"Are you crazy?"

"Don't get me wrong, I haven't made up my mind. I'm just trying to figure it all out, come up with some plan."

He taps one foot on the floor and fiddles nervously with the newspaper on his lap. "Have you talked to your mother?"

"No. I want to hear what you think first."

"Well, I can't tell you what to do. Maybe she can give you some advice."

Might as well ask the Pope or Martin Luther! I think bitterly. "Okay."

When Mother joins us in the living room, I propose a game of Scrabble, her favorite, hoping it might mellow her out a bit before I introduce the delicate topic. The game doesn't get far. As soon as I mention David's call, Mother starts trembling. "Why do you talk to him?" she demands.

"Well, he *is* Jonathan's father, so I have to keep in touch. Jonathan does have a right to know him."

She rises from her chair, places both hands on the table and leans forward, eyes sparking with fervor. In a high, crackling voice she declares, "Jackie, I have prayed fervently for you and your son, prayed that no harm come to you. I have prayed you would take Christ into your heart and accept His love and let Him guide you. I have prayed you would seek the Lord and ask His forgiveness for all your sins. The only way to eternal life is through the blood of our Lord and Savior Jesus Christ, who died on the cross that we might be saved. He loves you so much, Jackie." Her knuckles are white from clutching the table edge as her head wags back and forth. "All you have to do is accept His love. I have prayed for you to bring your son to the Lord and have him baptized in our church in the name of the Father and the Son and the Holy Ghost. I've been so thankful since you came back... so you can get your life straightened out."

Her voice grows shriller as she labors for breath. "And now before you've even had your son baptized ..." she stops to gather air, "you talk about going back there! After all you've put me through! First you marry an atheist ... then you run off with this David. I don't know how much more I can take ... This is my last word." Her chest heaves. "You are *not* going to take my grandson back there ... Don't even think about..." Her face has grown chalky as she gulps for air. Abruptly she turns and leaves the room.

The silence left in her wake is broken by the feeble clatter of Scrabble pieces as I put them in the box. "Sorry for spoiling the game," I mumble to Dad.

III

Next morning I awake to the sound of my brother's voice. I dress and take Jonathan downstairs for breakfast. He eats pieces of banana while I make tea. Snatches of conversation waft in from the living room: "she" this, and "she" that, but the rest of the sentences are inaudible. Of course Mother is confiding in him. They always stick together in family matters, a majority of two.

I slice Mother's homemade bread, put two pieces in the toaster, and find a pan to cook oatmeal.

"Any more coffee?" Rick's voice from behind gives me such a start that I spill the grape juice I'm pouring into Jonathan's cup.

I grab a sponge. "Just a minute, I'll check." Why can't he do it himself?

He leans against the kitchen doorway, cigarette dangling between fingers. Taking a quick puff, he flicks the ash into an empty packet he uses as a makeshift ashtray. Even slouching, he is much taller and looks down at me through narrowed eyes. One opens a little wider as he juts his chin toward Jonathan. "Hi there, little fella." He seems to use only half of his mouth for speaking. "I see Grandpa got some bananas for you. Like 'em, don't cha?"

From the highchair, Jonathan stares, mouth agape, fist clutching a chunk of banana poised midair. I hand Rick a cup. "Cream and sugar?"

"Nope, straight." He peers at the black liquid, swirls it around. "So what's this I hear about you goin' back to Jamaica? We're sorta wonderin' if there's somethin' wrong with you ..." His voice trails off as he looks up.

I put oatmeal in a bowl for Jonathan, add honey and milk. "What's your point?"

"Well, as we see it, if you have to fly this far to get away from that guy, he must be really bad. Going back would be crazy. So what's the deal?"

I take a deep breath while choosing my words. "First of all, I never said I'm going back. But I do worry about the long-term effects of separating Jonathan from his father, and I'm looking at my options."

"Come on! Going back there is just plain stupid."

"I'm not the only one involved here. I have to think about what's best for everybody. David loves Jonathan, but he gets carried away with discipline. Still, I have to be careful of overreacting. How would you feel if your wife took your kids away?"

"She'd never do that."

"Well, it's not as if we're strangers to corporal punishment. Remember how Dad used to beat you?"

"As if I could forget." He emits a half snicker, half grunt.

"I used to get so upset when he hit you, especially in the morning when he'd go up to your room to get you out of bed. Then we'd hear the screaming and kicking..."

"Dad's mellowed a lot since then. Now no one would believe how he used to go on."

"I'm glad to hear it. He never hit me much. Only twice that I remember."

"You had it easier 'cause he left it up to Mom to discipline you, and she'd just use her old wooden spoon. Remember the time we

152

got it away from her and hid it?" He chuckles, glancing sideways at me. I nod and smile. "Yep, took her quite a while to find it," he sniggers. "Meanwhile she didn't have nothin' to hit us with. That was great!" Abruptly his expression turns grim. "But this David, he's not anything like Dad. He just sounds mean."

"If I return to Jamaica, it wouldn't be to live with him. I'd try to get my old teaching job back and keep Jonathan with me. He'd just visit his father."

He zips his jacket and adjusts his cap. "Well, if you ask my opinion, I'd say Jonathan is a lot better off right here in Iowa where he's got plenty a relatives. He can spend time with me and my kids and with his grandpa on the farm. This is where your boy should be. Not down there with all them niggers."

I whirl around, slam utensils into the sink, run water over them, struggling for control.

"Bye, folks," Rick hollers as he pulls the door shut behind him. Through the window I watch him climb into his pickup, red neck hidden beneath his sheepskin collar.

I clean Jonathan's face and hands, lift him from the high chair. "Come, Big Guy, let's find your toys." Settling him on the carpet, I turn over the toy box, and balls, trucks, blocks, and dolls tumble out. He reaches for a string of red and green wooden beads and shakes it furiously. Dropping it, he crawls toward the stuffed Bugs Bunny and grabs it by an ear. I stack plastic blocks which he promptly knocks over, thinking the game immensely amusing.

Rick's performance is a stark reminder of why I left this place and why I can't raise Jonathan here. A city might be better. At least neighbors wouldn't be watching our every move, and schools would be integrated. I'll look for jobs in the Sunday paper.

At the supper table, Mother says sternly. "We'll be going to nine o'clock service tomorrow. I hope you're coming along."

"Depends how Jonathan is feeling. I shouldn't take him out in the cold until he's all better." I hate using him as an excuse. Why can't I summon the courage just to say no? I rise to clear the table. "Go ahead and have your bath. I'll take care of these."

"Oh!" She looks surprised. "Okay, thanks." She removes her apron and hangs it up.

I hand Dad a towel to dry the dishes while I wash. "I know we're really getting on Mother's nerves," I say. "Last night was too much. We have to leave. I'll look in the paper tomorrow for a job and a place to live."

"There's a house in town for lease. Just the right size. I can help you with the rent to get started."

"But there's no work around here. I'm thinking of looking in Des Moines…"

"If you're nearby, I can help more." His breath is on my neck, his hips press me against the sink cabinet. "A woman needs a man…"

"I'll have to see what jobs are available," I say as I squeeze the sponge and slip away to wipe the table. Quickly I rinse the sink and dry my hands. "Gotta check on Jonathan now. Goodnight."

I dash upstairs, his touch clinging like a cobweb to my skin. It all comes rushing back: the time when I was twelve, fresh, innocent, and probably irresistible. I've never thought of it that way before, but now it connects. That was in the kitchen, too, a Sunday afternoon while Mother was taking her nap. I was bored and looking for something to snack on. Suddenly he grabbed me, dipped me into a backbend, and planted a hungry kiss on my lips. As swiftly as it happened, he disappeared. I didn't tell anyone; just pretended it didn't occur. Tonight felt the same. Creepy. Again I won't tell.

In bed I toss and turn. Keep waking from a dream of someone chasing me. I never see who and can never get away, never get free.

IV

I go downstairs early the next morning, heat a bottle, and leave a note on the table: *Good morning. I'm keeping Jonathan inside today, so don't wait for us. See you after church. J.*

After they leave, I go back down. The thick Sunday *Des Moines Register* is on the table. Jonathan eats and plays while I read every single job ad, but they are mostly sales and business. I hate sales and don't qualify for the other positions. The only teaching vacancies are for science, math and special ed. Iowa certification requirements are so strict that I can't qualify anyway without more training, despite holding certification in Maryland. That leaves fast-food and waitress work. Things I did in college. Hardly adequate for supporting two of us. Discouraged, I take Jonathan upstairs and get dressed.

When my parents return, the classifieds lie open on the table. "Find anything?" Dad asks.

"No, and it pretty much covers the state."

Mother says, "I was talking to Margie Hoffman after church. You remember Margie, don't you?"

I don't. "Uh-huh."

"She works in the county office now, and she says once you become a resident, you can collect welfare checks and get food stamps. You only have to live here a month. Tomorrow you should go fill out an application to get the process started."

"Then you can move into that little house," Dad adds, "and we can help you—"

"Do you think I went to college and traveled halfway around the world just so I could bring my son here to live on welfare?" I regard them sternly, my anger rising. Probably everyone in town knows my story by now and has a plan for my life: welfare, food stamps, church, daily scrutiny. Next, the scarlet letter! My brother

155

never resorted to welfare, even when his girlfriend got pregnant and he had no job. The big mobile home they moved into after their hasty marriage, Dad paid for with cash.

"It would only be temporary," Mother offers.

"At least in Jamaica we don't need warm clothes or heat, and medical care is practically free so there's no need for health insurance. There are advantages…"

"You can't take Jonathan back there." Mother's voice rises. "I won't allow it!"

"Don't get upset. I'm not talking about living with David. I can get my own place. Remember, Jamaica is Jonathan's homeland. How can I deny him his birthright?"

"Is there anyone you can stay with?" Dad asks.

"Yes, a friend at school offered help if I ever need it. I'll call her tomorrow."

Through the night I keep rehashing the conversations with my parents and with David, two futures competing in my head. With the bleak job situation here it might be months, even longer, before I can find anything. And if I do, it will mean sending Jonathan to daycare. What will I tell him as he grows up? How can I justify him not knowing his father? In Jamaica it'll be hard to afford a nanny, and David won't help with expenses as long as Jonathan doesn't live with him. Just thinking about it makes me realize how dependent on David I've become. I really don't know how to survive in Jamaica on my own. Not here either.

On his next call David tells me how he's been running non-stop trying to keep the business going by himself. When he asks about Jonathan, I say, "His cold is better, and he's crawling all over the place. Mother got out a box of old toys for him. It's fun seeing his reaction to the things I used to play with."

"I miss you guys so much. Plus, I keep worrying. It's dangerous to have Jonathan there with atomic warheads pointing at him, poised to go off at any moment. You know the headquarters of the Strategic Air Command are right there in Nebraska, don't you? Globally speaking, that's at your back door."

"I don't really think about it."

"Well, that's not going to keep something from happening. You and Jonathan are much safer here. For his sake you have to bring him home. Believe me, I'll do anything you ask, if you'll just come back. *Anything.* I'm sorry for what I said about him making noise at the beach and all. You know I didn't mean it. I'll never hurt my boy again. You've really made me see what's important."

Surprised by his declaration, I try to remember exactly what Marie advised. Finally I say, "Well, we will only come back if you guarantee we can live in our own place, and you won't interfere. Once we get settled, we can discuss visitations and –"

"Whatever you want. Go ahead and make your reservations. I'll call back tomorrow night to find out when to expect you. I can't wait to see my son!"

"I'll think about it."

"Tomorrow then," he says, and we hang up.

Him actually saying he's sorry casts a different light on everything. I remember my breakup with Alex, how he pleaded with me to reconsider my decision to leave. But leaving had seemed simpler than entering the scary and uncertain path of reconciliation. Maybe it requires more courage to go back and work on things than it does to stay away. Hard as it is to admit, it's possible I did overreact to David's threat. He probably never had any intention of killing Jonathan. Of course not! My own fear caused all this confusion. How far am I going to carry it? Already I regret getting my parents involved. Better to admit the mistake and deal with the consequences than to continue in a wrong direction that might ruin our lives forever.

Tossing and turning, I recall an article I read a few months ago about Einstein which mentioned his rocky and irregular home life. He had several children, both in and out of wedlock, and overlapping affairs with women, two of whom he married. Does this go with the territory of genius and invention? Do I need to be more understanding, make allowances for David's needs? Is that the life of an inventor's wife?

V

Next morning I call the airlines. The soonest flight available is five days away. After booking it I feel better. Resolved to run no more, I'm determined to get our lives back on track, back in Jamaica. This time I will stand by the family I've created and keep my promises. Meanwhile, I have the jobs of making peace with Mother and of convincing everyone here we will be safe.

"Way to go, Jac!" David says when he calls and hears the news. "We'll make it work. I know you want to as much as me. I'll meet you at the airport. Can't wait to hold my boy!"

His warm enthusiasm is encouraging, but I wonder about his plan to meet us. When I try to call Karen and get no answer, I remember they've gone to England for the holidays. As the day for departure draws nearer I do my best to reassure my parents. "Please try to understand why I can't keep Jonathan here," I say to Mother. "I don't have the right. How can I ever explain to him when he grows up why he never knew his father?"

"This is a man you're not even married to!"

"By natural law we are. We have a child. Nothing can change that fact. I'm only asking you to try to understand—"

"The wages of sin—" she intones.

"Love, hope, charity, these three," I interrupt. "But the greatest of these is love." I reach out and place my hand on hers. "You know, Mom, I hope we can see each other a lot more in the future than we have these past few years. I want Jonathan to know his grandparents, too."

The most warmth she can muster is, "I'll never stop praying for you."

I hug her. "And I want you to know how much I appreciate your putting up with us."

When the day comes, she refuses to go to the airport, and my embrace doesn't even elicit a tear. In the car I tell Dad, "I really appreciate all you've done; just hope Mother isn't too hard on you after this."

"Hmph," he grunts and glances into the mirror as his foot touches the brake.

"I'll call and let you know everything's all right," I continue. "When we're settled, I want you to bring her to visit, so you can see for yourselves that we're fine. It will be good for you to get away from this cold."

"Your mother doesn't like to fly."

"Maybe she'll change her mind. I bet you'll both want to see how Jonathan is doing."

"We'll see."

On the flight I hold my sleeping son, feeling optimistic, though not without misgivings, about my decision. I'll just take a cab to the Sandman guesthouse. But if David shows up at the airport, I'll make it clear that our joint rearing of Jonathan needs to be negotiated. And I'll tell him my parents are coming to visit. This backup doesn't feel nearly as solid as Marie's, but I'm determined not to let him intimidate me.

Kingston 1971

I

Slanted rays of the setting sun greet us when I carry Jonathan from the plane. I raise my face to the painted clouds–plum, lemon, lime, mango–like fruits of the sky, spellbound overhead, as though awaiting a last glimpse of the fleeting ball of flame. I turn toward the terminal and see crowds of people flourishing banners from the upstairs balcony. Pretending they are welcoming us home, I return a hearty wave.

Inside I join a long customs queue, supporting Jonathan on my hip as I inch our baggage along with my foot. When we get to the head of the line, I spot David hurrying toward us. He pecks my cheek and reaches for Jonathan. Lifting him high, he gazes into his eyes. "Home to Daddy, Big Boy! Everything's okay now. You're back with Daddy." While I deal with customs, he tickles and plays with Jonathan but gets little response. Then he returns Jonathan to me, picks up my two suitcases and says, "Come on. The car's right outside."

He makes a path through the dense crowd. Reluctantly I follow, looking around for a place to talk, but nowhere do I see an empty seat or a private nook. Then we're at the car and he's loading my bags into the trunk. Three cars are lined up behind, waiting for us to vacate the space. He opens the door for me to get in, and before I'm settled he starts the engine and moves forward. Joining the line leaving the lot, he reaches over and tousles Jonathan's hair. "How does it feel to be home?" He glances at me.

"As I stepped off the plane I caught a glimpse of the gorgeous sunset..."

He's talking to the parking lot attendant. Cars behind us honk impatiently. He hands the man some bills, mumbling, "Set of thieves," and the tires screech as he accelerates and careens onto the road toward Kingston. "I found your car here the day after you left. Had to get Dougie to bring me out so I could drive it home. What a hassle you put me through! And that stupid note!"

"I didn't want you to worry..."

"It was a damn ignoramus thing to do! What do you think would have happened if the police had searched and found it before I did?"

"I don't know. I didn't think—"

"Exactly. You *never* think about the consequences of your actions."

"That's not true. I, I try to—"

"I'll tell you what would have happened. If your car had stayed in the lot more than a week, the police would have broken in and towed it. Of course, they'd look up the registration and read the note. In no time they would have been at my yard, arresting me on suspicion of abduction. Or murder. And what defense would I have since you didn't let me know where you'd gone? That note would damn me. I can't believe how selfish you are!" He grips the wheel, his voice growing louder as we bounce along the potholed road.

Feeling him looking at me more than the road, I clutch Jonathan, my eyes locked on the traffic ahead, unable to remember anything I'd planned to say. Finally I come out with, "We have a lot

162

to talk about. Both of us have wounds. We need to understand and forgive..."

"Bumbo seed!" He swerves suddenly to avoid a truck barreling down the middle of the road. I grip the armrest. "You think I'm going to understand the torture you put me through?"

I press against the door, instinctively trying to make more space between us. The rest of my planned speech seems to have blown out the window.

"What do you think has happened to the business during your little vacation? You just forgot about our customers, the people who depend on us. In Iowa, Jamaicans don't matter. But where do you expect the money for paying bills to come from if nobody takes care of business? You never thought about that on your holiday."

"David, I'm sorry I panicked and took Jonathan away. Now I've come back to keep my promise, but if we're going to be good parents, we have to find a way to trust each other. It'll take time, so for now it might be better if—"

"You're damn right! It's gonna take a *long* time before I can even trust you with going to the grocery store. Renae was a liar, and she was dumb. But you! I've never seen anybody so sneaky! You made a complete fool of me."

"Can't you get it through your head? I was afraid for Jonathan's life! Is that so hard to understand? Don't you know anything about maternal instinct?"

"Oh yeah! I've been trying to overcome it for most of my life. And now I have to save my son from the same smothering—"

"Turn up here," I interrupt as we near the turn-off to the guesthouse.

"What?"

"I have a room reserved at the Sandman."

He doesn't even respond, just keeps driving until he pulls into our driveway, slams on the brakes, and turns off the engine.

Without a word, he deposits my bags inside. I follow and hastily open one, fumbling to find the things Jonathan needs. I carry him to the kitchen, set him in the high chair, and open a jar of baby food.

Hearing music in the living room, I breathe a little easier. At least he's giving us some time alone. I speak softly and spoon custard into Jonathan's mouth, trying to sound reassuring while regrouping my thoughts for the discussion to come. When he loses interest in the food, I mix formula in his bottle, take him to say goodnight to Daddy, and carry him to his room. He falls asleep in my arms even before I lay him in his crib. I kiss him and gently close the door.

I find David in the living room and say, "Shall we talk now?"

"What do you have to say?" He doesn't look up from the amplifier he's adjusting.

I sit. "Well, I want you to know I came back here with Jonathan because you assured me you never meant what you said about killing him. I thought you sounded sincere, and I decided to give you the benefit of the doubt that I may have jumped to a wrong conclusion. If so, I don't want to deprive Jonathan of knowing his father because of my error. In other words, for the sake of our son I'm willing to assume I was wrong. That's why we're here tonight. But it doesn't mean—"

"So, from what you're saying I can assume you don't give a shit about me. You're just here to see what more you can get for your precious baby."

"That's *not* what I'm saying. Have you forgotten you begged me to bring Jonathan back to Jamaica?"

"Always going on like the martyr. Just like your mother. Why is it so hard for you to admit you love me? Always too goddamn selfish to let on you care about me."

"David," I shake my head, "it's not about you and me. It's about Jonathan..."

"You'd like to think so, but you've got it all wrong. Jonathan *is* because of *us. We* came first. Without *us,* there's no Jonathan." His features are absolutely calm. His eyes, cold. I stare transfixed, like Lot's wife, a pillar of stone.

He continues, "I know how women operate. After a man gives you a baby, he's disposable, like trash. Only your precious child is important then. The man becomes an inconvenience to be tolerated only if he gives you plenty of money, clothes, nice car, home, and fucks you good. You women make me sick," he snarls. Then his voice gets louder as he rises and stands, legs spread, in front of me. "I hope you got plenty of sympathy up in Iowa because you're sure gonna need it when I'm done with you." He glares down, hands poised at his sides.

II

I raise my arm, but not fast enough to block his fist. Blood spurts from my nose as I reel off the chair. Hands over my face, I scramble up, run to the bathroom, press a wet cloth to my nostrils. I hover at the sink, rinsing the rag over and over. Tears mingle with blood swirling down the drain. Twelve hours ago Jonathan and I were safe in Iowa. Now I'm cowering in the bathroom with a fractured nose. What an idiot!

The door opens. "Is it broken?" he says.

"I don't know," I mumble into the cloth.

"Move that rag and let me see." He grasps my shoulder and turns me toward him.

Trembling, I lower the cloth. He examines me from all angles. "Nope. Mine's been busted a couple times, but you're lucky ... this time anyway. Stop sulking now and come out so we can finish our talk."

I follow him to the bedroom. "Sit," he says, and I lower myself onto the edge of the bed. "You've made me out to be a monster to all your relatives, I'm sure. Told them I mistreat you and your precious baby. Went and made it impossible for me to ever get any respect from them, haven't you?" I keep turning my head to follow his pacing.

"You made a big mistake when you took my son away. You deceived me, so now you need to be punished because you can't live with the guilt." He stops and faces me. "You came back to be punished for your sins. Only then will you feel better..." He punches me in the stomach. I crumple over and choke as a bitter taste fills my mouth. He grabs my arm, twists it behind my back, forces me onto the floor. "You will never put me through that again. Never!" Still twisting my arm, he steps on my back, unbuckles his belt.

"No! No!"

"Are you sorry?"

"Yes, David! I'm sorry!"

His belt cracks across my buttocks. "If you ever take my son away again, I'll kill you. There's no place in the world that I won't find you." With the next lash I lose control, feel a pool of urine surround me.

"Stop! Please. No more! Please ..."

As he raises the belt again, I close my eyes and imagine myself hugging Jonathan in his crib, with the sweet smell of his hair against my cheek, like we slept in Iowa. I clench my lips, determined not to wake him.

III

"I hope you're not planning to go anywhere today with that face," David says as he enters the kitchen next morning. "Looks like a garden egg squashed on the road."

I won't be going out for weeks; you've seen to that! I fume inside, as tears well. But I swallow and manage to say, "I was thinking of working on the company books. Probably a lot to catch up on."

"Yeah. Should keep you out of mischief for a few days." He rubs Jonathan's head. "How's my boy." Then he pours a cup of tea and opens the newspaper.

When my face is nearly back to normal David says, "I know you're really trying, but you've got too much time on your hands. That's why Jonathan keeps clinging. You should get a job so you're not around him so much. We need to find a new helper anyway, so we may as well go ahead and get someone who can live in. Then you'll be free to leave for work early."

Let a stranger raise my son? I put Jonathan in his playpen and stoop to gather blocks strewn on the floor. "It might be hard to find a teaching job this time of the year."

"Nonsense. They always need teachers. Just put your mind to it."

So I train a new helper, Monica, a tall young woman, to our routines. Then I listlessly start a job search, consoling myself that the need to show up for work looking presentable might deter David from hitting me. Eventually I secure a part-time position at a small private school. The earnings are pitiful, but it meets his

167

demand to get me out of the house while keeping me away no more than four hours at a time.

IV

A letter arrives from Alex, asking for a divorce because, he says, "It hardly serves my interest to be married to a woman who has another man's baby." He offers to send the money from our mutual savings if I can get it done quickly in the Dominican Republic. He must have found a woman; else, why the rush? I contact the Dominican consulate and find it's faster and cheaper than a Jamaican divorce. David, confident our flourishing business will survive, says he'll go along, so we can get a vacation in the bargain. I schedule the trip during Easter break. Marie offers to keep Jonathan, welcoming the chance to fuss over a baby again.

In Santo Domingo the military are everywhere. Armed soldiers stand on corners and ride around in trucks the color of leftover guacamole. It's fun to discover how readily I can understand and speak the Spanish I studied in college but never really used. For once David lets me take the lead in talking.

One call to the lawyer, and the divorce is underway. A limousine with armed escort arrives at our hotel and carries us to a swank office suite. After completing necessary forms, Señor Medina explains we will need to drive out to the country in order to appear before a special judge. When we return to the limo David eyes the rifle and murmurs, "What's the deal with all these guns? We going into combat?"

"I suspect our lawyer has political enemies. Remember, this is a military dictatorship. Probably best for his and our protection."

Apprehensively we settle into the back seat. Flanked by David on my right and the guard on my left, I try not to impose on the wall of silence that encloses our protector; any distraction from his duty might prove fatal to us all. Medina, in front with the chauffeur, leaves the glass partition slightly open. As we speed along the highway in air-conditioned comfort, surrounded by tinted glass, David whispers, "I wonder if this tub is bullet proof."

"Sorta like working for the mafia again, huh?"

He grins slyly and puts his arm around me. I lean against him, making more space between myself and the guard, and try to relax.

During the long drive we come upon several military roadblocks, but when we are waved through without so much as opening a window, I wonder what special markings our car bears. Arriving at a mountain village, Señor Medina announces we're in his home district. David waits in the car while I go inside and tell the judge what Medina has instructed me to say. Raising my right hand in oath, I answer *"Sí?"* to several questions and explain my husband's whereabouts: *"El vive en otro país, en Canada, y no puede venir aquí."* He seems satisfied, and Medina quickly ushers me back to the limo.

When we return to the hotel he instructs us to remain in the country and call him in two days.

The next morning we rent a car and set out to explore the island. First stop is a beach hotel nestled beneath the tallest coconut trees I've ever seen. While I lounge in a hammock in my new bathing suit, David snaps pictures. Later he sets the camera on automatic and we pose together, arms around each other and kissing.

After dinner we listen to the band warming up and watch a few couples move onto the floor. "What kind of dance is that?" I ask, impressed by their performances.

"Tango. It's fun. I'll show you sometime, but not tonight. I'd rather go to bed with you. Come." He stands and pulls out my chair as I rise. If only he would keep treating me this way! Months have passed since he's mentioned my flight to Iowa. Maybe the worst times are behind us.

On the last visit to Señor Medina I get a document to send to Alex for his signature. When the law office gets it back, a final decree can be issued. As we leave, I say a prayer of thanks, feeling that somehow the divorce could be more significant than I expected.

V

"The test came back positive," I tell David nervously.

"Great!" he says. "Jonathan needs a little sister or brother. Then you won't have so much time to spoil him."

Relief washes through me. "You're glad?"

"Of course. You know I love kids." He caresses my stomach. "And I like seeing you pregnant. Turns me on." He dips me back, kisses my neck, throat, mouth.

This must be God's way of letting me know that coming back was the right choice. I'll train this baby better from the start; he'll have no excuse to hit her... or him.

I stop teaching in my seventh month and focus on transforming the spare bedroom into a nursery. Marie donates a cute wicker crib, and I make a ruffled skirt for it and matching curtains. I move most of my things into the room, planning to sleep there to avoid disturbing David with night-time crying and feedings. At a weekly exam Dr. Moore reports the baby is full term and tells me to check into hospital next day.

Once labor is established, David sits beside me and begins hypnosis, helping me to relax and flow with the contractions as they get stronger. Three other women are in the ward, each in different stages of labor. But only I have a man at my bedside, holding my hand, wiping my brow, feeding me lemon drops, and softly speaking words of encouragement.

Much sooner than with Jonathan, I feel an overwhelming urge to bear down. I tell the nurse to call the doctor, but she ignores me. Enduring one onslaught after another, I feel as if I'm single-handedly holding back a tidal wave. I keep saying, "It's time! Get the doctor!" but no one heeds.

Finally a nurse checks me. "Quick!" she cries. "Call the doctor! This one's ready."

The midwife rushes over and examines my progress. "Fully dilated," she shouts. "No time to get her to the delivery room!" At long last I hear the welcome words: "Go ahead. Push!"

Every muscle in my body synchronizes with the primal surges as David squeezes my hand. "Way to go, Honey. You're doing great!" Three pushes and our baby is born. "It's a girl!" he crows.

Within moments, a bundle tightly wrapped in soft white cloth is placed in my arms. I stare down into the darkest, deepest eyes I've ever seen. David puts his arm around me, and together we marvel. "Watch her eyes," I whisper. "They don't look like a newborn's. How can a baby look so wise?"

We take turns holding her while she gazes around the room as though thoughtfully surveying her new habitat. "Thanks for coming to live with us," I murmur, awestruck by how unlike a baby she seems, except for her tiny body.

The midwife commands, "Push again. We gots ta get da afterbirt out."

"But I'm not having contractions. Wait until they start again."

"No. We gots ta get it now. We ken pull and you poosh."

"That's not the way to do it." My eyes desperately seek David's support. "When the contractions start again, the placenta will come by itself. Don't hurry it."

Despite my objections, they keep tugging. Exhausted, I doze off. When I awake, Dr. Moore is there. "Congratulations," he says. "You did a fine job without me, but now there's a little complication. When the midwife was trying to remove the placenta, the cord broke and a piece stayed inside. Don't worry, it's not serious, but we can't leave it there. Removing it surgically will require general anesthesia. I'm going to scrub and prep now. The nurses will take you into the operating room. I've already told David."

"Oh, no," I moan. "Can't we just use hypnosis?"

"Absolutely not. I won't perform the procedure without anesthesia. I'm sorry, but there's no other way."

Soon after he leaves, David leans down beside me. "That asshole doctor," he seethes. "So help me, if anything else goes wrong, I'll break his neck. You know where he was while our baby was being born? At a cocktail party! Didn't want to be disturbed. The fucking bastard! For now I'm just being quiet and watching to make sure he does the rest of his job right, but once this is over ... I'm gonna sue him!"

"Where's our baby?"

"She's out in the hallway lying in a little basket. Anybody could come by and take her. And she looks cold. A while ago I went out to get some paper and a bottle of ink to take her footprints. Can't trust these idiots not to mix her up with some other baby. Be back soon." He squeezes my arm.

The next thing I remember is feeling intensely cold. I'm lying on a narrow table and the room seems to be spinning. "Help!" I cry, afraid of falling off. "Please, somebody, help me!"

David rushes in and grasps my shoulders. "It's all right, Honey. It's all over with. Dr. Moore says everything's going to be okay. Try to relax. I'm right here and our baby's fine. As soon as the paperwork's done, they'll take you both to the ward so you can get some rest. You sure need it. You've been through a lot. I love you, Honey." With his grip anchoring me, the spinning subsides and I drift off.

The next evening David brings his camera to the hospital and proudly snaps pictures of me holding our daughter. Then he says, "I'll take you home tomorrow."

"But... Don't come too early. I want to see the doctor first."

"Nonsense. I can't wait around all day for him. You're both fine. Just get a good night's sleep, and I'll see you in the morning."

David arrives before the doctor, quickly helps me pack and whisks us off. Driving toward home, I worry how Jonathan will react. Still a baby himself, he might feel threatened by the new arrival. "Do you think Jonathan understands what's going on?" I ask. "Did you tell him we're coming home today?"

"Don't worry," David says. "Everything'll be okay. He bloody well better behave himself."

When we arrive, Jonathan is playing in the back yard while Monica hangs clothes on the line. Before they see us, I whisper to David, "Here, carry her while I say 'Hi' to him." Then I call out, "Jonathan! Mommy's home. Come here, Big Boy!" I kneel and open my arms as he comes running.

Behind us David says, "Looky, Jonathan, see what we got. Come see your little sister." He crouches beside me, holding her at Jonathan's level.

Jonathan stops, stares quietly at the baby. He looks at me, at David, and then his face screws up with a loud wail. Hurling himself against me, he clutches my dress.

"Hey, what's the matter? Don't like your sister?" David snarls. "Ya need something to cry about again?" Cradling the newborn in his left arm, he whacks Jonathan's bare chubby legs, turning the skin crimson. Jonathan screams and runs for the back door. Halfway there he stumbles, falls face down on the grass.

"Stupid little bastard! I'll put him in his room. Here, take her." David thrusts the baby into my arms, grabs Jonathan and disappears inside. I stand holding my daughter, powerless to rescue my son. Ashamed to face Monica, I hurry into the house.

Each day I try a different name until we agree on Angela Hope. I love "Angela" because it means messenger, and "Hope" is the name of my favorite aunt. As I notice her calm adjustment to life, her keen observation of everything, and the ponderous depth of her eyes, I can't help thinking she possesses special gifts. Time will tell what.

Patiently I try to overcome Jonathan's horrendous introduction to his sister. When David is away I encourage him to touch her and hold her while he sits beside me. Petrified at first, he gradually relaxes and learns to bring clean diapers, get towels, help push the pram, and shake rattles to entertain her. Breast-feeding becomes a family affair with him sitting beside me and holding a storybook as I read to him while suckling her. However, I'm bothered by the feeling that there isn't enough of me for both of them and Jonathan is getting short-changed.

At night the moment Angela wakes, I leap from my bed, lift her up, and press her to my breast. I never get enough sleep, but it's worth it to keep her from getting on David's nerves. She shows no signs of gripe and seldom cries, so he has no reason to launch a discipline regimen.

Suddenly it's Christmas season. David and I decorate the tree, while Angela lies on the sofa in rapt attention to the lights and carols. "Look at her!" he exclaims. "See how her eyes focus on the candles. And watch her head turn. She's actually listening to the music!" The little angel has truly won Daddy's heart.

Jonathan stands in the doorway. "Come help Mommy and Daddy," I say, holding out an ornament. "You can hang this on the tree." He gazes at the tree, around the room, and then comes forward slowly, hand outstretched, and takes the carved reindeer.

Kingston, 1972

I

"Hey, Jac," says David the day after Christmas, "Dougie and the crowd are going to celebrate New Year's at the Sheraton. There's still some tickets left. Wanta go?"

"Isn't it expensive?"

"Sure, but we can afford it this once. Besides, the tickets include dinner and drinks."

"I don't have anything to wear..."

"So you can buy something. Don't skimp. I want you to look really good. Something sexy, but with class."

I search through several boutiques until I find the perfect dress—an exquisite red gown, embroidered in gold and accented with a slit up one side. It costs more than anything I've ever owned, but I can't risk not being dressed as well as the other women. I even buy matching gold evening bag and strappy shoes.

The afternoon before the party I go to a hairdresser. It has been so long that I've forgotten how marvelous it feels to have the girl massage in the shampoo. I close my eyes and enjoy every shiver running down my neck, across my shoulders, along my arms. If only it would last forever. But then she's rinsing. Next an aroma fills my nostrils. I raise my lids enough to see her squeeze something on her palms that smells like nectar of the gods. She rubs it on my scalp, works it through my hair. As the shivers start again, I close my eyes and swoon. When she's done, I move to another chair, carrying the memory of Nirvana with me, but as the stylist combs and trims, the shivers elude me. I wonder if hairdressers have any idea how their hands affect people. Maybe this, rather than appearance, is what takes so many women to salons every week. A clandestine way of paying someone to touch you. In the mirror I admire the upswept chic style, a perfect complement to my elegant outfit. I tip generously and rush home.

After getting the children settled for the night, I put on the dress to show David. His eyes widen as he lets out a long whistle. "Turn around." He views me from every angle and then pronounces, "Perfect!"

"I wonder if you'll think so after you hear how much it cost."

"I don't need to know. You look great. That's what matters."

Sitting at the vanity to put on make-up, I look at my reflection, try to dismiss the scars as the price of motherhood. Then I set to work, carefully applying concealer to the mark at the corner of my lip and penciling in the missing parts of an eyebrow. Mascara and eye shadow help to camouflage damaged eyelid tissue. Will our new year really be different? I can't help hoping.

As I poke through my jewelry case trying to decide which earrings to wear, David comes up behind. "Try this." He places a small box before me.

"What?" I open the lid and behold a pair of double hoop gold earrings. "Oh, David, they're beautiful! Thank you so much!" I put them on and rise for his inspection.

"Just right." He smiles approvingly and kisses my cheek.

Waiters stand at the ballroom entrance bearing trays of glasses filled with champagne. After a couple of sips, I begin to relax. At the dinner table they keep pouring wine and champagne, but I drink slowly and manage to maintain a mellow feeling without losing control. Before dessert, David stands and asks me to dance. I'm glad for the slow tune, a reggae version of "Red, Red Wine." Surrendering to his lead, I don't miss a step, even when he dips me at the end. The tempo is picking up when a friend of David whom I hardly know asks me to dance. I try too hard and end up stepping on his toe. Dougie is the partner I enjoy most. He guides me so firmly that it's impossible to make a mistake.

The music grows louder, reducing my obligation to make bright table conversation, so I just laugh along with everyone else at jokes the guys are telling, despite missing some of the punch lines. On the stroke of midnight we all toast the New Year and break into "Auld Lang Syne." I almost feel like I belong.

Then my breasts begin to throb. Fearful of staining my dress, I find David and he agrees to leave without delay. On the way home he says, "You looked great tonight; made me proud of you. I hope you had a good time."

"It was my best New Year's party ever." I squeeze his hand.

From the front door I hear Angela whimper. "Thanks, Monica," I say as I rush past her, unzipping my dress. I press my baby to bursting breasts, both of us grateful for the relief. Sitting in the rocker, I kick off my shoes and listen for the sound of David's car. Will he return to the party? Minutes pass but I don't hear the engine start.

I return Angela to her crib and peep into his room. Tux draped on a chair, he lies sprawled on the bed. For the first time since Angela's birth, I slip into bed beside him. Kissing his neck, I run my fingers along his thigh, across his groin, up his chest. He turns over, murmurs my name, and then is all over me. A happy new year indeed.

II

David's new friend, Marcus Pattern, runs an engineering firm. The two subcontract jobs to one another and have drinks together after work. I finally get to meet him when David invites him over for dinner. Friendly, warm, and intelligent, Marcus is easy to like. He talks a lot about his wife walking out and leaving two pre-teen children for him to raise. "Donna was only eighteen when we got married, and we started having kids right away," he says. "I was always the leader in the family. You know how it is. Now she wants to have a *career*." He rolls his eyes. "She's going to university to get her degree and doesn't want to be held back by family obligations. I can understand how she feels, but what gets me is how any woman can care so little about her own children! What do you make of a woman who chooses a career over her own flesh and blood?"

"I don't know," I shrug. "Guess I was lucky. I mean, I already finished college and worked a few years before starting a family."

"Your kids are lucky, too." He looks at me with undisguised admiration.

Wondering how much philandering his wife put up with before walking out, I say, "I'd like to meet your kids sometime."

"Well, you'll get a chance this weekend if you come with David to the christening of my boat. We're naming her *The Samba.*" He describes how he and a few friends designed and built a motor launch which they plan to use for dinner-dance cruises in the harbor. Only finishing touches remain.

The Samba's maiden voyage is gala, with a sumptuous spread of island food and crates of champagne. A calypso band plays as the boat glides across the smooth harbor. Couples dance on the deck and laughter reverberates in the cabin. Leaning against the bulwarks, I nurse my champagne. My daily exercise has worked, for I've managed to wear the white bell-bottom pants and green midriff blouse from the year before. David sidles up and whispers, "How is my woman still so sexy?" I smile as his arm encircles my waist and he spins me into the dance crowd. I follow the best I can as the band breaks into a lively reggae beat but wish I had practiced more at home.

After the set we join Marcus and his children. Despite my repeated attempts to draw them out, they refuse to smile. Not even food or music stirs their interest. He also introduces Desmond, his brother, who resembles a linebacker on an American football team, and so many others that I despair of remembering all their names.

The next week Marcus invites us to go on a weekend cruise, a test run of the craft before going commercial. Twenty some people are going, including his almost-ex. He wants Donna to come for the sake of the kids. Given their glumness the week before, I can understand. Since I have tapered off with breast-feeding, I figure I can spend a night away from Angela. When Monica agrees to do weekend duty, I start to prepare for the Saturday morning departure.

Friday night David doesn't show up for dinner. I finally give up waiting and put away the food. Then I finish packing and go to sleep in Angela's room. I don't hear him come in, but next morning his car is in the driveway. Quietly I do my routines of feeding the children and getting everyone dressed.

At 8:30 I fix David his usual tray with tea and newspaper. Excited about the cruise, I open his bedroom door and sing out, "Hey, sleepy. Wake up!" Then I stop in horror. A skinny black-haired woman in red panties is stooping beside his bed, straining to clasp her bra. David lies under a sheet. "Wait outside!" he blurts. "I'm not ready yet!"

The tea tray crashes to the floor. I stand petrified, my face burning as I gaze from one to the other. Then I run, slamming the door behind me. I dash through the kitchen and outside. On the back steps I crouch. Feel like retching, but my body won't. Sunshine fills the yard, bathing me with its warmth, but I can't stop trembling. "*Things fall apart; the center cannot hold...*" blares in my exploding brain.

III

Later–maybe five minutes, maybe a half hour–David appears. "I'm sorry," he says. "Didn't expect you'd come in so early. She's gone now. I'm really sorry."

"Sorry? *Sorry!*" The words explode from my lips. I rise and approach him. "You're going to be a lot sorrier than you ever imagined possible! This is my house, too! My home! I've had it! I'm not taking any more!"

"You've every right to be angry. I understand. Just let it out. It's okay."

"It's *not* okay!" I shriek. "Nothing's okay anymore. I HATE YOU!"

"Just listen," he says, holding his palm up like a preacher delivering a benediction. "That woman doesn't mean anything to me. Guess I got so drunk last night I didn't know what I was doing. Believe me, I was as surprised as you when I saw her in my bed. As soon as I woke up, I told her to leave. She's just a prostitute."

"A prostitute! You brought a prostitute into our home? With our children sleeping in the next room? YOU SCUM!" I slap his face. He doesn't recoil, doesn't lift a finger in self-defense.

"So now you have to *pay* women," I sneer. "Rather coming down in the world, aren't you?" Suddenly my protest feels futile. I don't even have the option of divorce. "But thanks for giving me this evidence. It'll be useful in family court for getting custody..."

"Jac, I'm so sorry." He reaches for my arm.

"Don't touch me!" I jerk away.

"You've got to believe me. I love you. I don't know how I could have been such an idiot. There's no excuse. But don't take it personally. It had nothing to do with you. I don't even remember coming home..."

"I wish you hadn't," I look at him contemptuously. "It's time for you to move out!"

"But Jac, this is the weekend of the cruise. You've been looking forward to it so much. I'm not going to let you miss it. I'll stay with the kids and you go."

"What?"

"It'll be good for you to have a break. You need a chance to cool off after all this. I'll call Marcus and ask him to pick you up."

"But I'm—"

"No buts. I'm sure Marcus won't have it any other way." He goes inside and dials the number. After a brief exchange, he opens the door and reports, "It's all set. Marcus will swing by in a half-hour. Just get yourself ready. I'll take care of everything here."

I shake my head. "I don't know if..." I look up, but he's gone.

Still in shock, I mechanically pile my boating gear on the verandah. Then I put Angela in the pram, help Jonathan into his pedal car, and walk with them around the yard. They sense something is wrong, so I try to explain. "Jonathan, Honey, Mommy's going to sleep on Uncle Marcus's boat tonight. Maybe next time you can go, too, but for now Daddy's staying home with you and Angie. I'll miss you, but it's only for one night." Getting away is exactly what I need, but *with* the children. And for good! On the boat I will figure out how.

Rather than brood over David's betrayal, I decide to make the best of being on my own. For once I don't have to sit in the cheering section, listening to his jokes and asking leading questions to massage his ego. I can talk with anybody I want about subjects that interest *me*. Though Donna's beauty is a bit intimidating, I join her on deck. "So," I smile, "I hear you're going to university. What are you studying?"

"Economics."

"Really. I took a few econ classes in college and actually enjoyed them. What do you plan to do with it?"

"I'm hoping to —"

"Mommy!" Her children dash over. "Look what Daddy gave us!" They are both adjusting new sunglasses. I rise to make room for them to sit beside her. Clearly they want their mother's undivided attention, so I drift away. Probably they're still hoping for reconciliation. Is this a preview of what's coming for us? I choke up, fight back tears as I climb to the upper deck.

"Hey," a male voice greets me. "Come on up. The weather's fine." It's Bob from Canada, Marcus's partner in the boat project whom I met at the christening party. I accept the drink he offers and together we enjoy the view of the harbor on one side and the Palisadoes Peninsula on the other as the boat skims along the smooth surface. We settle down on cushions and are soon talking like college students about books, philosophy, art, the cosmos. I enjoy the free-flowing exploration of ideas, even though on some points we don't agree. He's a big fan of Ron Hubbard.

"You ought to read what he has to say. He's absolutely changed my life," he raves. "Here, take this." From his bag he withdraws a dog-eared paperback copy of *Dianetics I*. "Believe me, it's worth reading. I see the whole world differently now."

"I'm sure it is," I smile, "but I've had enough of other people's philosophy. At this point, I need to figure out a few things for myself."

"That's the beauty of Dianetics; it gives you a framework for figuring out your own unique place in this crazy world that can be overwhelming when you don't have an anchor point. The backlash to religious fundamentalism has left a terrible vacuum. Dianetics helps people get past it."

I scoop up a handful of plantain chips. "Which religion are you recovering from?"

"Catholic, of course. The hardest one to get over. That's why I can't get a divorce. We've been separated for over two years, but my wife won't hear of it. If I divorce her, she won't be able to take communion. Could even get ex-communicated. For her that would be death. That's how much the church controls her. I miss my kids, but I just can't go back to the enslavement."

"Tell me about your children..." As he goes on, I realize how starved I've been for adult conversation. The quandary of my own family crisis churns silently inside.

We spend the night anchored near Lime Cay, far from city lights. I unroll my sleeping bag on the upper deck and lie down. In the pitch sky, the waning moon appears. Through the night I keep waking and marking the progress of the night traveler across the diamond-studded sky. Like it, I seem to be in an endlessly recurring orbit ... around David. Is it foolishness to think I can change orbits when even the moon can't?

Next day as *The Samba* returns to harbor I lean on the gunwale staring across the water. Marcus comes up behind and nudges my shoulder. "Penny for your thoughts."

"You don't want to know."

"Jac, David's no saint, but he does love you and his kids. That's a given, regardless of what else goes down."

"He told you what happened?"

"Not the details."

"I get knots in my stomach just thinking about it. I don't ever want to see him again. But I have to and it's killing me. I hate him so much!"

"What happened exactly?"

"He brought a whore to *my* home and slept with her while the children and I were right there!"

"Ouch! I never did anything that rotten to Donna, and she left me anyway!" He smiles wryly. "Now I understand why you don't want to go back. There's plenty of room in my house if you need a place while you sort this out."

"Thanks, but I can't with the kids.... I'm still numb; just don't know..."

"Whatever happens, don't forget them. Donna's disregard for our kids is what I can't get over. David's really sorry; I could tell on the phone. It's hard now, but maybe in time you can forgive him."

"Done that...too many times already. I can't ever trust him again. Anyway, thanks for listening. Maybe I will take you up on your offer."

"Any time."

"And thanks for the wonderful cruise. I really appreciate your letting me come."

"All my pleasure, I assure you." He squeezes my shoulder in friendly, big brother fashion and slips away.

As we near the yacht club, I can make out David's car parked beside the pier. Then I see him sitting on the dock with Angela in his arms and Jonathan standing beside him. Despicable ploy! Using the children to get near me. I hoped to ride back with Marcus and Donna, but now... My break is over.

IV

I grab my bag and climb from the boat. Immediately David's voice entreats me. "Jac! We're over here."

I walk over, ignoring him, and crouch to hug Jonathan. "Hi, Big Boy. Mommy's back. How are you?"

"O.K." he mumbles and points to his sister. "La La."

I run my fingers through his messy blond hair, kiss his grubby cheek. "Yes, you and La La came to meet Mommy. That's wonderful!"

Straightening, I come face to face with David.

"We all missed you and want you back home. I've done a lot of thinking, and I'm going to make this up to you."

I reach for Angela, but he pulls her back. "Get in the car. We have to talk."

I clench my teeth and glance around. People leaving the boat are scattering quickly. Marcus is nowhere in sight. I've stepped right into David's snare. As I watch him carry my daughter to the car, the image of Marcus's kids flashes before me. My children mustn't be torn like them, sacrificial lambs in our battles. This round I'll concede. I lift my bag in one hand, hold Jonathan's chubby fist with the other, and march to the car.

At home, David is Mr. Contrite, following me around the house, with a litany of apologies: "I was wrong. I'm so sorry. I'll never do anything like that again. I promise. Please believe me....This time I've learned my lesson. If you'll just give me a chance, I'll make it up to you. I love you, Jac. You and the children are everything to me.... This could be the turning point for us, if only you'll give me another chance." He hounds me, insisting he can't go on living without my forgiveness. So sincere, he seems to believe it himself. "You won't be sorry," he says. "I promise you."

When he finally lets me have some time with the children, I put them in the tub with rubber boats and ducks and fish. We have a splashing good time without worrying about getting the floor wet. Then I read them a storybook about an octopus, and Angela falls asleep on my lap. I place her in the crib, and lift Jonathan into his bed. "Do you want Daddy to come say Goodnight?" I whisper as I kiss his cheek.

"Okay."

I tell David and he goes in and does his tickling routine until Jonathan is gasping hysterically. It seems to be the one way they can interact safely.

Emerging from Jonathan's room, David takes my hand and leads me to the master bathroom. "Now it's time for you to relax," he says. The tub is filled with warm water and bubbles. "Sit here and soak. I'll shower in the other bath."

I lay back in the warm lavender-scented bubbles, gently plashing the water until it turns cool. Tying a short peignoir around me, I enter the bedroom. Candles and incense are burning, and soft piano music wafts from the stereo. David hands me a goblet of

187

wine. Clinking his glass to mine, he says, "Welcome home, Darling. Let this be the beginning of our new life together."

My final thought before falling asleep is, He's a Jekyll and Hyde. Maybe he can't help himself. If only we could get a professional opinion! But he'll never agree to any such thing.

Two days later David announces, "I have bad news, Jac. I'm afraid that prostitute... well, she really was the worst kind of whore. It looks like I got a case of the clap. We both have to go to the VD clinic for treatment."

My mouth drops open. "You mean I... I might have it?"

"I'm really sorry to put you through this, but we have to get this taken care of first thing tomorrow morning."

"I can't believe—"

"It's not such a big deal. I don't think you got it, but we can't take any chances. All you'll have to do is get a shot of penicillin and fill out a report."

Wishing I could wear a veil, I ride silently with him to the clinic, stoically suffering the ignominy. The workers treat me with courtesy, but I can imagine how they will later smirk and joke about the white bitch who can't keep her man satisfied—or even worse, white tramp spreading disease. My only aim is to get out of there without seeing anyone I know. Another step down on a seemingly bottomless ladder of degradation. If only I could avoid ever having sex with him again! Just run the business, raise the children, and stay in our separate bedrooms. That I might be able to endure.

All the way home he never stops talking about his latest plan for improving the energy output of his invention.

V

"You're spending too much time at home with the children. It's like you don't think about anything except who's going to poop next and wondering where I am. It's time you got out and found a job.

Here, look through the classifieds." David gestures at the *Sunday Gleaner* on the table beside him and takes a mouthful of ackee and salt fish.

"A job?" I put a johnnycake on Jonathan's plate and coax Angela to open her mouth for a spoonful of crushed papaya. "I can't leave the children—"

"That's just the problem! They need to fend for themselves more."

I refill their juice and hold Angela's cup while she drinks. As I go to the sink for cloths to wipe their hands and faces, David continues, "Why don't you sit down and eat? Where the hell is the maid?"

"The new one can't start until tomorrow. Remember?"

"Oh. Well, I hope she shows up on time. You gotta get going with your job search."

I remove Angela's bib, lift her from the high chair, and put her in the playpen. "David, we have no idea how this new maid is going to work out, and I don't think you realize how much time it takes to do the company paperwork, much less get a job."

"Bullshit. It's a proven fact that the length of time it takes to do a job is directly proportional to the time available to do it. That's the problem—not using your time efficiently. Be sure to read this today." He thrusts the employment section at me.

I get up and carry dishes to the sink. "I'll look at it later." I stoop down. "Jonathan, come, let Mommy tie your shoe."

"Believe me," David says, "it'll be good for you to get out of the house. Give you a reason to take better care of yourself." He disappears in the direction of his workshop.

I look down at my faded dress and sloppy sandals. Maybe he's right.

After responding to several ads in the paper, I get only one interview. But it goes well and I'm hired as a lecturer at the teacher training college. By then the new maid, Clemmie, is settling in.

Older than any we've had before, she makes me feel more confident about leaving the children with her. Only time will tell how long she'll last.

The working conditions at the college are superior to my previous jobs, as is the pay. I appreciate the academic environment where I can focus on content rather than discipline. The college uses traditional English texts, including Shakespeare, the Bronte sisters, Hardy, and the romantic poets, with a Graham Greene novel as the sole example of modern literature. Since Jamaica is now independent of Britain, I think students should read some of the literature produced by outstanding West Indian writers like Kincaid, Walcott, Braithwaite, and the Naipauls. But curriculum planning is not my prerogative, so I have to use the colonial texts. When possible, I make comparisons with contemporary regional writers.

The class is surprised one day when I distribute mimeographed copies of some Bob Marley lyrics and call him a bard. One student raises his hand and says, "Miss, I don't mean to be disrespectful, but this doesn't look like good English."

I smile. "Can you read aloud an example of a passage that you think is not good English?"

"Sure, most all of it," he says and begins reading:

> *No woman, no cry.*
> *Little darlin', don't shed no tears.*
> *No woman, no cry.*

"Thank you," I say. "And what do the rest of you think?"
Silence.

"Let's forget about words like 'good' and 'bad,'" I prompt, "and use the terms 'standard English' and 'dialect.'" I write these words on the board, and under the 'dialect' heading I copy the Marley lyrics. Then I ask the class how they would convey the same idea in standard English. Scattered chuckles come from around the room. "What's the matter?" I arch my eyebrows.

A young lady raises her hand and volunteers, "You can't show the same feelings in regular English, Miss."

"You may be right, but let's try," I coax. "Let's start with the first line. How could it be said in standard English?"

Poised at the board, chalk in hand, I wait until a voice says, "Please, Mother, don't cry."

"Good." I write it. "Okay, the next line."

I write as someone says, "Don't be sad, my dear. I don't want you to cry."

Everybody laughs when I ask for a volunteer to sing our translation.

"Not possible," a young man responds. "Marley's tune and words, they fit together."

"Point well made," I smile.

The next class we read two of Shakespeare's sonnets. The follow-up writing assignment is to compare and contrast the lyrics of one of Marley's songs with a Shakespearean sonnet of their choice. My turn for delight comes when I read their pieces, revealing nuances of their lives and customs which I know little about. Encouraged, I continue inventing methods and creating materials designed to foster pride in their national heritage, a pride I hope will carry over to the classrooms where they will eventually teach.

Arriving home from class one afternoon, I hear the phone ringing. "Hello," I say.

"Hi! It's Dad. We're at the airport."

"Dad? Where?"

"In Kingston!"

"You're kidding!" I gulp.

"No, I'm not. We just got through customs."

"Well, it'll take me a while to get there. Where exactly are you?"

"Don't bother coming out. We can take a cab. I have your address. See you soon."

VI

Worried about what David will say and do, I give Clemmie instructions for expanding the dinner menu. Then I rush around to make sure the house and children are tidy while wondering how to entertain my parents. It's the first time they have ever visited me in my home ... anywhere. Why now? What do they want?

When they arrive, I'm still in a fluster, but at least the house looks decent.

"This is unbelievable," I say as we exchange perfunctory hugs. "It doesn't seem possible that you're actually in Jamaica! But you must be tired. Come on in!"

I lead them inside and present their grandchildren. Angela observes wide-eyed from her walker and then throws down a toy for someone to retrieve. Grandma stoops to the challenge. Jonathan stands stiffly, clutching a matchbox car. When Grandpa kneels, he cautiously opens his hand and they investigate it together.

"Have a seat while I get some drinks." I indicate the chairs at the dining table.

"We've been wondering how you're getting along down here," Dad says. "And we wanted to see Jonathan again and meet our new granddaughter. So we thought coming unannounced would be the best way to keep you from going to any trouble."

A surprise ambush. Mom's idea, no doubt. "David will be so surprised!"

I pour tall glasses of limeade and offer one to Mother. "Thanks," she says, "but could I have mine without ice?"

"Sorry." I give it to Dad and pour another for her.

Dad drinks deeply and smacks his lips. "Delicious! What do you make this with?"

"Limes...from our tree. Come out in the yard and see it."

192

I pick up Angela, take Jonathan by the hand, and lead the way outside. Dad marvels at the abundance of tropical plants and wants to know all their names.

While touring the house, Mother comments, "You have a nice-sized place, but it's so plain. Don't you want to fix it up? This isn't how you're used to living."

I bristle but force a smile. "Guess our tastes are different. I don't like clutter. Now why don't you sit down and relax while I go check on dinner."

When David drives in, I race to the door. "My parents are here! They flew down and arrived without warning. They're staying for dinner."

"Great!" He turns and greets them with hearty handshakes. "I've been wanting to meet you, but wasn't expecting to today!" Then he inquires about their flight and offers to move their luggage into the spare room.

"Oh, no!" Mother says. "We can't stay here. You aren't married. We were hoping you could suggest a guesthouse..."

"Well, if you feel that way..." David glances at me. "Jac, what about the Sandman? It's nearby. Call and see if they have a vacancy."

"Okay." Relieved that he's ignoring her rebuff, I make the arrangements.

Then while I set the table and work with Clemmie to get the meal served, my parents play with the children and question David about his business. Over dinner, he volunteers to take time off from work the next day to show them around. I appreciate his offer since I have to teach all morning. Doing our best to put on a good appearance, we get through the meal without any reference to my runaway flight to Iowa two years before.

After dinner David calls Marcus and arranges to take my parents for a ride around the harbor on *The Samba*. Everyone says goodnight to Jonathan and Angela and I take them to their room to read a story before settling them in bed.

I return to the living room in time to hear Mother say, "Doesn't Jonathan talk yet?"

"Of course," I answer. "Didn't you hear him say 'Bye Bye'?"

"I mean real sentences, like other children his age. Your niece Diane is only a few months older and she can already—"

"Children develop at their own rate. Many don't speak till they're three or older. He'll talk when he's ready, and we're not putting any pressure on him about it."

"Well, I think he should see a speech therapist. At least get a professional opinion —"

"Nonsense!" David interjects. "Studies show that children who wait longer before they start talking are usually smarter. They take more time to think things out for themselves. Speech is really the beginning of thought control. Using words other people have made up and assigned meanings to actually limits what we can think. Jonathan's a smart boy, holding on to his own ideas for a while. Watch and see."

"I hope you're right." Dad sounds dubious. "But it's getting late. We better get over to the guesthouse."

"I'll drive you." I jump up and get my keys.

Next evening, I'm setting the dining table when David and my parents come in. They're exhausted because after the boat ride he took them for a drive into the Blue Mountains, so I hurry to get the food served while Dad takes Jonathan outside to play. David and Mother sip limeade in the living room as she jiggles Angela on her lap. While setting the table, I muse about how nice David was to give up a whole day of work to entertain them. Suddenly I hear raised voices and rush to the living room as David says, "What right do you have to come into my house and criticize how I live?"

"I did not criticize," Mother retorts. "I just asked if you accept the Lord Jesus Christ as your personal savior."

"And how is that any of your business?"

"Because these two little ones are my grandchildren."

194

"But they're *my* children, mine and Jac's. We decide how they live, not you." Looking at me, David says, "Your mother put this tract in our living room." He holds up *The Portals of Prayer*. "Thinks she can barge in here and tell us what to read, what to believe, how to raise our children—"

"That's it!" Mother rises and thrusts Angela at me. "I've had all I can take!" She trembles as the shrill timbre of her voice signals a gathering storm.

Dad appears, face grim. "What's going on?"

"Nothing, Dad," I say. "Please everybody, dinner's ready. You must be so hungry after your busy day of sightseeing." Tight-lipped, they follow me to the dining room.

David and I remain erect, eyes open while Mother and Dad bow their heads and he recites a blessing. Then I pass bowls around the table and dish up for the children.

"How was your day, Jackie?" Dad finally breaks the silence.

"Busy as usual. My students are nervous about mid-term exams, so we mostly reviewed. In the afternoon, Jonathan had his swimming lesson, and Angela came along to play in the kiddie pool."

"How's he doing?" Dad asks.

David answers, "A waste of money. The kid's too scared. He's never going to learn to swim unless he gets some courage."

"He did better today," I say. "Didn't cry at all."

"It's about time!"

"I never heard of children learning to swim when they're so young," Mother says disapprovingly.

Dad jumps in. "I think it's great. In fact, my father said the best time to learn is before a kid can even walk." He proceeds to describe the pioneers' tried-and-true method of throwing children off bridges to sink or swim.

Mother doesn't say another word until I bring out dessert. Tasting the lime pie, she turns to me with a look of amazement. "This is delicious! Can I get the recipe?"

195

"Sure. I'll write it down for you after dinner. It's from David's mother. If you can't buy limes in Iowa, lemons will work fine."

We get through the meal without another outburst. Quickly I write down the recipe and offer to drive them to the guesthouse. On the way Mother sputters indignantly, "That David, I can't believe him! No one has ever spoken to me the way he did. I just can't take any more of it. I'll go on praying for you and our grandchildren, Jackie, but I cannot set foot in your house again, not as long as he's there."

"Don't worry," Dad says. "I'll reschedule our flight so we can leave tomorrow."

He calls later to say he's gotten them on a morning flight. It's at the same time as my class, so I can't drive them to the airport, and I'm not about to ask David.

I leave early next morning and stop at the guesthouse to say goodbye and make sure they get a cab. Mother hugs me stiffly. "Just remember, Jackie, I love you." With puckered chin she adds grimly, "And so does Jesus."

"I love you, too." I say, fighting back the tears that goodbyes to her always provoke. For the past ten years every one of our encounters has ended with this same desolate feeling of failure and regret. The way she says "I love you" with a ring of profound disapproval lets me know she means she would love me if only I were different, and it is my fault for depriving her of that joy. Dismissing her as neurotic would be easy, but it does nothing to fill the emptiness inside. Why does she make it so hard? The feeling is undoubtedly mutual. And I've totally bungled this chance to enlist my parents' support; David now knows how ineffectual they actually are.

Kingston, 1973

I

Halfway through our bedtime reading of *The Cat in the Hat,* David bursts in. "Hi everybody! The most incredible thing happened today. You gotta hear this, Jac!"

Promising to finish the book tomorrow, I hustle the children off to bed. Then I turn my attention to his exuberant face.

"I know you'll think this sounds crazy," he says, "but bear with me. It's amazing." He holds up his hand as if swearing on a witness stand. "I was driving through the hills up in Clarendon. I'd bought a couple ounces of weed from a farmer and was heading back to Kingston when all of a sudden I turned off the road and started driving along a winding lane. It was like I had no control over where I was going. Vines and branches were everywhere, but I kept driving. Then I rounded a bend and saw a clearing filled with sunshine." He gestures expansively. "It felt like I'd gone through a tunnel and come out on top of the world." His eyes are wide, unblinking.

Trying to look attentive, I watch for cues of what he expects from me: *"I know some new tricks," said the Cat in the Hat. "A lot of good tricks. I will show them to you."*

"So I stopped the car and got out. I looked around 'n decided to sample my new smoke. I cotched on the hood to fill my pipe and took a few puffs."

I can picture his habitual pose, sitting with one foot dangling and the other leg bent, forming a triangle. One elbow would be propped on the raised knee with his hand holding the pipe while he leaned against the windshield.

"The weed was fantastic so I kept it going and walked over to the other side of the clearing where a log blocked the track. The sunshine was so bright I couldn't see much at first, but when my eyes adjusted I saw a man sitting quietly in the shade at the end of the log, as if he was waiting for me."

"Who was he?"

"Just what I wondered. For all I knew, could be a cop! And there I was, caught red-handed, but he just said, 'I've been expecting you.' How do you like that?"

"Strange."

"Yeah, but the funny thing is, it didn't feel strange. So I said, 'Well, here I am.' And he started talking, as though he'd always known me. I sat and listened. Don't know how long I was there. Could have been hours. He told me more about what's going on in this world than you'll ever read in any newspaper or book. And he's right—most of what we read isn't true anyway. Just a pack of lies to keep us under control."

David paces the room. The more he talks, the more animated he becomes. "We go around believing their lies and keeping their machines going and money flowing into their banks. Slavery hasn't ended. It's just hiding under the name of capitalism. Mark my word, if things continue the way they're headed, with greedy capitalists controlling everything, it'll destroy the whole world. As we speak, the bastards are building nuclear power plants all over America because they want to make themselves even richer. Nuclear plants produce plutonium, the most toxic substance on this planet. It has a half-life of two hundred and fifty thousand years! Do you know what that means? It kills everything it has contact with for that long! They want the power, but they don't know what to do with the by-product. Don't want it in *their* own back yards, of course. So you know what they're doing?" He reels, pausing to relight his pipe.

"What?"

"Sealing it in concrete vaults and dumping them in the sea! The vaults'll deteriorate and contaminate all the oceans. When that happens, we're all dead. It won't be in our generation, but what about our children, and our children's children? Those bastards don't care about the earth, people, or anything except their own rich asses. And we're all pawns in their power games!"

"He told you all that?"

"You haven't heard the strangest part yet. The sun was getting low, putting the whole clearing in shadow. I stood up and went to piss behind a tree. When I turned back, he wasn't there. Gone! Just evaporated. I looked around for a few minutes but couldn't find him, so I got in my car and drove out to the main road. Then I realized I didn't even know his name, so I went back to look for him, but guess what?"

"What?"

"I couldn't find the lane! Gone, too. Like it never existed!"

"Was it dark then?"

He whirls around, eyes round as poker chips. "I'm telling you, it wasn't there! I could *not* go back. Just like we can't go back in time. Don't you see what I'm saying? Today time and space became one. I must have walked through a time warp and it created a space warp. Once the time had passed, the place was gone. The warp had ended; there was no way back!"

"Amazing!" I tidy the books on the table, at a loss for what he expects from me.

"To put it simply, an angel appeared today and told me what's going on in the world. The question is, why? Why did he choose to reveal the Truth to me? Must be my invention. He didn't say anything about it, but I think he knows. Jac, he wants *me* to save the world from nuclear destruction. Somebody out there must know my invention is the answer. But I haven't been working on it as much as I should. I think he came to get me on track. Anybody can run a business and make money, but I shouldn't waste my time on that anymore. It's my job to save the world. But I'm not sure I can handle an assignment this big. I'll need your help. If I accept, we'll be in it together."

I stack the large books on bottom, smaller on top. "What do you think the job involves?"

"I can't be sure. Whatever we do, there are risks. If I take this on, I run the risk of failing. But if I don't, destruction is certain. So there's not really a choice, is there?"

"I guess not." I want to be supportive. But the intense glint in his eye reminds me of evangelists I saw years before in a revival tent where people were rolling on the ground. Then, too, I wanted to believe, but something didn't feel right.

Fired by the "angel's" message, David immerses himself round the clock in building an improved prototype of his invention which he is certain can extract energy from water with no toxic by-products. I help by revising, typing and mailing the patent application to a Washington attorney. Letters fly back and forth as we respond to his questions. It feels good to be helping David make a difference in the world. I love his concern, his caring enough about our children's future to try to do something about it.

II

The weekend before Angela's first birthday David's mother calls to ask if it's all right for them to stop by with a gift. I'm delighted she remembers. Despite wishing we could be friendlier, I have never called her except that one time to get a recipe, knowing David will consider it disloyal. "Hold on a minute," I say. "I'll check with David."

To my surprise, he says it's fine and even decides to stick around. Maybe this will be a new beginning, I hope, as I rush to tidy the children. "What do you want to put on for Grandpa and Gram?" I ask Jonathan.

He thinks for a moment and then pulls a red polo shirt from his drawer.

"Good choice," I say, slipping it over his head. "Want these?" I hold up denim shorts, and he nods.

"And how about you? What do you want to wear for Grandma Precious?" I pick Angela up and open her closet. "Let's find a pretty dress." Giggling, she stretches forward and tugs on a ruffly lime-colored one.

David greets his parents civilly and invites them to sit on the verandah. I rush to the kitchen to pour drinks. Jimmy admires the Lego structure Jonathan is building, and Precious convinces Angela to sit on her lap while opening her package.

After serving frosty glasses of limeade, I kneel to examine the gift. "What a sweet dolly! Thank you, Grandma Precious. You're so thoughtful."

"It's nothing much," she says modestly. "We just want dear little Angie to know we love her." We watch silently as Angela pokes and pulls on the doll's parts. Then Precious continues, "We have an announcement to make. We want to tell you ourselves rather than letting you hear from someone else."

"Hear what?" David asks.

"Well, as you probably know, we've been going to Toronto quite a bit the past couple years to help Renae with the children. Now we've decided to move there, and we've leased an apartment near them. We plan to go up in the spring."

"Wow!" I say. "This is quite a surprise."

She pauses and takes a swallow of limeade. Angela slips from her grandmother's lap, dragging the doll along. Jonathan goes "Buhrrrrr" as he rearranges cars and trucks around his Lego buildings.

"I can't imagine spending winters there," Precious continues, "so for the first year we'll keep our house vacant to use when we come back. We want to be able to see our dear grandchildren here, too, but for now Renae needs help with Wendy and Willie—"

"So that's why you're moving!" interrupts David. "To be with the children I'm not allowed to see because I'm such a rotten father! Take a look at *these* kids—do they look like I treat them bad?"

"Let's not get into all that," his mother retorts. "We mustn't ruin Angie's birthday—"

"You always have an excuse for glossing things over... never want to face the truth."

"Speaking of truth," his father speaks up, "I'd like to know how much you're sending to Canada each month for those children."

David glares. "Not a penny! I warned her I won't support them if I can't see them, and I'm sticking to it."

"At least you're honest. We've known all along that you haven't sent anything. We're the ones who have to provide for *your* children. You think that's right?"

David shrugs. "You get to see them whenever you want!"

"I believe the divorce settlement includes a court order for you to pay a hundred dollars a month or face prosecution."

"I haven't seen anybody come after me for it though. Let them try." He twirls around, arms outstretched, and shouts, "Here I am, world! I'm not hiding!"

"You're really begging for trouble, David. I have a good mind to tell Renae to get a subpoena to make you send money."

"Sure, Dad, go ahead. Keep meddling in other people's business. Never give a thought to being loyal to me! Always stand up for whoever's against me." David's voice grows louder. "You have the nerve to come into my house and start criticizing how I live. Bastard! I oughta punch you right in the mouth!"

"Stop it!" I leap up, jump between them.

Precious's voice trembles, "Enough, David! You'll do nothing of the sort. Jimmy, let's go." She rises.

"Yeah, you better," David sneers. "Don't worry, I'm not gonna hit the old fart. Just want to see him quake a little. Get him out of here and make sure he never sets foot in my house again!" He stands in the middle of the verandah, arms folded, legs spread.

I follow Precious to the car, murmuring, "Thanks for coming. I'm so sorry ..."

"We know it's not your fault, Dear. I don't know what possesses David..."

"And thanks again for the present. I wish we could keep in touch, but..." We look helplessly at one another as Jimmy, shaking – probably more from rage than fright–starts the engine and backs out of the driveway. I stymie the impulse to wave, knowing David will take it as befriending the enemy, and return to the verandah.

"Hypocrites!" he declares. "Always going on like they're so good and pretending they never do anything wrong. If you only knew!"

"Knew what?"

"The dirt they keep hidden. Like when I caught Dad screwing our neighbor's wife."

"What!"

"God's truth. I was walking to the neighbor's house one afternoon when I noticed our car parked behind some bushes by the road. I went over to check it out and through the window I saw Daddy humping away on top of Mrs. Winthrop. Couldn't believe my eyes! Didn't want to. Until then, I had really swallowed the crap they fed me about morals and honesty. But that showed me it was all lies."

"Did he see you watching?"

"No, he was too busy, like a hog rutting. Later when he got home I told everybody, loud and clear so even Mumsy could hear. But he denied it! Can you believe that? The jackass said I was lying! Never saw him so bullshit! And then he punished me."

203

"Punished *you?*"

"Yeah. Had the yard boy flog me. I'll never, ever forgive him for it! The brute flogged me with a stick until I was blue. And my father watched."

I shiver at the image. "How old were you?"

"About ten, maybe eleven. Not long after, they sent me to boarding school. They really couldn't afford it, but I guess the old man didn't want me spying on him anymore."

"Who did your mother believe?"

"She knew I was telling the truth but would never admit it. Very good at pretending things she doesn't like don't exist. But that's their problem. We won't have to worry about seeing them anymore."

III

A surge in the supply of guns sweeps across the island as Jamaicans prepare for the third general election since independence. The Labor Party's failure to meet rising expectations has caused widespread discontent giving the opposition Peoples' National Party a good prospect for winning. On the bloody campaign trail, PNP candidates promise to deliver justice and economic equality for all. They march to victory and straightaway begin nationalizing private enterprise. Hotels, factories, bauxite companies—one industry after another falls to government takeover. Rumors abound about the new Prime Minister being a personal friend of Fidel Castro. Fearful of a Cuban-style revolution, capitalists hustle to bag their money and get off the island. Before long most of the garish mansions on the ridges of Kingston's Beverly Hills are occupied by caretakers. Jamaica is bleeding—red blood and green.

The exodus of entrepreneurs and investment money affects our business. Several companies do not renew their contracts. Despite keeping bids to a minimum David can't secure any new clients, so we're forced to lay off a worker and sell a van.

As law and order crumble, politicians from the previous government flee, and citizens barricade themselves inside their homes. David's friends have guns to protect property and family, but he's not convinced that's the answer. Over the newspaper at breakfast one morning he says, "Here's another story about a burglar breaking into a house and using the man's own gun to shoot him. Just like the one last week. We may actually be safer without a gun."

"I agree," I say, trying not to appear too eager. I feel less threatened by outsiders than by the idea of having a loaded weapon in the house. What if the children got their hands on it? Or he did when in a temper?

He folds the paper and shoves back his chair. "Don't wait dinner for me tonight. Marcus and I are working on a job at the airport and we can't stop till we're done. I don't know how long it'll take."

"Oh. Thanks for letting me know."

Having only one class to teach, I get home early. In the afternoon I fix a picnic supper for the kids and spread a blanket in the back yard. We eat and play leapfrog until dark. After their baths I read "Jack and the Beanstalk," pointing to the words as I say them. Angie mimicks me by pointing to pictures and laughing. Jonathan, thinking her naughty when her hand covers words I'm trying to read, keeps saying, "Stop it! Stop!"

"It's okay," I say, but I can tell it really bothers him. She notices, too, and is all the more mischievous. Impatient with the bickering, I hustle them off to bed. Then I stack some Herbie Mann and Botticelli albums on the record player, and open up *A Brighter Sun,* a novel that's been on my "to read" shelf far too long.

I'm in a deep sleep when the phone rings.

"Sorry to wake you, Jac," David speaks rapidly, "but I'm in a little trouble and need your help. Don't panic. Just listen carefully; I only get one call. I'm in the lock-up at the Trench Town police station. You got that?"

"Trench Town!" The worst part of Kingston. "What's going on?"

"Can't go into details. Only got a minute. Marcus and I are both here. Desmond—you know, his brother—is on his way over to you. He needs cash to bail us. Take the money out of the box in my trunk and give it to him. Understand?"

"Okay."

"One more thing," he pauses. "We've both been beaten pretty bad. I just hope it doesn't get worse. You need to know in case we don't get out of here alive. See you soon, I hope, but I'm not sure how long this'll take. Gotta go now."

"Okay." I put down the phone, but remain immobile on the edge of the bed, stunned by his words. Fear in David's voice is an unfamiliar sound. What were he and Marcus doing in the roughest and poorest area of the city? Why are they in jail? Who beat them? Questions crowding my mind, I get the money.

Even though I'm expecting it, the loud pounding on the door makes me jump. Desmond, a member of the National Guard Reserve, wears his firearm boldly visible in a waist holster. That coupled with his burly 220 pounds commands respect in all quarters. His take-charge attitude gives me assurance he can handle everything.

"These guys are lucky you're coming to their rescue," I remark.

"I don't know what this country's coming to." Desmond shakes his head. "Can't trust anybody. It was the police who beat them up—at least that's what Marcus implied on the phone, but he couldn't explain. Don't worry. I won't leave without 'em."

I give him the envelope. "Good luck."

"Thanks. I'll need it. It's a good thing you had this cash on hand because I'll probably have to pass a few bribes. Okay, later." He turns and disappears into the dark.

It's mid-morning when David drives into the yard with a large dent on the side of his car. As he gets out his shirt hangs open, buttons missing. Bandages are on his head, hand and chest. Walking stiffly he enters the house and eases himself onto the sofa. I rush to pour juice and fix some bun and cheese.

"Just what I need," he says wearily.

I sit and watch him eat. "What a night!" He shakes his head ruefully. "Marcus and I were driving over to Port Henderson where we'd heard about a good party with reggae band and all. It was late, so we took the shortcut through Trench Town. Suddenly a car comes barreling out of a cross street without slowing down. I braked and swerved, but it caught the passenger side door, right where Marcus was sitting. Good thing I dodged, 'cause a direct hit could have killed him. We jumped out, only to see two guys coming out of the other car with guns drawn. They tell us to put our hands up and frisk us. When they find a gun in Marcus's leg holster, one starts talking about shooting us."

"My God!"

"Just then two police cars come screaming up, sirens blaring. They block the street, and a bunch of uniformed cops run over. I yell, 'Officers, help! These guys are gonna shoot us!' but one of them clobbers me with a billy club. That's how I got this concussion." He touches the bandage on his head.

"Why did he hit you?"

"Well, I found out later that the vehicle that crashed into us was an unmarked police car. Plainclothes cops were chasing a stolen car when they sped through the stop sign. They had already radioed for reinforcements. That's why the squad cars arrived so soon. The uniformed guys thought we were driving the stolen car. Things got mixed up real fast. Finding the gun on Marcus was reason enough for them to shoot us right there, 'cause they could always say he pulled it on them."

"Another reason not to have a gun."

Ignoring me, he continues, "As I started coming to, first thing I felt was a barrel against my temple and a boot on my stomach, pinning me to the ground. I heard the gun cock and opened my eyes. The cop looked at me, but couldn't do it. He pulled the pistol away, said, 'Shit, he ain't worth it,' and kicked me in the ribs with his steel-toed boots."

"Oh, my God!" I touch his thigh gingerly, unsure of where all his bruises are.

"I curled up and just lay there. Marcus was pleading with the cops to check his gun registration; said he'd left the license in his car. Finally he managed to convince them to give us the benefit of doubt and take us to the station rather than shoot us right there. I tell you, the angel was with us, 'cause things could have gone either way."

"Incredible." Momentarily I toy with a fantasy of how our lives would be different if the policeman had pulled the trigger. But he didn't, so it's fruitless to speculate. David survived and now expects my sympathy and comfort. "I'll run a bath for you," I offer. "Then rub some liniment on those aching muscles."

David and Marcus talk about suing for wrongful arrest and brutality, but the lawyer they consult tells them the courts in Jamaica are so overloaded it could take up to three years to get a hearing. David finds it hard to accept the reality that in his own country he no longer has the protection of law.

"I can't take this," he says, sounding more discouraged than angry. "Four more years of chaos before another election. I don't want to see how bad it'll be by then."

I think he's over-reacting. My everyday life hasn't changed drastically, except for rising prices and more rudeness in public places. But apparently that gun barrel at the side of his head made quite an impression.

IV

"Take a look at the article in here about Australia." David hands me a *Time* magazine. "The climate is mostly tropical, lots of beaches, good schools. I've heard some Jamaicans have moved there because the immigration policy isn't so restrictive as it used to be. I think we should check it out."

I glance at photos featuring beach scenes, koalas, and uniformed school children, mostly white. Though I have no interest in emigrating, I'm mildly curious about the faraway place. Still I don't take his interest seriously until the day he comes home with startling news that Dougie is moving his family to Florida.

"Oh no!" I cry. "When?"

"He's going up next week to look for a job."

"I thought they were doing so well."

"They were ... *before* the election. Marie doesn't feel safe anymore, and business has really slowed down. Dougie's afraid of getting laid off. Everything's changed."

Our discussion continues as news reaches us almost daily of another business closing or another family leaving. Karen and Tom have moved to California. Mrs. Edmondson's sons have gone to Australia, but she is preparing to move to Cayman. Two teachers I met at the college are seeking work in Barbados. Desmond plans to go to Belize. Marcus, like Dougie, is considering Florida, but he's concerned about prejudice there. Our world is unraveling at an alarming rate.

David and I agree Canada's too cold and the U.S. is too racist, so we decide to request visa applications for Australia. Information in the immigration packet fuels his excitement and even piques my interest: thousands of miles of pristine beaches; diverse population with recent immigration from the Caribbean, Latin America, eastern Europe and Asia; vast stretches of uninhabited land; superb diving on the Great Barrier Reef; booming economy; good public services including health care. It sounds too good to be true. Then I discover a policy prohibiting visas to unmarried couples with children.

"Well, guess it's time for us to do it," he says. "What do you think? Shall we give the Aussies what they want?"

209

"Get married just for a visa? Like a shotgun wedding? We shouldn't let bureaucrats coerce us..."

"We gotta be realistic. Marriage is just a scrap of paper. Why let it stand between us and a good future for our children?"

"Well, it's hypocritical..."

"Stop dreaming. The whole middle class is pulling out. The longer we wait, the harder it'll be. At least now we still have resources to sell, so we can afford to settle elsewhere. By this time next year, that might not be true. The government could even freeze assets, take over bank accounts. That shit happens."

I nod ruefully. "They've done it to corporations, so individuals could be next."

"You better believe it. Things could get much worse. If we agree that Australia looks like the best place, we'd be fools to let a technicality like marriage stop us."

"I suppose you're right," I sigh. It might be better to arrive in Australia married and respectable, and it'd be better for the children as they start school. The fact of David even considering it shows his commitment, and maybe he'll treat me with more respect if I'm his wife.

David makes an appointment with a justice of the peace and brings home a license application for me to sign. Since it's just for immigration, we decide not to tell anyone. I put on sandals and a lilac-colored dress I normally wear to school. David wears his usual working clothes—bush jacket and chino trousers. Casually, as though going to the bank, we leave the children with the maid. The procedure takes about two minutes. After signing the documents, we go to a bar in New Kingston.

When our gin and tonics arrive David says, "Well, Baby, here's to our future. Australia here we come!" Raising our glasses, we clink them and drink the tangy liquid. "Remember," he looks at me pointedly, "this makes no difference in our relationship. Married or not, you can't put me a leash on me."

The response to our visa application is prompt but inconclusive. We've passed the first hurdle, but next we have to be interviewed at a consulate. The closest ones are in Trinidad and Los Angeles. David thinks it would be an unnecessary expense to travel to either place and back to Jamaica. "Let's just buy one-way tickets to L.A., get visas from the consulate there and go on to Australia," he says. "We meet the requirements. No way they can turn us down."

"But if we sell off everything, we'll have nothing to come back to. What if we get stranded in California?"

"Always the defeatist mentality," he glowers. "When will you ever learn? The key to success is to expect success!"

We set a target date of mid August and prepare for departure. I have photos taken for the children's U.S. passports. Little Angela's picture looks sweet and demure, bright-eyed and eager for life's adventures. Jonathan's photo shows the image of a shy and tense child, fearful of looking directly at the world. David's cruelty has taken its toll. I just hope that in a new place with less stress he won't be so harsh

Money from selling office equipment, tools, cars and furnishings seems ample for traveling and resettlement. We pack half a ton of personal belongings in shipping crates and stay with Marcus for the last two weeks. As the immigration official at the airport stamps the departure date in my passport, I am amazed to note it is five years to the day since I first laid eyes on this enchanting island.

Australia, 1974

I

The sun is nearly setting when the pilot announces our approach to New South Wales. I hoist Angela up to the window and peer out at the most amazing geological formations I've ever seen. Mesmerized, I gaze at the awesome islands, surf, rocks, cliffs, and brilliant red rooftops racing by below. Even before landing, I'm in love with this land, feel as if I'm coming home. Here I will stay...forever.

Customs lines are a mile long, but when we reach the end David finds a taxi that drops us at a hotel in the Bondi Beach area of Sydney. Hardly conscious, I manage to get the kids undressed and into bed before I pass out from exhaustion.

Next morning Jonathan and Angela are ravenous. I let David sleep and take them out to find a restaurant. Dazzling sunlight engulfs us. A broad beach stretches along the opposite side of the street. Rolling surf reaches a crescendo a few yards offshore and then collapses, lazily licking sand at the water's edge. Surfers dot the undulating horizon. Screeching seagulls swoop to grab food and soar away clutching booty.

We enter a small restaurant offering "Full Australian Breakfast" for $1.95, and a young blond waiter takes our order. He returns carrying plates laden with lamb chops, fries, sautéed onions, thick slices of tomatoes, sunny-side eggs, toast and marmalade, and a pot of tea. While we eat I notice the waiter hovering nearby, observing us more closely than seems necessary. Eventually he comes over and says, "Do you remember me?"

Startled, I look into his eyes, study his features. "Mario? From The Academy?"

He bursts into wide grin. "Yes, Ma'am!"

"I can't believe it!" I rise and hug him. "How long have you been here?"

In amazement we share reports of the different paths which led both of us to this distant spot at the same time. He's eager for news of current conditions in Jamaica. I want to pump him for information about Australia but soon notice his boss eyeing us, so I give him a warning signal. "Let's talk more later."

"I'm here every morning. Spend the rest of the day surfing." He smiles as the children wrap leftover toast in napkins for the seagulls.

Even before we reach the beach hundreds of seagulls are circling and diving. Angela keeps chasing them, but Jonathan soon figures out he can get closer by sitting still.

I can't get over the encounter in the restaurant. It has to be more than coincidence—traveling halfway around the world, only to be greeted by a familiar face. What are the odds? There are dozens of eateries we could have walked into. Why that one? It must be a sign I'm in the right place, that in some mystical way I have indeed come home.

Back at the hotel, I tell David, thinking he'll want to meet Mario, but he says we don't have time for socializing right now. "We have to figure out where to live."

I open the newspaper. In addition to reports of labor disputes, raging bushfires, and the posturing of politicians, it has a feature story about Australian families traveling around the country on "working holidays" while they live in caravans. I show David and he thinks this might be a good solution until we find a place we like. He decides to go car shopping, and I take the children to the beach.

Two days later we arrive at a campground in the Sydney suburb of Parramatta pulling an eighteen-foot caravan behind our Holden station wagon. The van has a small bedroom for the children and a kitchen with a booth for eating which converts to a double bed for us. It's crowded, but other campers give us tips for making improvements. David buys an awning and attaches it to the side, greatly expanding our living space, and at a yard sale I get a table with folding chairs to use under the awning. I also buy tricycles, toys, books and plastic phones for the children. The park, nestled beneath pine and gum trees filled with birds that sing all day, has a playground, pool, store, book exchange, and lots of children.

While we await the arrival of the ship carrying our belongings, David hires a lawyer to prepare an Australian patent application, and he embarks on a search for companies to produce his invention. He usually insists that all of us go along on his drives around Sydney searching for manufacturers to approach. I try to keep the children occupied with books, crayons, and their phones, and I love to watch them sitting on opposite sides of the back seat, receivers pressed to their ears, chatting away. Angela's sweet high voice sometimes sounds incredibly grown up, making me feel smugly satisfied when she uses words like "proper," "explain" and "ordinarily." Jonathan talks more on his phone than he does directly to people, but he speaks too softly for me to hear specific words.

II

Sometimes David goes into the city alone at night. One evening after tea, he announces, "I'm checking out King's Cross tonight. Don't wait up."

After making up our bed and getting the children bathed, I sit in their room and read a picture book with stories about kangaroos and adorable little koalas in eucalyptus trees. Imitating the animals, they giggle and hop around until the caravan rocks. I keep shushing them not to disturb the neighbors and fall asleep before they do.

Next thing I notice is noise in the other room—movement, whispers. Alarmed, I sit up just as David's face appears in the doorway. "You left the light on," he hisses and switches it off. "Don't bother to get up. I just brought a friend over for a drink. We won't be long." He closes the door.

Through the thin walls I hear murmurings, feel movements. Who's out there with him? I plug my ears, but going back to sleep is impossible, for soon the whole van starts jiggling. So this is what the children have to put up with when we're.....Oh, God, No! How could he! Please don't let them wake up! I huddle on a corner of the bed, grasping the mattress as though it's a life raft as the van rocks back and forth. Why won't he stop! Tears pour down my face; I can't believe this is really happening! What kind of woman would do such a thing? Just when I think I can take no more, the swaying stops. Then mumbling, footsteps, running water. The outer door opens and closes; a car starts. Slowly my fingers release the mattress and I breathe again.

I'm shell-shocked. Here hardly two weeks and already he's at it, destroying any hope that our new life will be different. The humiliation is one thing, but the thought of him squandering our dwindling savings on a whore terrifies me. If only I had escaped in California while we were waiting for our visas to be approved! Could've taken the children, found our own place. But there he'd been decent. Really made me think things would be different. Now I have no place to go. I can't help fantasizing a car accident. People die in them every day; why not him?

Hearing the outside door latch, I freeze. Then he opens the bedroom door and hisses, "Come out here!"

My heart sinks. Why can't he just leave me alone? But I get up quickly to forestall him raising his voice. When he tries to kiss me, I turn away, stifling a choke as my nostrils take in the smells of alcohol, smoke and the other woman.

"You little shit," he sneers. "Jealous again. Don't you ever learn? How many times do I have to tell you to stop trying to control me? If you love me, you'd want me to have what I need. But it's obvious you don't care. After all the time and work I put in to help you get your head straight, I don't understand why the hell you can't…"

I don't even try to follow his tirade, but the longer he talks, the more agitated he becomes, like a simmering pot nearing the boiling point. I only pay attention to the volume. What if he wakes the neighbors? Any moment someone might bang on our door. Then he hisses "Pay attention!" and slugs me.

I stagger against the stove. The next punch hits my stomach, propelling me onto the bed. I double up in agony. He grabs a kitchen knife, leaps on top of me, straddles my body with his knees, and presses the weapon to my throat. I freeze, all senses tuned to the edge of the blade, terrified I'll feel blood. He pins me in the corner and seethes in my ear, "Don't ever let me see this attitude again; you hear?"

I can't speak or move.

"Answer me! Or so help me God, I'll *have* to kill you!" He presses harder.

I picture the children with no mother. Will they think that I abandoned them? How will they cope? A tear trickles from the corner of my eye. "Umhum," I moan without moving. The pressure increases, and as I try to draw back into the bed, warmth trickles down my neck. The blade against my skin becomes more insistent. I lie paralyzed, afraid even to swallow. The thought of the children waking up to a bloody massacre… The clock ticks. Far away an owl hoots. Gravel crunches as a car passes. Suddenly he withdraws the knife, tosses it on the floor. "Get out of here before I finish you off!"

I press a dish towel to my bleeding neck, grab a robe, and stumble barefoot out the door. In the communal bathroom, I wash the cuts and press folded tissue against them. Then I hide in a toilet

217

stall till the bleeding stops. Eventually I go outside and wander in the cool darkness until the sky turns gray and kookaburras in the gum trees announce a new day. Finally I take refuge under our awning and when I hear the children stirring I slip inside to look after them.

III

In the afternoon David brings a pile of mail and hands me a letter from Iowa. "So, you've been writing to your parents. What do they have to say?" he demands.

I open it and read aloud, rushing through the initial weather report. Then the bad news: Grandma has died. Over details of the funeral my voice falters and tears spill down my cheeks. I fumble to open the enclosed obituary.

David snaps, "Not one word in there about me! Like I'm not part of the family?"

I shrug. "But when we got married, we agreed not to tell anyone, so I haven't mentioned it—"

"You idiot!" His slap sends me staggering as the letter flies to the ground. "Since when does marriage make a family? After all I did for them in Jamaica, and they still act like I don't exist! It's your fault, always telling them terrible things about me." He is off and running. I sit petrified, hoping the neighbors won't notice.

Eventually he decides, "If I can't be part of their family, then you aren't either, or our children. Is that what you want?"

Convincing my parents to accept him is as impossible as getting him to change. I feel like a prisoner buried in a pit, sheer walls towering on all sides with a single ray of light far above, just enough to let me know I'm alive.

"I won't tolerate this anymore. You gotta prove your loyalty," he continues, but I can't focus on his words, much less devise a solution. Grandma ... she never even saw Angela! If only...

"I bet you haven't told them about my inventions either."

218

Shut up already! "Okay, David. I'll write to them."

"And tell them what?"

"You'll see." I blow my nose, wipe my eyes, get out paper and pen.

Dear Mother and Dad,

Much as it saddens me to hear of Grandma's death, I appreciate your letting me know. But I can't accept the way you continue ignoring the existence of my husband, the father of your grandchildren. When you were guests in our home David did everything he could to make sure you had a good time in Jamaica. The least you could do is include him in your letters. But if you keep refusing to accept him in our family, then you may as well disown me. And if you hold on to your prejudiced attitude, be prepared never to see your grandchildren or me again. If that's your choice, I suggest you have a ceremony like the Amish do when someone leaves the clan: write my obituary; disown me in your will; have a burial service; consider your daughter dead. Remember, if you do write again, please make sure it's to all of us. Thank you.

Jacqueline

I show him the letter. "I don't know about that 'dear' crap," he says but seems mollified for the moment.

I consider dropping it in a trash can but am afraid he'll figure out my deception when the next letter arrives from Iowa. I carry it to the mailbox, and before putting it in, I add:

P.S.: I loved Grandma and am sad she's gone, as I'm sure you are, too. How I wish she could have seen Angela! Don't take all of the above to heart, but please be polite to David. It's very important.

As I stuff the envelope through the slot, reality hits me: I'll never see Grandma again! I hurry to a secluded bench as a wave of sorrow engulfs me. Every time I try to stop the sobs, more pour out. Only exhaustion stems the tide. Then a cloud of desolation settles upon me. I've played into his hands again; now indeed I am utterly alone.

IV

When the ship arrives with our things, we unpack the crates and fill the storage space in our caravan. Days become shorter and temperatures drop, making evenings inside the unheated van uncomfortable. Exasperated that he can't get anyone interested in his invention, David says, "I've had enough. Let's go north where it's warmer. I hear a lot of Jamaicans have settled in Cairns."

"How far is that?"

"A long haul. Could take a couple weeks, and we don't have much money left. The sooner we start the better."

As David drives, I pass food and drinks to him and the children, search for radio stations he likes, and keep track of our route on the map. Across New South Wales and into Queensland I try to anticipate the children's needs to keep them from annoying him.

"Our money is nearly gone," he says after checking into a caravan park on the outskirts of Brisbane. "One of us will have to find work."

"Shall we look in the want ads?"

"I already did. Nothing interesting. Besides, this doesn't look like a place I want to live."

"Maybe we can get something temporary and then move on."

"Gotta go farther north. Not warm enough here. Trouble is, we barely have enough money left for gas and food, much less emergencies. It's risky to keep going."

"Plus, we have no way of knowing if there will be any decent work available there either." I know the idea of taking a job is abhorrent to him after running his own business for years. The last thing he wants is someone bossing him around. And it certainly doesn't chime with his concept of the "mission" that the angel gave him. The thought of his getting depressed makes me nervous. "Maybe I can get a job," I venture. "I'll look in the weekend paper tomorrow."

I get the paper before he's up, scan the employment section, and find some possibilities. While he drinks tea, I say, "It looks as if the Ministry of Education here in Brisbane hires for the whole state of Queensland."

"Really."

"Yeah. All of the school openings have the same application address, just different box numbers. All in Brisbane."

"Hmm. Anything in your field?"

"Well, the ad for high school teachers is general. Just says 'openings in all subjects.' Then it lists 'Tablelands, Fraser Coast, and other locations.' Maybe worth checking out."

"What's the address?"

"George Street. I think it's downtown."

"Find it on the map. We'll drive over first thing tomorrow. Get your documents ready. Transcripts, recommendations, all that stuff."

I'm not comfortable walking in without an appointment, but David insists I must "be aggressive." I put on my most professional-looking outfit—a forest green shirtwaist dress with white ribbing—and pack all the relevant documents into a leather bag that matches my white pumps. As we drive into the city David preps me. "When you find the office, ask to see the person in charge of hiring. Make sure you get to talk with someone who makes decisions."

"Okay."

"Don't take any bullshit. We're counting on you. Meanwhile, I'll get some food for the kids and meet you in the park across the street in an hour. But don't rush. Take as much time as you need. I know you can do it."

As David stops in front of a grandiose building surrounded by acres of grass, I smile at the children's somber faces and reach back to squeeze their hands. "Have fun, Guys. I'll see you later."

I climb the broad granite steps leading to a columned portico. Inside, I soon find the teacher placement office. Surprised by the absence of any waiting line, I fill out an extensive application form and then I'm shown into the office of Dr. Hoyt who seems to be in charge of staffing. A friendly, sun-tanned man with a hint of gray hair, he has the appearance of one who spends weekends sailing and playing tennis or cricket. After inviting me to sit, he delivers a quick summary of the centrally organized education system in Queensland which includes a vast network of home schooling done via two-way radios. His questions about my experience and college coursework are easily answered. Nodding thoughtfully, he says, "I have several openings that might be suitable. Would you rather work in Mareeba, Atherton or Cairns?"

"I'm not sure where Mareeba and Atherton are."

He gets up and moves aside a curtain revealing a huge map of the state studded with different colored pushpins. "The red pins represent vacancies in English." He takes a long stick and points to a red near the top of the map. "This is the one in Cairns, and here's the one in Mareeba," he moves the stick to the left. "And this is Atherton." He moves it down. "These are on the Tableland. Nice farming communities, whereas Cairns on the coast is more of a commercial center, with some tourism."

"Could I have a little time to discuss it with my husband?"

"Fine. That'll give me a chance to place a couple calls to the U.S. to verify your transcripts and teaching experience. So check with your husband and come back this afternoon to let me know your preference. I'll also need to know when you can start working, so I can notify the principal."

I report to David who checks the map and points to Cairns. "Looks like about sixteen hundred kilometers. Tell them you can start working one week from today."

V

We roll into Cairns on Sunday afternoon and check into a caravan park. Road-weary and overwhelmed by all the strangeness, I try to psyche myself up for work the next day. It won't be easy to get ready with the inconvenience of shared showers and toilets. And I have no desk or quiet place to read and make lesson plans. I set only one goal for the first day: to arrive on time. After a hectic morning rush, I barely make it.

I instantly like the feel of the rambling two-story school building with verandahs for hallways. Reminds me of The Academy in Kingston. I'm assigned two freshman and two senior classes. The first day I don't have to teach, so I get settled at my desk in a shared English department office, meet a few colleagues, and begin preparing lessons for the rest of the week.

David gets a loan from a local bank to tide us over until my first paycheck, and he looks after the children while I'm at school. But he soon becomes fed up with the confines of the caravan and goes looking for a house to rent. He finds a dilapidated but charming bungalow called a "hi-set" which, like most houses along the coast, rests atop pillars out of reach of floodwater. The open space beneath can be used as garage, workshop, and play area during rainy season.

When he becomes bored with the daily routine of childcare, David gets a part-time job repairing electrical appliances and finds a babysitter to leave the children with. But the work is tedious, so he keeps driving around, trying to make contacts. With a population of more than thirty thousand, Cairns is a bustling business center and the heart of commercial and recreational fishing in North Queensland, but it has no industry apart from tourism and agriculture. Hence, little demand for David's skills. Eventually he locates several people from Jamaica, but there is no evidence of a Jamaican community, as most of them do not know one another.

The only apparent form of social life is the nightly beer guzzling in hotels. We try out the one where teachers congregate after work, but neither of us finds beer drinking a compelling recreation so we don't become regulars.

At school I become friendly with another English teacher who recently got married. When I suggest inviting them over for dinner, David likes the idea. I feed the children early that night and put them to bed before the couple arrives. The lasagna and Chianti I serve hit the spot, since they are of Italian background. After we eat, the men disappear. She helps me clean up the kitchen and then we sit in the front room talking shop. She strikes me as extremely confident considering it is her first year teaching.

After they leave David says, "Did you notice anything unusual about them?"

"You mean the way she and I sat in one room while you men stayed in another?"

"What did you make of that?"

"Reminded me of my parents' social life in Iowa. Surprising to see the same custom here. Maybe it stems from the practice of sending boys and girls to separate schools."

"Maybe. But there's more. I got the impression they were expecting some partner swapping, just waiting for us to make the move."

"But how could that be? They just got married!"

"Well, your little school friend is *very* attracted to me."

"Oh." She did seem exceedingly gay in his presence but I'd dismissed it as nervousness.

"But he sure didn't get any encouragement from you, so we won't be receiving an invitation to their house. Would be a waste of their time. You're too boring," he sneers. Then he stomps off to the bedroom and slams the door.

I don't follow. Hoping he'll fall asleep before I go in, I pull on a sweater, slip outside, and sit on the verandah, looking at the stars. His cheating is hard enough to bear, but now it feels like he wants to use me as bait for ass trading. Here under the Southern Cross, half a world away from Alex, the same thing happening. What's wrong with me? Am I really that boring in bed? Or are David and Alex right? Is it not in man's nature to be monogamous? Is the notion just a lie perpetuated by Christianity and romance novels? Why can't I get over this longing to be cherished by one man alone? Am I a victim of men or a victim of the propaganda? Night dew settles, mixing with tears trickling silently down my cheeks, washing away any hope for new beginnings that Australia promised.

The next week David comes home with tickets he bought from a neighbor for a Saturday night dance. It's a fund-raiser for his veteran's organization. On the morning of the dance, we stop by the man's yard. A fascinating array of pets are wandering around or peering from cages—peacocks, snakes, iguanas, parrots, flying foxes, cockatoos, monkeys, wallabies, even a crocodile. Monty, a large slightly-balding man with a German accent, greets us. His wife Coretta isn't home, but he invites us inside, offers juice and coffee. Swords, knives, guns, and preserved heads with glassy eyes adorn every wall. As soon as manners allow, I finish my coffee and get the children back outside for a tour of the menagerie.

That night at the dance, I notice Coretta as soon as she enters the hall on her husband's arm. They twirl around the floor, her blue sequined gown catching the eyes of everyone. Soon the band breaks into a tango, leaving them alone on the floor as they deliver a polished performance. At the end of the dance the glitzy couple approach our table. Coretta's buxom chest heaves above a low-cut bodice exposing a grand canyon of cleavage. With a lacy hanky she dabs at perspiration beads on her brow and with her other hand she rapidly vibrates a silk fan. We hardly get through introductions before David whisks her away for the next dance. I sip wine and try to make small talk with Monty. His favorite topic is "de vor." So proud of his wounds. I wonder if he is one of those Nazis who fled the trials. Perhaps too young, but still ... When he suggests we dance, I rise, hoping he'll stop boring me with battles.

David keeps refilling my glass and pulls me onto the floor a couple of times when Monty is dancing with his wife. The place gets more crowded and the band louder until conversation becomes impossible. Finishing another set with Coretta, David returns to the table, leans down and says in my ear: "We're all leaving together now. Coretta's coming with me; you ride with Monty."

What? I teeter to the door, realizing I drank too much. Outside, I feel Monty grasp my arm. As he steers me across the parking lot, our car zooms past. "Where'sh David going?" I slur as Monty helps me into his car.

"Oh, don't vorry 'bout him," the German answers. "Just relax. You vit me now and I take goot care of you." He seems to be driving slowly and deliberately, so I lay my head back, eyes closed. When he shuts off the engine, I look up and see we're in his yard. He gets out, opens my door and says, "Come, I help you inside."

"But I have to get home. The children—"

"No vorries. David's dere, vit Coretta. You spend night vit me. Yah." He takes my hand, pulls.

The scum! He arranged a swap! I plant my feet on the floor, refusing to budge.

Monty puts his arm around my waist, pulls me up. I wrench away. He lunges at me, stumbles, goes face down. I run. Run, without looking back. Don't know if he is following me or still on the ground. Maybe he's hurt. Maybe so. I keep running–along the road, up a hill, around a corner. Our house comes into sight. My chest heaves, burns. I slow down to a walk. Our car is parked under the house. David must be upstairs, and Coretta with him. I open the car door, slide inside, close it softly.

A hint of dawn is tinting the sky when I see Coretta leave. I wait a little longer before creeping up the stairs. Inside, I shower and dress, knowing the children will soon wake.

It's lunchtime when David gets up. As I serve him a plate of beans on toast he says, "Did you have a good time last night?"

"I don't really remember. Too much wine."

"So tell me, how is Monty in bed?" he persists.

I can feel my face burning. "I don't want to talk about it."

"I don't mind telling you about Coretta—"

"I have work to do." I make for the back door and run down the steps to where the children are playing. "Hey, guys, can you give me a hand? Throw stones in the buckets and I'll carry them up the hill. Okay?"

"Can I use my truck?" Jonathan asks.

"Sure." I heave a fist-full of stones into his truck.

VI

"It's a waste of time for an inventor to be repairing toasters," David complains as he drives me home from school. "I shouldn't be frittering away my days on a stupid job any moron can do." He drives slowly, as if he has nowhere to go. "Should never have sold my lathe in Jamaica. If I had it, I could be building a new model of my nozzle or at least making improvements to the old one."

"Let's take a look," I say, opening the newspaper folded on the seat. "I've seen tools advertised before." I scan the classifieds. "Nothing today, but you never know when something will show up."

A couple of weeks later I'm reading the newspaper during lunch duty when I notice an ad listing tools for sale, including a lathe. But I forget to mention it to David until the weekend. When I finally remember, he's furious. "Why didn't you tell me sooner? It's bound to be gone by now!"

"I'm sorry, David. I just forgot. Besides, I was reading somebody else's paper, so I couldn't just take it. And I've been too busy with midterm tests and grades this week to think about it again until now. I'm really sorry, but we should still check it out. Maybe it hasn't sold yet."

"A waste of time. You've screwed me again."

"It's worth a try. I think it was Tuesday, or maybe Monday." I rummage through our pile of newspapers and pull out the one I want. "Here. The ad doesn't have a phone number; just an address. It's in Stratford. That's not far. Let's drive over."

"What's the use? It'll be gone," he says glumly, but I hustle the kids into the car. He follows, still insisting it's a wild goose chase. I unfold a map and direct him, all the while praying silently: *Please, God, don't let it be gone. I don't care if it's any good or not; just let it be there so he can't say I made him miss a great deal. Please pull out one of your miracles. If ever I needed one, it's now.*

I wait in the car while he goes to the door. If only I'd told him sooner. I don't know what possessed me not to. I didn't intentionally withhold the information. It was just my own stupidity. But why should it be my responsibility? Why can't he read the ads himself? After all, *he* isn't working full time. Despite all my excuses, the fact remains–I screwed up and he knows it. *A miracle, God. Please! You know I wasn't trying to sabotage him.*

Too soon, he returns. Empty-handed. I freeze. Getting in the car, he announces with a voice of steel, "I'm not even going to hit you. What's the use? But I can't take any more of you sabotaging my life and the future of the whole world. My inventions are the answer to the world's problems, but you don't care. Or maybe you really don't want me to succeed. I don't know which one but I can't tolerate any more of this!"

His voice rises as he starts the engine. "You make it impossible for me to succeed. I've put up with your shit because you're the mother of my children, but it's got to stop!"

"What kind of lathe was it?"

"What difference does it make?" His eyes blaze. "The point is, you didn't tell me. You don't care about me, or my invention, or our children's future! You're useless when it comes to important things, and hitting you doesn't work anymore. It helps for a while, but you always go right back to the old ways. The world can't wait forever for my inventions! I have to face facts: the effort I've put into you has been a waste of time."

With every word I feel smaller. I want to dry up, blow away, disappear. But he keeps up the harangue, tugging at his hair while driving jerkily along the road. "You're nothing but a burden. I can't let you stand in the way of my success any longer. When we get back to the house, pack your stuff and put it in the caravan."

"What?"

"I'll drive you to one of the parks. You can live there."

"With the children?"

"You crazy? You don't deserve them. Obviously you don't care about their future. Anybody can wash clothes and cook food. That's not love. We'll get along much better without you causing problems all the time."

"David! I know I made a mistake, and I'm sorry. But believe me, I just forgot! That's the truth. If it wasn't, I wouldn't have told you about the ad today. I was really hoping it would be a good lathe and you could get it. But we missed it, so we have to move on. Maybe try forgiveness. That was Jesus's key—"

"And look what it got him! I know, you'd like to see me strung up on a cross, too."

As I open my mouth to object, the car swerves, rocks, skids, throwing me against the dashboard. A truck, barely missing us, screeches to a stop. Two men leap out and stride menacingly toward us. I turn to check the children who have tumbled to the floor, while David opens his window, offers apologies.

We continue homeward, both sobered. "See what you just did!" he declares. "We all could have been killed back there! Goes to show why we can't afford to have you around. Nothing but trouble. So pack your stuff. I want to get this over with."

Back home I move like an automaton, going through the motions of packing. The children watch expectantly, as if I'm going to fix the problem. I can't meet their eyes.

David loads my bags in the caravan and tells everybody to get in the car. When we reach the park he says, "Go in and rent a space. You can say goodbye to your children while I unhitch the van."

I fill out the registration and pay with a check. Seeing both of our names on it, the cashier glances at the form and looks at me quizzically. "Just you?"

"Yes," I say, then grab the receipt and rush out. The car door swings open.

"Get inside," says David.

I obey, staring ahead. A lump paralyzes my throat. David buries his face in his arms crossed over the steering wheel. I can't bear to look at the children who are perfectly quiet, and I can't think of a thing to say that will make any difference. Can't even tell the children when I'll see them again. But before I get out I gotta make him agree to let me visit them, like on weekends. At least we'll have something to look forward to. That's it! I won't get out until he agrees. He can't start hitting me right here with people walking by every minute.

"Mommy," Angela's voice breaks the silence. "I have to potty."

Clutching the steering wheel with both hands, David bangs his head against it, moaning, "I can't do this. It's not going to work. I can't live with you, but I can't just dump you here like a stray cat. Go get your money back. Is there a bathroom inside?"

"Yes." I grab Angela's hand and pull her along. After taking her to the lav, I get the check back and return to the car.

He starts the engine and inches forward, fuming. "You make me feel like I don't even want to bother living. I'll never be able to succeed without a good woman to back me up. And you're ruining the children's lives, too. What kind of future do they have to look forward to if my invention never gets off the ground? The way things are going, the whole earth will become a nuclear wasteland. Is that what you want for your kids?"

I gaze at the road ahead, have no answer. Nothing makes sense.

"You're worse than useless. Actually you're a *minus quantity* in the universe. Just wipe out the good I try to do. The world's a worse place for you being here. You're a blot on the earth! An insult to the planet! What a fool I was to bring you to Australia! To think I was even idiot enough to marry you!"

His diatribe continues nonstop until we reach the yard. Then he says, "Feed the kids and send them to their room for a nap." He disappears into the bedroom. It's not like him to discontinue an argument without reaching some resolution, even if it takes all night. Is this just a break between rounds?

I grill cheese sandwiches and pour juice for Jonathan and Angela. "Eat quietly," I whisper, holding a finger to my lips. "Daddy's tired and needs to sleep." My attempt to force a smile is futile. They nod and hungrily devour the food. When they finish, I wipe their faces and fingers. "Time for your nap, now," I say and hustle them to their room.

I sink wearily onto a chair at the table and drop my face on folded arms, overcome by shame. The children deserve so much more. We should have done something special today! Like take a ride on the old restored railway to Kuranda that Jonathan has wanted to do for weeks. Every day we drive by the station but always have more important things to do, or fights to finish. Instead, just another wasted day. If only I'd told David about the ad! How could I be so stupid! Maybe he's right about me ruining their lives. His words echo in my ears: "*The world's a worse place for you*

231

being here. You're a minus quantity in the universe!" And I'm also a minus for the children. All this bickering and never any fun. I have to face it: I am ruining their lives.

Then I think of something David showed me in the medicine chest back in Jamaica. Did it survive the trip across the Pacific? I go to the bathroom and open the cabinet. Reaching behind the hydrogen peroxide, my fingers grasp a brown glass bottle labeled "Sodium Pentothal." I twist off the cap. It's still nearly as full as when he told me, "*There are several lethal doses in here.*" I shake a few blue capsules into my palm and stare. Then I put them back in the bottle, screw on the cap. *Just do it,* a voice inside urges. *If you hesitate, something will interfere and the children's torture will go on and on. Don't be a coward!*

I rest the bottle on the sink and use the toilet. He's right, I think. The children would be better off without me. They won't have to hear any more of these horrible fights, even worse now than in Jamaica. I'm not a good mother. All I do is try to keep them quiet. It's no way to live. While I wash my hands, I wonder who he'll blame for everything when I'm no longer around. And who will do all the things he's too important for? When I'm gone, maybe then he'll realize... But it will be too late. He's going to regret not having shown some appreciation sooner.

Bottle in hand, I return to the table and slump on a chair. He didn't even remember my birthday last week. After six lousy years, he still can't even tell me "Happy Birthday!" I pretended it didn't matter, but suddenly the hurt takes over. I try to muffle my sobs with napkins, keep blowing my nose, but the tears won't stop. I've never felt so alone. "He won't get another chance," I sniffle. "Never, ever! He's going to be so sorry!"

I stand, fill a glass with water, pick up the pills, a pad of paper and a pen. Tiptoeing downstairs, I go behind the house, climb inside the caravan, close the door. I pour a handful of capsules out of the bottle and stare at them. Then I pop them into my mouth and swallow. Then another handful and another. When the water is gone, I sit on the bed and write.

My dear family,
Thank you, Jonathan and Angela, for giving me so much happiness. I'm sorry I haven't been a good mother. I'm leaving you now so your lives can be better and you won't have to keep listening to the terrible fights. I always have and always will love you, and I'm so sorry I have failed you. David, you won. I leave you everything–the children, your freedom, and the peace to finish your invention. No longer am I in your way...

I slump, lose control of the pen.

VII

From far away a woman whispers: "Look! She moved. I think she's waking up."

So cold. Where am I? Can't open my eyes. My brain only registers coldness, hard metal, strange sounds, antiseptic odor. "I'm cold," I moan. "Please...so cooold!" A soft blanket. What a relief! But I can't stop shivering.

"Don't roll over," someone says. "You're attached to tubes; mustn't pull them out."

"Where am I?"

"Intensive care. You've been in a coma for three days."

I can't comprehend.

The next thing I hear is David's voice. "Jac, you're awake! Thank God! My prayers are answered." He squeezes my hand, kisses my forehead. Through half closed lids I look momentarily into his intense eyes, see nurses fussing around me, then drift off.

When I wake again, I'm in a ward. I keep drifting in and out of sleep, my dreams full of bizarre images in neon colors, like a gallery of abstract psychedelic art. During intervals when I'm conscious David explains how I got to the hospital.

"After my nap," he says, "I didn't see you anywhere but decided to unload the van anyway. When I opened the door, there you were, slumped on the bed. I told you to help me carry the suitcases, but when you tried to lift one you stumbled. I noticed your eyes were dilated, and when I spotted the bottle of *Sodium Pentothal*, nearly empty, I realized what you'd done. I carried you to the car, shouting at the children to jump in. Every second counted. I didn't know if you could last the thirteen kilometers to the hospital, so I kept shaking you, trying to keep you awake. By the time we reached the emergency room, you'd turned blue. They put you on life support immediately. Later they said you weren't breathing because the drug had paralyzed your chest muscles."

"I don't remember anything."

"Figures. The doctor said you took enough pills to kill three people your size. By the end of the second day, he told me that if you remained comatose for three days, it was hopeless. Anyone who survives after that will be a vegetable, so he recommended taking you off the respirator. I spent the night crying and praying." He grips my hand. "I've never prayed so hard in all my life."

Propped up in bed, I struggle to stay conscious.

"I couldn't let them turn off the respirator, so I told them you squeezed my hand, and the doctor agreed to keep you on the support a little longer. And praise the Lord, you woke up! It's like I willed you back to life!"

"How are the children?" I'm ashamed to ask, given the ordeal I've put them through, but I have to know.

"Of course, they were upset, but they're fine since I told them yesterday you woke up. They wanted to see you right away, but I said they'd have to wait till tomorrow."

"Tomorrow?"

"Yeah. I'm taking you home. No reason to stay here any longer."

234

I drift off, back to the alien world of flying images which never stop changing shape and color.

Next day David shows up carrying a bag. "Here, put these on." He thrusts a pile of folded clothes at me. "And here's your toothbrush and comb so you can clean up."

"But... the doctor says I have pneumonia."

"Just a complication from the respirator. Nothing serious. You can keep taking penicillin at home."

"I don't think the doctor's ready to—"

"I've taken care of everything. Just get dressed."

At the front desk I sign a few papers without bothering to read them and accept a card with an appointment for the next week. Then I follow David to the car.

"I called your principal's office and told them you were in the hospital from breathing toxic paint fumes," David says as he drives. "They're expecting you back next week. That's all the sick leave you have. But don't count on any special treatment from me because of this stunt. You're lucky I'm bringing you home. You did a stupid thing and I don't want to hear any more about it. Don't try using this to manipulate me. Get that clear before you go inside. If you want to see your kids again, you have to agree."

My heart sinks as I nod numbly. Nothing has changed. Maybe worse is ahead. I recall that horrific night in Kingston after I brought Jonathan back from Iowa. When we reach the yard, I open the car door but hesitate, ashamed to face the children. What did he tell them? What are they thinking? Feeling? How can I expect them to understand when I don't myself? Can I ever make this up to them?

They come running, and I can feel David watching, listening as I kneel to hug them. They're satisfied to hear I'm "all better" and demand no explanation. We go inside, and as I fix lunch they chatter about the cassowary mother and chick they saw in the

235

neighbor's yard while I was gone. Then I tidy their room, put laundry in the washer, and get them to help me pull weeds from the garden.

The hallucinations taper off as my body continues expelling the drug, and I finally get some real sleep. Back at work I use the lies David provided to explain my absence.

When I go for the hospital check-up, the doctor says the pneumonia has cleared up; then he sends me to another office to see a psychologist. My heart leaps! Will we be getting family counseling? If only! Despite all David's accusations and despite my recent act of madness, I don't feel the least bit crazy. However, I've often wondered if David might be, but I've never been able to get him to a counselor or psychiatrist; hence there is no impartial assessment. Maybe now …

The receptionist calls my name and shows me into the psychologist's office. I can't fool him about the cause of my hospitalization but I do hold back on disclosing events that triggered my action, knowing David will kill me himself if any social services get involved. Eventually the doctor says, "I know these things are painful to talk about. You probably need more time to reflect. I'll schedule another appointment for next week. Okay?"

I nod. "Can my husband come in, too?"

"Eventually, but first I want to spend more time with you. I'm going to give you a couple of questions to think about before our next meeting. First, can you imagine doing a similar thing again? Why or why not? Secondly, try to think of some other way you could have handled the situation. We'll work together to figure out better solutions." Smiling, he lifts one eyebrow, inviting agreement.

"Okay. Thanks a lot." I rise and reach for the appointment card.

David is pacing in the lobby. "What took so long?"

"I had to wait to see the doctor. Then after the exam, he sent me to a psychologist."

"What! What did you tell him?"

"Nothing. He just got my name and stuff." I shrug.

"Good. No sense running off your mouth about our private business. Those shrinks are all a bunch of psychotics. They go into the field to sort out their own problems."

"He wants to see me again same time next week."

"Cancel!"

VIII

While I was in the hospital David found a new babysitter. She lives in our neighborhood, so I can walk over to get the children after work. Stephanie, a petite woman, has twin boys of her own. She is well organized and always smiling. Her home has a nice feel–clean, bright, lots of plants, a safe yard with sandbox and toys. Jonathan and Angela even like her cooking.

One day when I go for them, Stephanie presents me with two finger paintings they did. On Jonathan's I see a tiny brown craft on a huge mass of blue. Angela's is multi-colored overlaying swirls that look like the tracks of figure skaters. After admiring the paintings, I roll them and carefully place them in my bag. Then I thank Stephanie, clasp a small, chubby hand in each of mine, and head home.

"What did Stephanie bake today?" I ask.

"Granola bars," says Angela.

"You like them?"

"Um, a little good."

Jonathan adds, "Not as good as the cookies yesterday. *They* were yummy!"

"What kind?"

"Peanut butter with chocolate on top."

"I remember when my mother used to make those," I say. "I liked them, too."

We pause to sniff a clump of frangipani flowers beneath a tree. While I kneel to scoop a handful of the aromatic petals into my bag, Angela and Jonathan dart over to a nearby hedge. Straightening, I see them coming toward me with hands behind their backs. "Surprise!" they shout, each whisking out a huge crimson hibiscus blossom.

"For you, Mommy!" Angela glows.

"You like them?" Jonathan peers up timidly.

I sink to my knees. "Of course, I like them. They're gorgeous!" I pull them close. "And I *love* both of you!" I kiss Angela's cheek on my left and Jonathan's on my right. When I release them, they thrust the flowers into my hands and run ahead, zigzagging before me, stopping to investigate whatever catches their fancies. I trail behind, carrying my love bouquet, hoping they won't notice the tears in my eyes.

Overwhelmed with gratitude, I reproach myself. Why couldn't I see before how blessed I am? Clearly I have been given another chance. And this time I won't throw it away. The answer to the psychologist's first question is easy: Never, ever will I kill myself. Regardless of what David says, I now know I have significance in the world. Nothing can make me bail out on my children again, no matter what!

But the psychologist's second question is harder. If another situation arises—and it's bound to—how will I handle it? Somehow, somewhere there has to be a solution. I don't know what yet, but I *will* find it. Maybe that's enough for now, just knowing I won't give up. Still, I have to be careful. David and I are in a life and death struggle. For the first time, the enormity of what I did hits me: It's a miracle that my children aren't motherless right now! I look up the road to where they have paused. "Race you!" I shout, and they speed off with squeals of delight.

After passing the poster outside the grocery store for the umpteenth time, I finally take one of the tear-off address slips and slide it in my pocket. I've always wanted to try yoga, but never did anything about it. Now here's a class right in the neighborhood. But what will David say?

I wait until after dinner to tell him and am surprised when he doesn't object.

On the day of my first class, I cook dinner early and serve the kids. Then without eating, I rush to the church where the yoga group meets. Soft flute music and a scent of burning jasmine greet me as I enter a dimly lit space where several bodies are lying on mats spread around the room. Much as I try to mimic the instructor, it's impossible to coax my body into all the strange contortions. But the conscious breathing makes me feel relaxed and big inside, and the guided meditation is so divine that I don't want it to ever end. After class, I walk to the car, tingling with energy. Again I have that sense of coming home. This time home to myself. I must return.

I buy a black leotard, make myself a special foam mat covered with purple and blue flannel, and go to class again the next week, and the next. With the help of a yoga book, I practice postures, breathing, and meditation in the spare bedroom between classes. The mat becomes my life raft on a choppy sea.

IX

As Christmas nears, we have to stop swimming at the beaches because of sea wasps, a jelly fish that inundates coastal waters and is reputedly the most deadly creature in the sea. Warning signs are posted on public beaches alongside bottles of methylated spirits. The only antidote, it has to be applied within seconds of an attack. Most Queenslanders don't go near the beach during this season, but we still like to walk along the shore and play in the pools left by the receding tide.

One Saturday we go to a beach near Buchanan Point. As I watch the children build a mountain of sand, David says, "I'm going to try to get a good shot of Double Island." Camera slung over his shoulder, he waves and heads south along the shore. When he returns, a young man carrying a bucket and a net is with him.

"Say hello to Neil," David says and introduces us.

Neil explains his net is for catching small fish to use for bait. "I'm going fishing on the reef tomorrow so I need a good supply."

He notices Jonathan's wide-eyed interest. "It's easy. Wanta give it a go, Mate? Come on." Neil wades out. Jonathan hesitates, looking from me to David.

"Go ahead," David says.

Over the next hour, we all get lessons on how to cast a bait net, and Neil fills his bucket.

In the shade of a coconut tree, I spread a beach blanket, take our lunch out of the cooler, and invite Neil to join us. "It's all right," he shakes his head. I already had brekkie."

"But this is lunch, and we have plenty," I insist, handing him a paper plate and cup. "Orange juice or iced tea?"

"Juice is fine," he gives in, grinning shyly, and helps himself to an egg salad sandwich.

A lifelong Queenslander, Neil is an encyclopedia of information about the beaches and reef. Patiently he answers our questions about sea snakes, crocodiles, sharks, and sea wasps. Then he invites us to go out in the boat with him the next day. "Huraay!" the children cry.

On Sunday we come home with several coral trout that Neil shows us how to filet. We can't get over their size, giants compared to what we speared in Jamaica.

Reef trips with Neil become almost a weekly affair. Jonathan catches his first fish on Neil's boat. He has a hard time pulling the whopper in, but with Neil's help, he holds on, slowly reeling until Neil scoops it up with a landing net. He always gives Jonathan a job on the boat and teaches him new nautical words every time we go out. He quickly learns to read the instruments and sometimes helps steer. One day when Jonathan is steering, Neil goes up to the bow to roll in line. Suddenly he shouts, "Turn to starboard! It's too shallow here!" But the boat is already brushing bottom.

Terrified, Jonathan freezes at the wheel, as though steeling himself for a blow. But Neil just says, "Relax, Mate. We can get out of here. No worries. Move over and let me show you."

On future weekend trips, Jonathan becomes Neil's shadow, following everywhere he goes.

<h1 style="text-align:center">X</h1>

"I've decided to start my own business," David announces as I get into the car.

"Oh?" I twist to deposit my books and bags on the back seat. "What kind?"

"Hypnotherapy."

"But what about your invention?"

"I'll keep working on it, but I need contact with people, too. Should be a helluva lot more interesting than vacuum cleaners and toasters."

"Wouldn't you get more business doing electronics on your own? I mean, how many people have even heard of hypnotherapy, much less be willing to spend money on it?"

"I know I'll have to do some educating at first. Maybe start with a newspaper article; get someone to interview me. And I'll run a little contest or pass out coupons. Maybe reduce rates for an introductory offer. I'll need your help with promotions."

In my spare time! "Okay."

"It'll be interesting to see how something like this catches on. People here aren't exactly sophisticated, but they're not closed-minded either. With the right publicity, it could take off."

All I can picture is how he will blame me when things don't go well. "I'm glad you're going to get your own business started, but with all this," I motion to the bag full of notebooks, "I can't be much help. Tonight, for instance, fifty exams to mark."

He scowls. "I know you don't want me to succeed. If you had things your way, I'd spend the rest of my life fixing ceiling fans for old ladies."

"I'm only being realistic. Don't want you depending on me for what I can't provide. Besides, you're more creative than me about things like promotionals."

"That's true."

"But I'll be glad to check your spelling. And maybe I can help with decorating the office. Where's it going to be?"

"Don't know yet. I looked at a couple places today, but the locations aren't right. Too noisy. I need privacy and quiet. No distractions."

At least he's not thinking of setting up shop in our house.

He progresses rapidly in the next couple of weeks: office, furniture, business cards, and an interview published in the paper about therapeutic benefits of hypnosis. I make drapes, pick out potted plants and pictures.

Elated when people start calling, he spends hours on the phone explaining how hypnosis can help with nail biting, bed-wetting, obesity, smoking, insomnia, gambling… A few people make appointments, and I breathe a little easier.

"Dinner's ready!" I call. "Get your hands washed."

The children come running and climb onto their chairs. As David saunters in, he announces, "I had a shiatsu treatment today."

"A *what?*" I sprinkle dressing on the salad and toss it.

"Shiatsu. It's sort of like massage."

"Oh?" I dish up for Jonathan and Angela and pass the salad to David.

"It's a Japanese thing. Like acupuncture, but they use finger pressure instead of needles. I've seen it advertised in the paper, but didn't know what it was. Then this afternoon I noticed a sign in the arcade and stopped to ask about it. Sounded interesting so I decided to try it out right then and there."

"How was it?" I lean over to cut Angela's spaghetti.

"Fabulous! I bought a book to learn how to do it and I've been studying all day. When you finish cleaning up, come in the bedroom so I can try it on you."

"How long will it take? I have lesson preparations to do, and the kids need baths."

"Always everything else before me," he glowers.

I shrug, refusing to be bossed.

"Well, hurry up and get that stuff taken care of because I don't want to be rushed. I'll keep studying until you're ready."

"Who wants mango ice cream?" I ask.

"Me!" the kids sing in unison.

After tucking them in bed, I join David, leaving my class prep for the morning. He hands me a book. "Here. Read the passages aloud that describe the techniques while I do them." He flips the book open and points to the heading where I should start, *Pain in neck, shoulder and arms.*

"Okay, here goes. 'Using four fingers of both hands lightly press and rub keiraku numbers two and three, beginning at the base of the skull and working up toward the ears and downward...'" As his fingers follow instructions, the most amazing sensations shoot through my body, as though he is puncturing and draining deposits of tension. I sigh, "This is incredible. I've never felt anything like it. Just using your fingers?"

"Yeah. Fantastic, isn't it? Imagine feeling that all over your body!"

"It's very intense, but doesn't actually hurt."

"I know. Amazing. The Japanese have used this therapy for centuries. It's just starting to catch on now in other parts of the world." He rubs his palms together vigorously. "Lie on the bed now so I can work on your back. Read the next section."

While I read, he presses points along my spine. Then he says, "I'm thinking of using this with hypnosis. Not everything can be treated with words alone. Sometimes I feel like for certain problems, I need to do more. This might be the answer."

"Don't you need to have a license, since this involves touching people?"

"Who'll know the difference? I'm not going to advertise it or charge extra. It's just an add-on to a regular hypnosis treatment."

Obviously his mind is made up. I close my eyes and enjoy the rest of the massage.

One night when Neil is having dinner with us David starts telling him about how his treatments are changing peoples' lives. I express concern about him discussing clients, but he insists there's no ethical issue if he doesn't mention names. Much as I appreciate him deriving satisfaction from his work, the extent of his excitement bothers me. It's as if he gets a high from wielding power over peoples' minds.

After dessert, the men move into the living room, and the children go outside to play. While cleaning up the kitchen I overhear David say, "You'll never guess what the most common problem with women in Queensland is."

"What?" Neil says.

"Frigidity."

"Really?"

"Yeah, and that causes all sorts of other things like headaches, backaches, obesity, chain smoking, even cancer. Name a woman's ailment and I bet it's related to frigidity."

"No way!"

"I know it sounds far out, but I swear that's what I've discovered. *Every* woman who comes to me is frigid. Most are married, but their husbands spend nights at hotels drinking and are too smashed to satisfy a woman when they get home. Others go off in the outback and screw sheep or whatever they can find to stick their pricks into. I hear stories you wouldn't want to know about.

These women are so frustrated they're nothing but a bundle of nerves; immune and nervous systems totally out of whack."

"So how does hypnosis help?"

"That's why I added massage to my treatments. Had to find a way to get their clothes off."

"Stop putting me on!" I picture Neil's look of disbelief.

"I'm not! Once they undress for the massage, it's not hard to get them relaxed by rubbing their thighs a little, and then they get so hot from listening to my voice that they're begging for it. I swear, absolutely begging for my cock! All I do is give it to them and let them stick it in. Believe me, Man, some of these women haven't had a good dick for years. They're desperate by the time they reach me. Can't get enough. One orgasm after another. They love it!"

"Come on! You're not being straight with me," Neil protests.

"Oh yes I am! But I'm only giving them what they need in order to treat their ailments. Once they have a few orgasms, they start to relax, so we can take care of other problems. Until their sexual needs are met, nothing else gets through."

"I don't believe it!" Neil insists. "You can't have women just come in off the street, lie down, and let you ball them."

"I know it sounds far out, but the fact is I'm helping these women, unlike doctors who don't bother to get to their real problems. I'm there for them, like a psychiatrist or minister, only I give them what they *really* need. It's risky, I know. Someone might report me, or a jealous husband could... "

I can't bear to hear anymore, so I empty the sink and slip out the back door. What must Neil think of me now? I'm the wife of a man being paid by women to screw them! And what are other people thinking and saying? I have no way of knowing who is involved. Maybe a cashier at the supermarket, or the mother of one of my students, or the wife of my principal! Not only will they laugh at me, but if word gets out, there'll be a scandal. I'll lose my job. How can he not realize the danger! I sink onto the steps, cover my face with my hands. If I say anything, it'll just be another battle.

245

"Mommy," Angela touches me. "Can you tie my shoe?"

I look up. "Of course, Honey." I make room for her. "Sit here. I'll even show you how to do it yourself. Let's start with the left one. Take the lace and hold it like this ..."

XI

Neil is at our house one evening when David puts a stack of Herbie Mann, Elton John, Bob Marley and Neil Diamond albums on the record changer. He fills his pipe with a mixture of tobacco and ganja and passes it around, but we both decline. After drawing a few puffs, he dims the lights and lies down on the carpet. When the albums finish David sits up and shakes his head. "I just had the most incredible vision! A spirit brought me a message. Did anyone else see it?"

"No," we answer in unison.

"So it just appeared to me. That figures." He nods. "Okay, listen up. I've been chosen to save the world from extinction." He pauses. When no one speaks, he goes on. "The spirit said it won't be an easy job and success is not guaranteed, but I'm the best one to do it. There'll be ridicule and opposition. I don't like the responsibility, but how can I refuse? If I accept, we'll be in it together, Jac. What do you think?"

I sigh. Didn't we already make this decision in Jamaica after he saw the angel in the mountains? "What will we have to do?"

"It requires total commitment, putting Mankind first. Like Jesus did. I've been spending too much time on other things. Now I've got to get serious and build a model of my invention that *proves* it can deliver free energy. A prototype they can't turn down. It'll be dangerous. Oil companies don't want it, so they'll try to shut me up. I'll have to be careful and smart. Actually notoriety might be my best protection, so I have to get my message out in public. If everybody knows about it, they won't be so fast to kill me."

Neil gets to his feet and stretches. "Well Mates, I gotta go; work in the morning. I'll leave you to make your big decision." At the door he whispers, "I'll call tomorrow."

When I return to the living room, David says, "I have until tomorrow night to think this thing over and give my answer. You have anything to say?"

"Let me sleep on it."

David accepts the challenge and receives another message about the mission. "Even though a prophet is without honor in his own country," he explains, "the spirit says my people should have first chance to benefit from my invention. So I'm going home, and taking the children with me. Since you like Australia so much, you can stay here or come along. You don't have to decide right away; it'll take awhile to get organized."

I feel numb, can't respond, can't process. All I can do is hope that this too will pass. Later, while lying awake in bed, I recall a feature published in the Jamaican *Gleaner* a couple of years before about a sociological study of cannabis done by the university. It included anecdotal reports about the traditional method of introducing boys to ganja. An elder would observe adolescents taking their first puffs and interpret the different reactions. Some got energized, others got sleepy, some became loquacious, and a few hallucinated. Those in the last group–particularly the ones who saw a little man dancing–were identified by the elder as boys who could not tolerate cannabis and they were forbidden to use it. Being a boarding school boy, David had missed out on all this, but I suspect he would have been designated as one who should not use it. Though I can't remember anything about it in the article, I wonder if it's possible that the traditional initiation doubles as a way to detect who's disposed to mental illness?

David works harder than ever on his prototype and gives up his office. He says we can't afford daycare anymore and keeps the

247

children at home. Jonathan becomes the assistant who holds the nozzle for Daddy's experiments and turns the water on and off. Sometimes David brags about what a great helper his boy is. Other times he curses the child brutally. Angela keeps herself entertained by drawing pictures with crayons and playing with the kittens she has adopted. The biggest excitement of their day is when David lets them take turns sitting on his lap and steering the car when they come to pick me up after school.

On Saturdays I usually make pancakes for breakfast. One morning I spread apple butter on the children's and dribble syrup over them. Next I fix my own.

"What are you doing, Mommy?" Angela puckers her face as she sees me spread mayonnaise on my pancake and then roll it around a leftover sardine.

"Want a bite?" I offer it to her.

"Noooo!" she shrieks in alarm.

I chew and swallow. "How about you, Jonathan. Shall I fix you one like this?"

He shakes his head vigorously, his mouth too full to speak.

"You don't know what you're missing!" I prepare another sardine roll-up.

After the children finish eating, I sit down with my cup of tea and glance through the weekend newspaper. Noticing the date, something clicks in my mind, and I go to the calendar on the wall. I flip back two months before I find the last date I marked my period. "Oh, my God!"

David is livid. "Terrific timing! I take on the biggest job of my life, and you go and get pregnant! I warned you my family can't always come first anymore. I have responsibilities to the world. If you're trying to make me give up this commitment, forget it! And don't expect me to carry the burden of supporting everybody!"

"I won't be sure until I see a doctor. I'm just sharing my suspicion—"

"Suspicion! Don't bother me unless you're certain. I don't have time for distractions. This is the biggest challenge of my entire life! But how could *you* understand? You've never done anything difficult or creative. You don't know what it's like to really care about anything or anyone except yourself. You can't think past what's inside your own belly!" His hand strikes my face and I see an explosion of fireworks as I fall backwards onto the sofa.

I roll over, filled with rage. Then I go limp and pray silently: *Please, God, don't let him hurt my baby.*

XII

At the end of the month he gives the landlord notice.

"But, David," I say, "everything we've been hearing about Jamaica sounds even worse than when we left. How can we possibly manage there now?"

"That's why I have to go! They need me. That's the messenger's orders. My job now is to get my invention ready. I'll be shown what else to do when the time comes."

"Meanwhile we need to eat and have a place to sleep. Spirits might not think of such things... I mean, without physical bodies—"

"Are you mocking me?" he glares.

"I'm just wondering what the plan is. I don't know what to pack..."

"Stop trying to confuse me. It's simple. We'll take the caravan back to Sydney. All you have to do is decide whether or not you're coming."

Knowing his resourcefulness, the absence of a practical plan doesn't worry me so much; the real problem is I don't want to leave Australia. And if I'm pregnant, by the time we reach Jamaica, I won't even be able to work.

When David starts selling our furniture, I hand in my resignation to coincide with the end of the school term. I can't let him take the children without me. Neil becomes morose over our pending departure. I know he thinks we're abandoning him, and it feels that way to me, too.

David has a plan to mollify Neil and explains it right in front of me. "There's this nice girl who came to me for hypnosis to treat her eating disorder, but she hasn't overcome her virginity problem yet. I think you two would hit it off." He holds out a slip of paper. "Here's her name and number. Give her a call."

"What makes you think I'm not capable of finding a woman for myself? Keep your damn number!" He rips the paper and lets the bits fall to the floor. "You're crazy, Man! I gotta go. If I stay around any longer I might hit you!"

"Good idea, coward. If you start a fight with me, you won't be able to walk out of here!"

Neil turns to me. "I'll be back later to see the kids off."

I nod, biting my lip. If only he would take a stand! Maybe somehow we could prevent David from taking the children. But he ignores David's challenge and strides to his car without looking back.

Just as we finish packing Neil shows up. He hugs me and whispers, "So long for now." I fight back tears, unable to speak. He kneels in front of the children, places little sailor hats on their heads, and says, "If you want to see somebody again, never say 'good-bye.'" Picking Angela up, he hugs her tightly for a moment. Then he puts her down and squeezes Jonathan's shoulder. "See you later, Matey."

David comes over and shakes Neil's hand. "Thanks for everything, Brother."

We get in the station wagon. David starts the engine and pulls the heavily laden caravan slowly out of the yard while Neil leans against his car, waving. The children and I stretch out the windows, hands fluttering, until we lose sight of him. As we pick up speed on the road, I leave the window open so the breeze will dry the tears I can no longer hold back.

XIII

"Stop it, Jonathan!" David commands, his eyes focused on the rearview mirror. I turn around to see my son slowly withdraw his thumb from his mouth. With his left hand, he grasps the right and forces it into his pocket. After a few minutes I open the cooler to get out drinks and pass around little bags of popcorn.

"Where's my harmonica?" David says, gaining speed on the Bruce Highway. I take it from the glove compartment and hand it to him. He eases into Bob Marley's catchy "I Shot the Sheriff" melody while I, disheartened that Neil made no move to prevent our leaving, pretend to look at a map. If only he'd said something! Given some sign that he loves me! But how could he? I never let him know I would leave David for him. And do I really love him or just need a protector? Besides, it's ridiculous to expect a young man like him to take on two children and a pregnant woman... How foolish of me!

"How far do you think we can get today?" David intrudes on my thoughts.

"Well, it's nearly ten now, so we shouldn't have any trouble making it to Townsville. If the road is good, maybe we can get as far as Bowen or Proserpine. Let's see if they have any caravan parks." I pull out the guidebook.

As Cairns becomes more distant, my thoughts turn reluctantly to a perilous future rather than dwelling on Neil and the life that might have been.

Speeding south from Brisbane, David says, "My plan is to spend some time in Sydney before heading to Jamaica. I have a much better prototype of my invention now, so I want to find a manufacturer before we leave. Could provide some money to help with expenses back in Jamaica. We'll live in the caravan while I do the patent application and look for a company. Don't have to be in any rush to leave. And this'll give us time to look for good travel deals. What do you prefer–airplane or ship?"

"Ship," I say promptly. One of my lifelong dreams–to sail across an ocean–could it really happen?

Only one caravan park has a vacancy. Its facilities are inferior to the one we stayed at previously, but we spend little time there anyway. Every day David has something for me to help with–searching through phone books, making calls, guiding him as he drives to different addresses, typing and mailing letters, accompanying him to meetings. We continually drag the kids around in the station wagon, and make them wait for hours. I hate it but don't complain, lest he suggest we leave them alone in the caravan.

Eventually he negotiates a contract with a company interested in the oscillating shower nozzle application of his invention. He will work with them for six weeks perfecting the design for mass production. I'm relieved as I look forward to spending some peaceful time with the children. But alas, it doesn't work out that way. David has to drive an hour each way, so he leaves early and returns late, exhausted and irritable. Perpetually on edge, he yells at me in the mornings and hits me in the evenings. I'm so embarrassed that I keep the children inside most of the time in order to avoid people's stares and questions.

After two weeks of this, he goes out to get the mail on a Saturday morning and comes back shouting as he waves a paper in front of my face. "See what you've done now! Gone and gotten us evicted! It's all the damn noise you keep making. I don't have time for this horse shit! How am I supposed to concentrate on my work with you nagging me all the time? And when am I gonna relax if I have to spend weekends looking for another park?"

Alarmed, I grab the paper and sink onto a chair to read it as his tirade continues.

"I can't believe the things you do just to make life difficult for me! This is all because of you blabbing your fucking mouth. Bitch! It's time for you to get a taste of what real trouble is. Bring the kids. We're going for a ride."

I slip a knee-length muumuu over my head, grab fruit and bottles of water, and hustle the children to the car. David drives to a thickly wooded area and parks. "Wait here," he instructs Jonathan and Angela. "Mommy and I are going for a walk." We get out. "That way," he points toward a path and nudges my behind.

Unable to imagine where we're going or why, I follow a winding path through gum trees and down a slight incline. Fallen branches and wild undergrowth filled with nettles gradually obliterate it. I fear we might already be out of earshot of the car.

When I halt and bend over to pick stickers from my sandals, he says, "Okay, far enough. Find a tree you really like and put your arms around it."

Perplexed, I numbly obey. The woods are lovely and quiet except for birds chattering above. What kind are they? I look up at their large bodies, black with white spots. Maybe magpies . . .

"Close your eyes and hug it real tight," he says.

Whack! Something strikes me from behind so hard that my legs collapse and my clinging arms scrape against the bark.

"Stand up and hold on," he snarls. "That's just the beginning."

Pain sears my thighs as I struggle to rise. I turn my neck and see him grasping a limb about five feet long and three inches in diameter with several protruding knots.

"Turn around and close your eyes," he snaps and clobbers my buttocks.

I clutch the tree as if it's my baby's lifeline as he swings again and again and again....

Puffing, he finally says, "That's all...for now anyway. Let's go."

I crumple to the ground, crying uncontrollably, from fear as much as pain.

He tugs on my arm. "Get up. We have work to do. Gotta find a new park today. Monday I have to be back at work and won't have time for anymore of this bullshit."

I rise to my knees and pull myself up by the tree. As I hobble along the path, choking back sobs, he seethes behind me, "If I have to drag you out here again, it'll be a lot worse. Just remember that."

Cleverly he's managed to batter me without leaving a visible mark or a witness.

In the following weeks I redouble my efforts to placate him, but I can no more know what might set off a tantrum than I can predict at what spot in the night sky a shooting star will appear. He smokes marijuana every night and sometimes even in the mornings before going to work, claiming it helps him relax, but I suspect the opposite. My thickening waist is more difficult to camouflage, and I can't help worrying he might actually want me to lose the baby.

We make reservations on the *Marconi*, an Italian liner, and get required vaccinations. David finds buyers for our caravan and car, and we pack belongings for shipping. I feel a little better after getting our passports stamped with permits extending our immigrant status in Australia for two years. Can't imagine not being back long before then, but I regret that our baby won't be born here.

The excitement of boarding ship with all the confetti and streamers partially overshadows my sadness at leaving. As the *Marconi* inches away from Circular Quay, I stand at the rail with hundreds of passengers, waving to throngs of well-wishers on the dock. Gaining Sydney Harbour, the ship moves faster. Then it hits me. My chest heaves, and tears spill over. "Goodbye, Harbour Bridge," I whisper beneath my breath. "Goodbye, Opera House. Goodbye, Bondi Beach." Too rapidly the cherished landmarks wane in the distance. *We have to come back,* I cry inside. *We just have to!*

Jamaica, 1976

I

Three weeks of paradise, sailing across the Pacific. I spend hours sitting on deck in my muumuu, reading, sipping drinks, chatting with fellow voyagers, watching the children in the pool. They love the water slide. Won't stop even when their skin becomes sodden. Observing the expanse of deep blue for weeks on end without ever seeing another craft makes me appreciate Earth's vastness. By the time we reach the Panama Canal, my throat is sore and I feel feverish, probably from overexposure on the windy deck. After moving through the canal locks, we disembark and fly to Jamaica.

The island we return to is shockingly different from the one we left two years before. As political factions vie for power, we hear gunfire all over Kingston. Throughout the nights helicopter searchlights sweep through neighborhoods. Gunshot explosions keep waking us. We move from one rooming house to another, but everywhere is the same.

Despite martial law and curfews, Bob Marley goes ahead with plans to perform at the Smile Jamaica concert. To our shock, we hear on the morning news that he and three others were shot while rehearsing in his own yard, less than a mile from our old home. Two days later he performs anyway with a bullet in his arm, accompanied by his wife, Rita, her head bandaged from gunshot wounds.

"This city has gone mad!" David declares. "We better head for the country where things aren't so out of control. Gotta figure out what's really going on and how to fix it."

We load our bags into the rented car and set off early the next morning toward Port Antonio. "I'm going to look up my uncle Sid," David says. "He has a big place and should be able to put us up for a while."

He tunes the radio as we drive. DJs keep spinning records by Marley and the Wailers like "Songs of Freedom" and "Get Up, Stand Up." There are frequent news updates, but so far no gunmen have been detained.

My sore throat is now a full-blown cold with an incessant cough. "Stop that!" David says. "You sound disgusting. Uncle Sid will think you have TB."

"I can't help it," I wheeze and pop another cough drop into my mouth.

"It's all in your mind. But if you go on like that, you'll kill the baby in your belly."

I keep holding my breath trying to stop the tickle in my throat but can't suppress the hacking that erupts from the pit of my chest, convulsing my whole body. I cough, hold my breath until I explode, then cough again. I worry if the baby is getting enough oxygen as David keeps passing cars even on curves and hills.

Though shocked to see us, Uncle Sid, a short, muscular, brown-skinned man with silvery hair, graciously invites us to stay. Next morning at the breakfast table he says, "I've got the perfect cure for your cough," and hands me a plate with a grapefruit cut in half. "Eat one of these three times a day, and you'll soon be well. My trees are bearing so we have plenty. And put this on it." He sets a jug of honey in front of me. "Fresh from my hives."

"Thanks." I taste the grapefruit. "This is delicious! It's so sweet, doesn't even need the honey."

"Put it on anyway. Honey's packed with vitamins."

I follow his prescription, and in a couple days the cough abates. As we prepare to depart at the end of the week, Sid hands me a quart of honey and puts a box of grapefruit in our car. "Keep eating these every day," he says, "and you'll be fit in no time."

Hugging him, I whisper, "Thanks, Uncle Sid. Thank you for saving my baby."

We drive to Montego Bay and on to Negril. The trip takes longer than normal because David keeps stopping to question people. Next we spend a night at Carambola, David's ancestral estate near the west end of the island which we visited a couple of times before going to Australia. David treasures memories of childhood days spent there, but this time he can't relax. "I gotta get back to Kingston," he says. "That's the hub of the action. It may be dangerous but it's where I'm needed most."

Back in Kingston, we move into a two-bedroom furnished duplex. Soon David becomes convinced the CIA is instigating and supporting the political warfare devastating the island. "It's my job," he says, "to drive them out."

Every day he drives around asking questions and giving speeches, usually insisting the children and I accompany him. I feel he's using us as protection, hiding behind my skirt and their innocence. He enters areas where people gather, like outdoor markets and fishing docks, and randomly strikes up conversations. His provocative statements soon incite disagreements and lead to raised voices that draw onlookers. After attracting a gathering, he climbs atop a wall or car and launches into a speech. Pet topics include the CIA plot against Jamaica, his marvelous invention, legalization of marijuana, and sexual freedom. He sometimes imitates the Rastafarian dialect, calling himself "I and I" and referring to Jah, the Rastafarian name for god. "Ras Tafari!" is his newest exclamation.

One day we drive into the Blue Mountains and stop at the inn where he took my parents for tea. Overlooking the city, the inn boasts more than a 180 degree view of the southern half of the island. To our dismay, the former proprietors are nowhere to be seen. Two shiny four-wheel-drive vehicles are parked behind the inn. An American youth is working on one. In his gregarious style, David starts a conversation with the young man, volunteering personal information and asking questions.

The youth invites us inside where we meet several more young Americans wearing jeans and army fatigues. Gradually David's tone takes on a sharp edge. "All this fancy stuff," he sweeps his arm to take in the sound equipment, cameras, telescopes, televisions, diving gear, and expensive clothing strewn around the place, "who pays for it? You expect us to believe mighty America is so prosperous that any kid can buy whatever they want? Or could it be that you're living high off the taxpayers?"

Our hosts silently exchange glances.

David smiles. "Hey, how would you like to try my smoke. Bet you don't have any this good in America." He pulls a bag from his pocket and loads his mini bong.

"It's all right, man," says a burly character wearing a sleeveless t-shirt exposing a collection of tattoos. "We don't need anything from you. In fact, it's time for you to move along."

I look at David, then the front door, and grasp the children's hands as a deafening roar shakes the room. Through the plate glass window we see a helicopter descend on the front lawn. A man in fatigues enters the house carrying an automatic rifle.

I hustle the children out the door and dash for our car. David is right behind. We exit the yard in a cloud of dust thrown up by our spinning wheels. Speeding down the mountain, David declares, "We found them, Jac! That's CIA headquarters! They have the best location on the island for watching everything and directing their whole operation. Now we've got to expose their plot to the people. They know we're onto them, so we have to move fast before they try to shut us up."

"You didn't tell them where we live?"

"Course not. First we'll contact the Defense Force. Then we'll put an article in the newspaper. I'll try to make an appointment with the Prime Minister while you write a letter to the editor. We gotta make haste."

I write a letter to *The Daily Gleaner* and after two rewrites David signs his name and sends it. Excited when it gets published in the weekend edition, he calls several radio talk shows to describe the CIA operation he has discovered on the mountain.

A week later I see a display ad in the newspaper showing the mountain lodge for lease. "Hooray!" David cheers. "We did it! Kicked their asses out! Things should settle down now so I can concentrate on getting my invention ready for the people."

I'm skeptical of his CIA theory. More likely, the inn occupants are members of a drug smuggling operation. Of course, there's the possibility they're involved in both types of covert activities. Why not make a little profit on the side while using taxpayers' money to thwart post-colonial national development? Whatever the truth might be, I don't discourage him from perceiving their departure as a personal victory.

Furious when he can't get through to the Prime Minister, David turns to the opposition. He contacts the former Minister of Industry, the Honorable Roland Fairweather, and makes an appointment. After careful preparation, he displays the patent applications and demonstrates several versions of his invention including the oscillating shower nozzle, an irrigation device, and a model which he thinks has industrial uses. The politician is impressed. More meetings ensue and eventually they sign a letter agreeing to be business partners in marketing the invention. David

259

will continue refining his prototypes and demonstrating them to potential manufacturers. Fairweather will supply contacts and fund the operation, including a stipend for our living expenses. The initial payment covers expenses for six months. The agreement is reached just in time to save David from looking for a job.

When Fairweather brings several American representatives of the Western Gulf Corporation to Jamaica to see the inventions, David insists I accompany him to the meeting at a New Kingston hotel. While we're still setting up the demonstrations Fairweather enters with his coterie of expensively clad and manicured businessmen. After brief introductions, they sit, cross their legs, and look at David expectantly, ready to be impressed. David launches directly into an account of his heroic exposure of the CIA operation to destabilize the island. Then he attacks the U.S. government and the capitalist system for exploiting third-world countries as the listeners exchange glances and shift impatiently in their seats. Before he gets around to demonstrating his devices, they rise and walk out. Fairweather rushes after them, trying to explain away his role in inviting the delegation to waste their time and money on a crackpot.

David turns to me in a rage. "I brought you along to keep me on track! You're the one who's supposed to know how Americans think. If I wasn't saying the right thing, you should have stopped me! Why can't I *ever* depend on you?"

While he raves, I focus on repacking the equipment. If I tell him what I really think—that he's made a great shower nozzle, but it isn't going to save the world, and that his intensity and wild exaggerations always alienate people—he'll strangle me. Better to let him be mad for what he considers negligence. At least we have enough money for my impending delivery.

II

I try to prepare Jonathan and Angela for my absence by showing them how to fix peanut butter and jelly sandwiches, mix drinks with Milo powder and milk, and open cups of yogurt. I don't want them using the stove, but they can help themselves to fruit, and six-year-old Jonathan can pour cereal and milk. I ensure the cupboards and refrigerator are well stocked and keep up with laundry, knowing I might leave any day for the hospital.

While I read to the children I let them touch my abdomen so they can feel the baby kicking and rolling around. "I know it's a girl," Angela says confidently. "I just know!"

During a routine exam the doctor discovers complications and tells me to check into the hospital immediately. After labor is induced, I rapidly become fully dilated and am wheeled into the delivery room. As the baby's head emerges, the doctor shouts in the middle of a contraction, "Stop her! No pushing! Stop everything right there!"

David squeezes my hand, "Don't bear down. Just breathe shallow. Relax and breathe lightly."

Relaxing is out of the question, but I hold on, flutter breathing like a hummingbird, for what seems like half an eternity, only vaguely aware of shouts, curses, and banging reverberating around the room. Focused on my breath, I don't know what's going on.

"All right!" the doctor says at last, "Let her go! Push now. Push!"

Within moments the most gorgeous baby girl I have ever seen is placed in my arms. I press her to my breast, and she immediately starts suckling.

David follows us into the recovery room, bursting to tell me what the commotion was all about. "When her head appeared, the doctor saw the cord was wrapped around her neck. If you'd continued pushing, the blood supply through the cord would have been shut off. Air couldn't get to her lungs either, so she would have suffocated before she was even born, or her brain would have been damaged."

"She's soooo perfect," I coo to the bundle snuggling contentedly in my arms.

"The doctor called for scissors to cut the cord, but the nurse handed him one right out of the sterilizer that burned a hole through his glove. He dropped it on the floor and shouted for a new glove. When he got it, she passed him another scissors which did the same thing. That one he threw across the room. The third try, he finally got one he could hold onto and cut the cord. I've never seen a doctor sweat like him. Or curse nurses like he did! He's one fantastic doctor!"

"Amazing." I smile down at our sleeping beauty. "I'd like to name her Sydney. What do you think?"

"Sounds fine."

"How about Sydney Lynne?"

"Sure. Go ahead and register her that way."

His quick approval surprises and also disappoints me. He didn't even ask why I like the name, as if he doesn't care. I picked "Sydney" while we were aboard the *Marconi* realizing it could work for either a girl or boy. The only difference would be in the middle name. It was the first and last place I saw in Australia, the land of her conception, and I hope the name will bring us the good fortune of return. The second significance is in appreciation of David's wonderful Uncle Sidney who saved my life and hers with his fabulous grapefruit. Her name will forever remind me of his kindness.

Two days later David announces that I've languished in the hospital long enough. Reluctantly I pack my things, gather Sydney in my arms, and follow him out.

When we get home, I discover he has installed an automatic washing machine. "Thank you!" I say, moved by his thoughtfulness. "This'll make my life so much easier."

Angela and Jonathan are eager to see and touch their sister. I hold her on my lap while they sit on either side and exclaim over her fascinating tiny parts. Jonathan counts her toes and fingers. Angela strokes her silky head, asking, "Can she see me, Mommy? And can she hear us?"

"Yes, Honey, just watch."

A pang of guilt hits me as I recognize how bleak their lives are. They have few toys now, not even tricycles, but make do by entertaining themselves with things they find in the yard. I recall the fine schools we tried to get Jonathan into a few years back. Now that's out of the question. No money, and who knows where we might be living next month? It's all I can manage just to keep them fed and clean.

III

Sydney is a few weeks old when David reports that his friend Marcus is returning to Jamaica with a new American wife. Next day he meets them at the airport and brings them to our house. Marcus hugs everybody and passes out gifts to Jonathan and Angela. Proudly he presents his wife Liz and their baby son, six months older than Sydney. I serve refreshments as we exchange stories of the past two years, filling in the many gaps left by sporadic correspondence.

After divorcing Donna, Marcus hired an American *au pair* to help him with the children. When she got pregnant, he put the children in boarding schools and flew with her to California where they got married. Now he and Liz are back looking for a boat to buy and live on. David tells about the progress with his invention and his courageous exposé of the CIA. Both are disillusioned with

American lifestyle and sad that the dismal business climate in Jamaica makes life here untenable.

Liz and I exchange baby stories for awhile, but she is clearly exhausted from their journey. "I really need to rest," she tells me as she rises and approaches Marcus. "Excuse me, but I'm worn out; I think we better get going—"

"Stop interrupting us!" David rebukes her. "Can't you see Marcus isn't finished with his drink? And maybe he wants another. We're old friends; got lots to catch up on."

"I'm sorry, but I'm exhausted and so is—"

"Go lie down if you're tired. Nobody's stopping you, so quit interfering with us. Don't they teach you anything in America about respecting a man?"

"Lay off, David!" Marcus interjects.

"I'm serious," David persists. "Your woman has a lot to learn."

"I'll have you know," Marcus retorts, "that Liz has her bachelor's degree in anthropology. She knows a lot more than you give her credit—"

"Bachelor's degree, my ass! You think that impresses me?"

Liz says, "Let's go, Marcus. I didn't come here to be insulted."

Marcus gets up. "She's right, David. You can't speak to my wife that way. If you don't want to drive us, I'll call a cab."

"Don't bother; I'll drive you. If you're happy with letting a woman run your life, it's all right with me."

"For Chrissake!"

"All right. All right. I'm sorry. Calm down, everybody." David rises. "Let's go."

Liz glares at him but says nothing as she marches out the door. My face burns with shame.

IV

I'm still breast-feeding Sydney after dinner when David says, "Hurry up. I can't wait all night. You know I need you to type this addendum to my agreement with Fairweather."

"I'll be right with you," I say, patting her back. As soon as she burps, I lay her in the cradle, then go to the typewriter and insert a sheet of paper. "I'm ready."

"Here," he hands me a pad. "Type it exactly as I've written, but all double spaced."

Soon after I start typing I hear Sydney cry. She's still hungry. Unnerved, I keep making mistakes and having to use the correction tape.

"Pay attention to what you're doing," David says. "I'll take care of her." He goes into the bedroom. A moment later her cries get louder and then become shrieks.

I rush in and see him striking her back with a switch. "Stop! Don't hit her!" I force myself between him and the cradle. "She's still hungry! You rushed me, so she didn't get enough—" I reach for her, but his fist sends me reeling and I see spinning lights as I crash to the floor.

"Stop interfering, like you know more than me about children!" He grabs my hair, shoves me onto the bed, lashes my legs with his belt as Sydney's cries get louder. I roll off the bed, scramble toward the door. "Not so fast!" His foot rams my belly. I double up, gasp for air. Sydney sobs jerkily. Straddling me, David glares down with belt in hand. "Go in the bathroom and clean yourself up. At this rate our work'll take all night."

I struggle up, stumble to the bathroom, wash my face. Through a crack in the door, I can see the back entrance to the house. Leaving the water running, I slip outside. The dark air is fresh, a blanket of peace filled with fragrance of night-blooming jasmine and the chorus of tree frogs. I want to run. He'll have no idea

265

where to find me. But I have no idea where to go either. No friends here now. I take another step into the welcoming darkness of cool black air that inhales me into its lungs. Into this cavern I can disappear. But when the sun rises, what then? I look back to the dimly lit house and barely make out the open louvers of the room where Sydney is. Next to it, breeze stirs the curtain in Jonathan and Angela's room. If I go inside, David is bound to go on haranguing me for hours, sapping my energy, confusing my thoughts. Another wasted night.

Above me a dark cloud moves quickly away like a curtain opening on stage and a half moon appears. I gaze up. Father sun is off gallivanting on the other side of the world while mother moon reigns here, surrounded by their night sky children. Jonathan, Angie, Sydney—my stars. I go inside, turn off the water, sit down at the typewriter.

Fairweather rejects David's proposal to extend their partnership, and he refuses to send any more money. "We'll give up the house," David says, "but not the car. Need transportation. We'll find a cheaper place on the north coast."

Island Tour

I

After a tedious journey over the mountains, we enter a beautiful estate on the north coast and drive past luxurious villas surrounding a golf course. "Looks like Mafia headquarters," David says. "Might be an interesting place to live. Most of the houses seem empty. Shall we capture one?"

"What do you mean?" My stomach cringes.

"Just pick one and move in. How do you like that big white one on the hill?" He points. "Or you prefer the pink one over there with the little cupolas?"

"We could get killed messing around this place."

"They're not doing business here anymore. For once in your life, just loosen up!" He drives through an open gate and along a driveway lined with royal palms. We enter a wooded area, round several curves, and suddenly come upon a less ostentatious two-story frame house. It is surrounded by decks and overgrown croton hedges interspersed with clumps of bougainvillea, gigantic wild ginger, bird of paradise blooms, and a plethora of entangled vines–a hungry jungle intent on reclaiming its territory.

David stops the car. "Wait here while I look around."

When he disappears around a corner of the house, Angie tries the door handle. "Can we get out, Mommy?"

"No. You heard Daddy say to wait here."

"But I have to pee!"

"Me, too," says Jonathan.

I sigh. "Okay then. Get out one at a time and stay on this side of the car so no one from the house can see you."

While they're watering the grass, I put Sydney on the driver's seat to change her diaper and then press her to my breast. No sooner are both children back in the car than David appears, grinning broadly.

"The door's unlocked," he says, "but nobody's inside. Looks like somebody lives here 'cause there's food in the fridge, but it's old. And the grass hasn't been cut for weeks. This place needs someone to take care of it. Shall we give it a shot?"

He's serious. I groan inside.

"One closet has a few shirts, but there's nothing in the other bedrooms, so some dude must live here alone. We can move our things into the two empty rooms. That way, if the guy comes back, we won't be in his way. For all we know, he may only come here a couple times a year. It's a shame for this place to go to waste."

"I ... I really don't think—"

"The worst he can do is throw us out. What do we have to lose?" he shrugs. "Besides, everybody's doing it. Most of the houses in Beverly Hills have been captured."

A few days after we move in, the children and I are returning from a walk when we see a jeep in the yard and David talking to a man standing beside it. He looks to be in his thirties and has reddish hair with a complexion to match. David hails us. "Come over and meet Peter. Just got back from England."

The owner of the shirts. My heart sinks.

After introducing us, David gestures expansively, "Did you notice how good the yard looks? You wouldn't believe what a mess it was when we got here, so I cut the grass and raked the leaves.

And wait'll you see how Jac cleaned up the house." He seems on the verge of inviting the man into his own home.

Peter grunts; his eyes shift nervously from David to me to the children behind.

"Go on," David gestures toward the house. "Take a look." They go inside. I park the pram by our car and keep the children nearby to be ready for a hasty departure.

Minutes later David opens the door and beckons. As we enter he says, "Peter likes the way you cleaned everything."

"Great!" I try to look upbeat. "I haven't done anything to your room—"

David interrupts, "She can even do your laundry, and she's a fantastic cook."

Peter shakes his head, "I'm seldom here for meals—"

"Wait until you taste her pies and bread! Worth coming home for—"

"Mommy can make everything," Angie beams.

"From the mouth of babes!" David chuckles. "Yeah, Man, you need help with this place. I can fix those leaking faucets and the broken toilet—probably needs a new valve. And the security lights, some of them don't even come on. I'll repair all those things, and it won't cost you a thing, except for materials."

Peter sighs. "I have a man who comes here once a week. He's supposed to keep an eye on the place, fix things—"

"Well, he's sure not doing his job...if you don't mind my saying so. This place deserves better."

Peter's initial look of incredulity has been replaced by cautious skepticism, though I suspect he's wondering which political gang we belong to. Eventually he reveals that he travels a lot and spends little time in the house.

"It's obvious then, you need a caretaker, and here we are!" David shrugs his shoulders, palms up. "What do you have to lose?"

Still looking dubious, Peter agrees to give the arrangement a try, but stipulates, "No loud music when I'm home. And you'll be responsible for replacing anything that gets broken." He looks pointedly at the children.

Shelter we have, but little else. David can't set up a workshop and quickly tires of yard work. His persistent presence makes us all tense, so I escape every morning by putting Sydney in the pram and taking the children on long walks around the golf course.

One afternoon while Jonathan and Angela are napping, David, more restless than usual, insists that I walk with him. I push Sydney in the pram and listen as he vents his frustration at the loss of Fairweather's support. Unwilling to accept that the deal is over, he keeps searching for an angle to win him back. Glad to see his rancor directed at someone other than me, I hold back from cutting his threads of hope even though I think it preposterous to expect the man ever to give him another chance.

When we return to the house, David heads for the kitchen to make a sandwich. Soon he calls, "Where's the guava jelly? It was here yesterday."

"I don't know." I follow him into the kitchen. "Maybe behind some other jars." I search and find the peanut butter in its usual place but no jelly.

"It's goddamned annoying when a man can't even have a sandwich to fill his hungry belly! I want to know who took it. Jonathan! Angie! Come here!"

The two rush in and stand at attention, hands clasped behind their backs. Both deny knowing anything about the missing jelly. Wide-eyed Angela confirms, "It was there a little while ago when we made sandwiches."

"Oh, so you guys had peanut butter and jelly this afternoon, huh?"

"Yes, Daddy," she answers while Jonathan nods.

David opens the pantry door, turns on the light, and scrutinizes the floor. He bends down and picks something up. "Look what I found. A piece of glass! What got broken?" Silence meets his inquisitorial gaze. The children stand paralyzed, white as milk, even their lips drained of color. David goes outside and opens the trash barrel. From it he pulls a paper bag. He untwists the top, peers in and brings it into the kitchen.

"You lying little thieves!" he explodes. "You broke the jelly and then lied about it! Which one of you did it?"

Still standing with hands behind their backs and eyes riveted to the floor, no one breathes.

"It has to be one of you. I don't care about the friggin' jelly anymore; I just don't want a liar in my house. Speak up! Who's gonna tell the truth?"

Chin quivering and head bowed, Jonathan mumbles, "It broke when I was tryin' to make my sandwich and–"

"So you're the liar! I figured. Just like something you'd do–break it and then lie about it! Ya little shit! I'm not even going to beat you. Just get out! I won't have a ras clot liar in my house. Get out of here!"

Jonathan raises his eyes, his face a portrait of bewilderment.

"You heard me! Get out. Now!"

"But Daddy," Angela pipes up, "it was an accident. He just–"

"Stay out of this!" David snaps and turns to Jonathan. "You have it too good around here. If you can lie to your father, it's time to find out what the real world is like. Just walk out that door, Boy, and keep going. You're on your own now."

I pat Sydney's back and jostle her on my hip, trying to keep her crying from adding to the chaos. Silently I pray, *Please God, please send Peter or someone to stop this.*

Jonathan moves toward the screen door, opens it, steps outside. He hesitates and then heads slowly toward the driveway. David breaks the silence. "Well, what's everybody waiting for? He's gone. Get dinner ready." He disappears into the bathroom.

Angela edges over to me and asks in a tiny voice, "Can I help, Mommy?"

I look at her but can't focus. "Umm, let's see. Just stay here with Sydney. Give her some water." I put her in the pram and hand Angie a bottle of honey water.

Then I dart out to the deck and glance around. No Jonathan. Down the steps, across the yard, along the driveway I race, desperate to catch him before he reaches the main road. What if he wanders into the woods? What if someone picks him up!

The gate to the road looms ahead. Oh, my God, don't let me be too late! I yank it open, look right, left. Then I spot a small figure, standing forlornly behind a tree.

"Jonathan!" I run to him. "Thank God!" I crouch, grasp his shoulders, look into his eyes. "I'm so glad you waited here. I was afraid I'd lost you!" I hug him, stroke his satiny hair. "You can come home now. Daddy was just trying to teach you not to lie." I stand and take his hand. "Come. You can tell Daddy you're sorry."

Silently he allows me to lead him to the house.

As I open the door, David appears. "So you sneaked out and brought him back!"

"He's sorry, and he understands now. Don't you, Jonathan?" I look at him to telegraph encouragement.

He nods vehemently, but doesn't meet his father's gaze.

"We'll do it your way, then. He'll have to be punished." David seizes Jonathan's arm and drags him onto the deck. He grabs a broom and swings it. The handle breaks on Jonathan's legs. Infuriated, David picks up a rake.

"No! Stop it! Don't!" Angela and I shriek. Sydney wails. I lunge for the rake, wrestle with David, fall to the floor. He kicks my stomach. I double up, gasping for air.

David clobbers Jonathan with the rake. He crumples to the floor, but David keeps hitting him. Angela screams hysterically. Finally stopping, he snarls, "He's all yours now. Do what you want with him."

I crawl to my son moaning on the floor. His legs are bleeding. I fear his back is too, but don't want to hurt him more by lifting his shirt. I touch his brow and murmur, "I'm sorry, Jonathan, so sorry."

"Is he dead, Mommy?" Angela whispers.

"No. Thank God. But he's hurt bad. "I've got to clean him up and get him into bed." I look around. Sydney is crying. "Please, Honey, can you pour some juice in her bottle?"

"Okay, Mommy." Angela rushes to the refrigerator.

Trying not to touch his pummeled flesh, I carry Jonathan upstairs, and lay him on his bed. With a pan of warm water, hydrogen peroxide, soap, cloth and towel, I gently clean his injuries while assuring him he'll be fine. But I keep wondering how he can ever trust me again. "I'm going to get you something to drink," I finally say. "I'll be right back."

I rush downstairs and fix a tray with a glass of water, cup of milk mixed with Milo, crackers, three baby aspirin and a piece of aloe. He drinks the water and takes the aspirin. I rub aloe on his cuts. After he has a few sips of the Milo, I bring Sydney up and sit to nurse her. Angela kneels beside Jonathan, feeding him crackers while gazing at his cuts and bruises. When he falls asleep, we steal from the room.

For three days he mostly sleeps. I carry him food, dress his wounds, try to comfort him. I search the few books I have for information on treating contusion, and when he can bear it, I start massaging him to ease his pain and stimulate healing.

David disappears after the fracas, but I don't delude myself that he's gone for good. All too soon he returns with a stray dog. He claims Astro is a phantom dog with special powers to appear and disappear, and he brags how Astro follows him everywhere, as though the dog's devotion proves what a great guy he is.

Peter doesn't like having a pet around, but stops short of forbidding it until the day he enters the kitchen just in time to see Astro pulling food off the table. The dog runs out the door with Peter in pursuit. He throws a rock and hits him. Hearing yelps,

David comes running and proceeds to castigate Peter for his cruelty to animals. I watch as the two go nose-to-nose exchanging epithets. If only they'd start slugging, David would get a thrashing! But the row climaxes with Peter proclaiming, "I want you out of here! All of you. Everything out in three days, or I call the cops."

II

The next morning David goes in search of shelter and doesn't return until sunset. "I got a fantastic place!" he reports. "It's called Jericho. Overlooks the golf course and has a pool, but the off-season price is a song. Even has caretakers. We're moving tomorrow."

At least there will be people around, witnesses.

At Jericho David sets up a makeshift shop and resumes working on his invention. Finally I can focus on home schooling for Jonathan and Angela. I buy a roll of newsprint and tape it to the wall as a substitute chalkboard. In large colorful letters I write the alphabet and post pictures cut from magazines to illustrate words beginning with each letter. On flash cards I print words and numbers. We decorate shoeboxes and fill them with crayons, scissors, pencils, paper and paste. The plan is to follow a regular schedule of having "school" for two hours each morning while Sydney naps.

Vera, the caretaker, lives in a cottage near the gate. She is available to cook and clean, but we can't afford her. Jonathan and Angie sometimes go over to her rooms, so I caution them not to become nuisances. One day they bring a plateful of tamarind balls home. Concerned, I go investigate.

"Don't worry youself," Vera laughs. "Dose pickney don't cause no trouble. Dat lickle Angie, she talk so good. When I give dem a taste o' dis or dat, it just cause I likes to share wid dem."

"You're very kind," I say, "and I really appreciate it. If you're sure you don't mind, I won't stop them from coming, but please don't hesitate to send them back home if they get in your way. And thanks for the tamarind balls. They're delicious." I return her plate. "Here are a few slices of fresh cornbread I thought you might like."

"T'ank you, Ma'am, t'ank you."

"Please, just call me Jac."

"Yes, Miz Jacs." She nods and smiles, unable to violate the ingrained use of titles to denote class distinctions.

Eager for Angie to become a good swimmer like Jonathan, I give her lessons whenever possible. One afternoon as I approach the pool carrying Sydney, Angela calls, "Guess what, Mommy!"

"What?"

"I can swim!"

"Really? Show me."

"Watch." Without armbands, she descends the ladder and paddles across the pool. At the opposite edge, she turns to bask in my applause and praise.

"That's wonderful! How did you learn?"

"Just did it. See!" She crosses the pool again.

Jonathan, who has been doing surface dives at the deep end, returns to the shallow water. "It's about time," he says. "She's almost five!"

"I'm so happy you both can swim now!" I say. "You're very brave. But I still want you to *always* go in the pool together. Never alone. Understand?"

"Of course," he replies.

"Yes, Mommy. Watch me again!" Angela splashes away.

I sit on the steps, dangling Sydney in the water as they continue swimming and diving. Reflecting on how independent they're becoming, I try to picture how life must appear from their perspective, imagining the world that swirls around and buffets them: A father who is dynamic, demanding, exciting, enthusiastic, affectionate, but also critical, intimidating, unpredictable, and brutal. A hard-working mother who is a great cook, patient, comforting, health conscious, and an avid reader, but also cowardly, weak, unimaginative, and lacking confidence. Where does that leave them? Will they become self-reliant and strong, or insecure, maybe mean?

"That was a beautiful dive," I call as Jonathan's head emerges. "Hardly any splash. Can you do it again?"

"Watch me, Mommy!" Angela shouts, teetering on the edge of the pool. She pinches her nose with her fingers and leaps far out, creating a huge splash.

When her head pops to the surface, I clap loudly. "What a brave girl!"

"Watch me again."

"I'm watching all the time. My two dolphins."

As I sit on a step below the water's surface, Sydney kicks and splashes water in the security of my lap. If only I could create more memories of good times like this with them. Everything's so different from what I intended. So far, they're wonderful kids, but in the long run, the bad could override what I've done right. And as Jonathan gets older, he may feel obligated to protect me from his father. I can't let that happen.

A raft tethered at one side of the pool carries David's newest project, a musical water fountain using his special nozzles. Electronic signals synchronize moving water that is illuminated by flashing lights. Every night he works on it, determined to get his dancing fountain performing well enough to convince Fairweather to renew their contract.

That night David says, "I'll give Fairweather one last chance. If he still can't appreciate how great this invention is, then I'll find someone else who does."

He puts on a Herbie Mann album while I sit, prepared to give constructive feedback. But the constantly moving bright colors against the background of the night sky strain my eyes, and I nod off. A stinging slap nearly knocks me out of the chair. My hands fly to my face as I struggle to keep from falling.

"Useless bitch!" David snarls.

"I, I'm sorry. It's just the lights; they strain my eyes. It's my astigmatism…"

"Stigmatism, my assitism! This is my last chance to win Fairweather back. And you sit there sleeping! Get me a glass of water."

I go for his water and fill my own glass with ice cubes, hoping that chewing them will help to keep me awake. When I return, he has on a Pink Floyd album. He sits at the control panel, fine-tuning settings, striving for the perfect adjustment. I try to make helpful comments, try to sound convincing.

"No, no, no!" he slams his fists on the table. "Lies don't help me to improve! It's obviously not as good as last night, but you didn't tell me, so I've over-adjusted. Now I have to get it back to where it was before, and that's not easy. You're worse than no help!" He switches off the fountain lights and pulls the raft to the side of the pool. "Bring the torch over so I can see what I'm doing."

I grab the light, and hurry to the pool edge where I train the beam on his apparatus. After making some changes, he returns to his command post on the terrace and continues adjusting the controls.

Hearing a hungry cry, I jump up. "Sydney's awake. I have to feed her."

"Always some excuse. Hurry up and get back here."

When I return, the fountain is leaping twenty feet in the air, exploding into a cascading umbrella of droplets, all reflecting the colored lights pulsing with the music. "It's fabulous!" I say. "Looks alive. Don't change a thing."

"You're just saying that because you want to go to bed."

"Believe me; it's perfect."

"Then this is it, Baby. It's Fairweather's last chance. Once he sees this, I don't know how he can refuse. I'm not even going to call first. We'll just load everything in the car and drive over. I'll set up a display in his pool that'll blow him away. He won't want to lose the chance to be in on this. You'll see! Let's leave first thing tomorrow."

I hope he's right. We're down to our last hundred dollars and the rent is already overdue. If this doesn't work, we'll have neither home nor car.

III

Only servants are there when we arrive at Fairweather's mansion. The cook recognizes David and does not object when he says we'll be spending the night. We park our bags in a guest room, and I help carry the fountain apparatus to the swimming pool. David sets up his display while I watch the children in the kiddy pool.

After the fountain is ready, David dons his trunks, dives off the board, and swims a few laps. Climbing out near me, he remarks, "That board's too low. I want to do some high flying." He gazes around and his eyes fix on a flat-roofed two-story wing of the house near the shallow end of the pool. "Dare me to jump off there," he points, "and fly into the pool?"

"Of course not!" I catch my breath, heart racing. "I'm not going to dare you to kill yourself."

"Oh, so you don't believe I can fly?"

"You're not a bird or a plane… or a kite!" I try to keep it light.

"Well, if Jesus Christ could walk on water, I ought to be able to fly. It would be a sure sign of my powers. A sign I'm the chosen one, don't you think?"

I fidget, hating how he keeps putting me on the spot. "I suppose it would, but remember the line of scripture that says, 'Thou shalt not tempt the lord thy God.'"

"Good point!" He eyes me with surprise. "So you can think after all. Should try it more often." He turns and paces around the pool, lighting and puffing on his pipe. Then he snaps his fingers, "I've got it! This isn't really tempting God. It's more like testing my faith. Like when Isaac—or whichever bloke in the Old Testament—was told to sacrifice his son. That's how God tested his obedience. So maybe God is testing my faith in His power to make me fly. Looking at it like that, I'm not tempting Him, am I?"

I shrug. "Did God ever promise you could fly?"

"It's not the flying; it's the faith. God must be testing my faith to see if I'm worthy of greater deeds, greater powers. Tell you what, before I go up, I'll measure how deep the water is. Bring me a tape."

I get a yardstick from the kitchen. Checking the water nearest the building, he says, "Thirteen inches. That's plenty if God wants me alive. And if he wants me to die, he can have me. Now watch, Jac. You're my witness." He heads for a ladder by the house.

As he climbs to the roof, I stare, dreading he might be seriously injured. I'll be blamed—due to my inadequate faith or something—and have to look after him. I don't worry that he'll be killed. He's not that foolish. After all his experiments with water, he probably knows something about surface tension that I don't.

He prolongs the agony, strolling around the flat roof, talking loudly and attracting the servants' attention. When he has four witnesses, he finally walks to the edge, spreads his arms, bends his knees. He won't really do it, I think. He's going to find some excuse...

But then he leaps. As he soars out over the pool, I gaze paralyzed. His body plunges downward... What the fuck! I never thought he'd really...

Smack! He belly-flops with a terrible explosion of water inches from the edge. Water cascades onto the surrounding cement. If the blow didn't kill him, he might still drown...

Then an arm moves… and a leg. He raises his head and slowly, painfully crawls from the water.

When Fairweather arrives home, David raves about his amazing flight, as if it proves his worthiness as an inventor. Despite our rudeness at barging into his home, Fairweather graciously invites us to dinner, agreeing to watch David's demonstration afterwards. But his time is limited since he has to be back in the legislature early next morning. We eat, and then while David and Fairweather go out to the pool, I bathe the children, read them "Anancy the Spider" stories, and get them settled in bed.

Fairweather is gone when we get up, but he's left a note asking David to stop by his office in the afternoon. The neutral tone reveals no clue as to his opinion of the fountain. I take the children for a dip in the pool, but David is too edgy to let us enjoy ourselves. We have a hasty lunch and drive downtown. I wait with the children in a park while David walks to the government office building.

He returns sooner than I expect. "Get in the car," he says dourly. As the doors close, he lets loose. "That cock-sucking mother fucker! He said 'No!' Refused to give me another cent. The ras clot, pussy-licking, thieving bastard!" He clenches his fists, pounding the air. "I'm gonna tell everybody in Jamaica about his lies and thieving! The CIA has bought him off. The fucking traitor!" He buries his head in his arms draped over the steering wheel. I hold my breath, awaiting more eruptions from the roiling volcano.

When he finally lifts his head, he speaks solemnly. "I'm sorry, Jac. I've let you and the kids down. I don't know what to do anymore. I've tried *everything*."

He sounds so despondent, so remorseful, that I think he's going to break down. "Don't blame yourself," I say. "I know you've tried hard. It's difficult to provide for the family *and* develop your invention at the same time. But you could do it if you just had the right financial backing."

After a long silence, he speaks in a stern, deliberate voice. "I have no choice now. He's driven me to it. I tried, I really tried to do it the right way, but the Prime Minister wouldn't listen, and the opposition has just betrayed me, so I have to turn to the criminals for support. I warned you this might happen, but I don't think you took me seriously."

"What are you getting at?"

"I'll have to steal a car."

"What!"

"I don't see any other way. The rent's overdue and we can't pay for this car anymore, but we can't get along without one either. I can't possibly do my work or get my story out if I don't have transportation. Trouble is, I could get arrested."

"It's not worth it."

"But there's a bigger picture. If I get arrested, I'll go into court. A judge will hear me, and newspapers will print stories about me. It's another way to get my message out. I didn't want to do it like this, but I don't see any other choice now after Fairweather—damn his soul!—has let us down."

"If you want a story in the newspapers, why not go directly rather than through the courts? Try Thomas Paine."

"Paine? Why him?"

"Well, everybody reads his column in *The Gleaner*. And he lives in Portland. Didn't Uncle Sidney say he knows him?"

"Yeah. They're both officers of the Banana Growers' Association."

"Maybe Sidney can put in a word, at least get you a chance to meet him."

"You're right! Why didn't I think of it? Let's find a pay phone and give Sid a call."

He drives to a hotel and goes inside to look for a phone while I take the children to the bathroom and change Sydney's diaper.

When we return to the car, David says, "I got through. Sid's going to contact Paine and will call tonight to let me know. We better head back to Jericho."

It's dark when we reach the house, and the children are sleeping. The headlight beams reveal a piece of paper tacked to the front door. David gets out to read it. "Shit!" he roars, crumpling the paper and heaving it into the bushes. "Those bastards don't give up!" He looks up and shakes his fists, shouting, "Why, God! Why do you put me through this?"

Returning to the car, he seethes, "Those mother fuckers locked us out! That bailiff note says our stuff is in the pool shed. We've got one week to get it out. Now I can't even answer the phone when Sid calls. Damn them! Let them all rot in hell! Where are my children supposed to sleep tonight!"

"The car's fine," I say. "The kids are already asleep."

"I've got to talk to Sid. We'll have to drive into Ochy and look for a pay phone."

I feed Sydney while he makes a call. Returning to the car, he reports, "Paine is out of the country. Won't be back for a couple of weeks. Guess we'll have to spend the night in the car and try to sort out this mess in the morning."

After a fitful night parked near the tool shed, we're jerked awake by a tapping on the window. Blazing sunlight is heating the interior of the car. Men stand on either side, peering in. "Shit!" David swears and lowers the window. "What do you want?"

One man flashes a badge; the other whips out an ID card and holds it for David to read. "Avis. I see. You want to kick my children out to sleep on the ground, so you can take your tinny car back. Go ahead and take it, but we're not getting out."

The man with the badge opens his holster and grasps his gun handle. I start rummaging and pulling possessions from under seats, out of door pockets, from every crevice, stuffing them into my straw bag. Jonathan and Angie, now awake, help by passing books, toys and cups from the back.

David lights his pipe and exhales slowly, forming smoke rings. A smile flickers across his face as he eyes the men and shakes his head. "You pathetic creatures. May God forgive you. You know not what you're doing." He taps his pipe upside down, puts it into his pocket. "You," he extends his chin toward the Avis man, "how many pickney dem you have? How would you feel if someone did this to your pickney?"

"Sorry, Man. Only doin' me job."

"I know. The capitalists own the lot of you. They've bought Jamaica body and soul. You're their henchmen, sent to destroy the one man who can save the whole country. And you don't even know what you're doing." He turns and looks at us. "Whadayasay, Guys, shall we let them have their pile of scrap metal? I don't think it's worth fighting for, do you?"

"No," I say quickly, "let them have it." Wide-eyed, Angela and Jonathan nod vigorously.

"Okay," David says to the men, "we've decided not to give you any trouble. But I have one favor to ask. On your way back to Ochy, if you see an empty taxi van along the way, could you send it up here? Tell the driver there's a job for him at Jericho."

"Sure, Man. We'll see what we can do." The Avis man pulls an envelope from his pocket and unfolds the yellow copy of a contract.

David opens his door; I follow suit and lead the children toward the pool. We use the toilet in the shed and wash with water from a hose. Amongst the helter-skelter pile of our belongings I find clean clothes and a package of disposable diapers kept for emergencies.

Suddenly I hear the spring of the diving board, followed by a resounding splash. When David's head breaks the surface of the rippling water he swims to the edge and hoists himself out laughing. "That's the way to take a quick shower!" He springs to his feet and, stark naked, does a series of jumping jacks. Running in place, he calls, "Get me some dry clothes. We gotta get this stuff out to the driveway and be ready for the van."

"What are we going to do with it?"

"Take it to Carambola."

"Carambola?" I can't imagine arriving there with all our belongings. The estate, left in trust by David's ancestor, is for descendents to use but *only* for vacations.

IV

We arrive late in the afternoon. The long steep driveway seems rougher than ever as we bump past the giant bamboo along one side. Rounding the final curve, we come into view of the gleaming white three-hundred-year-old great house. Built by the sweat and blood of slaves, the august stone structure stands majestically on a cliff overlooking the Caribbean. The van stops beneath an ancient naseberry tree, the trunk of which bears scars inflicted when it was used as a whipping post for errant slaves. Now the base spawns benign ferns and philodendrons.

Servants gather round, amazed to see us and so much baggage. "Mr. David, how long is you folks stayin'?" asks Miss Connie, the chief housekeeper.

"Permanently," he says to everyone's astonishment as glances are exchanged. "We're taking over. This is my place and my family has a right to live here."

No one argues, but I can imagine how the announcement will have them all abuzz once we're out of earshot.

"What's this about permanently?" I whisper to David as we climb the stairs. "I didn't think that was allowed."

"Times are different now. The spoils go to the bold. Why wait around to be told what we can have? It's time to take what's rightfully ours."

"But what about other heirs? How can they come if we're here?"

"They don't need to. Most of them live abroad in their big fancy houses in Canada and California. We're the ones who need shelter. But don't worry. I'll call Philip tomorrow and tell him we're just staying for a few weeks while I look for a place in Negril. I'll ask for a loan, too. Gotta have a car. He'll give me the money, just so no one can accuse him of letting his nieces and nephew starve."

Feeling weary and grubby, I unpack things to bathe and feed the children and hustle them inside. The interior is a virtual museum, furnished with heirlooms gathered from around the world–Tiffany lamps, grand piano, exquisite china, spinning wheel, Persian carpets, four-poster canopy beds, a huge collection of hand-carved walking canes, all manner of crystal, brass, silver, marble and wood adornments, and statuary which could have once stood in the court of the Sun King. On former visits I spent hours examining treasures and asking David questions about them. The thought of living here now makes me nervous since the place is impossible to childproof.

With the money from Philip, David buys an old Vauxhaul station wagon. He parks it under the naseberry tree and spends several days fixing and replacing parts. Finally he announces, "She's ready enough. Pile in everybody. We're going to Negril."

The car performs well, and we're soon at the beach. I arrange our towels on the sand and take the children into the water. David disappears amongst bathers along the surf. When he returns, two people are with him. "Hey, everybody," he says, "meet Tracy and Jack." He smiles expansively. "They're coming back to Carambola with us."

"Hello," I say, wondering how long they'll be staying but don't ask.

"These folks came here searching for answers, and they found me," he says. "This is only the beginning; more are coming. We're gonna make our place paradise on earth!"

On the drive to the estate they pass around reefers while David expounds on the perpetual motion potential of his invention and his social agenda for Jamaica. But within a week the novelty of Tracy and Jack wears thin, and David expels them. He then goes in search of more converts for his commune and brings a Canadian couple to the yard. After two days they leave of their own accord, but I get blamed.

"You did it again," David says as I wash breakfast dishes, "going on like you don't want to sleep with him, just like with Jack. If you'd set a better example of living free, we could get something going here, but you're so damned repressed! I go to so much trouble to set things up and you keep ruining it with your narrow-mindedness." Whack! His slap sends me reeling, and I grasp the sink edge to keep from falling.

Steadying myself, I say, "Did you know Miss Connie is sick?"

His mouth opens, then closes. He frowns. "No. What's the matter?"

"She had a spell last night. Gall stones, they think. She's in terrible pain. I think you should go for a doctor."

"Oh. I'll see how she is first." At the door he pauses. "It's just as well they left. She wasn't all that good anyway."

I resume rinsing the bowls. Tomorrow I'll have a black eye. Even Carambola isn't a safe place anymore. I used to feel protected by Miss Connie's presence, but now it appears that witnesses no longer matter.

David goes for the doctor and stops at the post office where he picks up a certified letter. In it Philip informs him he is in violation of the restriction against permanent occupancy by heirs. Unless we vacate forthwith, he will be banned forever from the estate. David crumples the paper. "He's a fool if he thinks his legal games will scare me! Fuck all of them! This is my home now and I'm staying!"

"How does he know about what's going on here?" I ask.

"The Headman, Cy Carter. He's the snake in our midst. I've never trusted him. Bet he's been sending telegrams."

David sets up his fountain in the lily pond in front of the house and resumes working on his invention. I take the children on treasure hunts and to the garden with me so they won't distract him. Every afternoon we visit Miss Connie in her room. Despite her pain, seeing the youngsters seems to give her a boost. Then a notarized summons arrives announcing the estate trustees are taking the matter of our illegal occupancy to court. Three security guards appear. Headman Carter informs David they will be occupying the estate round the clock, pending outcome of the court proceedings.

"Let's just go with the flow," David tells me. "If they want to provide free security, it's fine with me. I don't like having people around watching what I do, but we'll make the best of it. Who knows? Maybe I can win them over."

He proceeds to deliver lengthy discourses to the guards about his invention and his plans for saving Jamaica. They listen to his speeches and watch the fountain but remain on duty. Their presence becomes so distracting to David that he can't concentrate. "If they don't get out of here soon," he declares in exasperation, "I'll use obeah on them."

"What do you know about obeah?" I ask.

"My great grandfather used it to keep slaves in line, and there's an obeah man in the village called Crossways. He says it keeps thieves away from his fields. Mainly jealous women use it to get back at their men, but people use it for healings as well as for revenge. Think I should ask Crossways to get rid of those guards with it?"

I shrug. "Would probably cost a lot."

"I'll try to work out a deal with him. I'm sick of these cock-suckers breathing down our necks. Gotta take the bull by the horns."

In the morning he brings Crossways, a short, sturdy man who looks like an ordinary farmer, to the estate and shows him around. Afterwards, David talks loudly within earshot of the servants about the man's work. "If those guards don't leave soon," he declares, "I'm gonna set obeah 'pon dem."

When they are still there the next day David says grimly, "I've warned them, but they refuse to budge, so we're going through with it. Tomorrow."

V

Just after sunset Crossways arrives with bottles of water, a variety of powdered substances, and seven candles, one for each person to be removed. David has decided to make a sweep and get rid of the caretakers as well as the guards.

After the children are in bed, we help carry Crossways' bundles, bottles and candles to the upstairs parlor of the creaky old house. We then move to the front verandah where David has set up the control center for his dancing fountain. He connects wires to the pump near the lily pond, and we settle down for a performance. Rainbow-colored water shoots into the black sky in endless configurations. The speakers blast out one album of music after another—Herbie Mann, Pink Floyd, Bob Marley. David huddles at the control panel, making adjustments to improve the performance of his queen while passing around the ganja pipe. At midnight, Crossways rises and says, "Time to begin."

David shuts off the fountain and we move into the dimly lit parlor. I turn around and catch my breath, startled by the transformation in Crossways' appearance. He now wears an ankle-length black and gold striped robe; his head is wrapped in a purple turban. Barefoot, he walks with dignified authority. David has put on his show; this is Crossways' time.

Following his instructions, we place a table in the center of the room, put three bottles of water on it, and make wax pools in seven places to stand the candles in a row. The Obeah man lights the candles and begins to chant softly in no discernible rhythm or pattern while accompanying the incomprehensible syllables with elaborate hand gestures. He grasps different bottles and glides his hands over them, gazing intently into the apparently clear water. A persistent sea breeze rattles the wooden louvers and presses through the cracks, causing the candle flames to leap and bow wildly until one gives up and dies. Crossways mutters, "Dat's de old woman."

"Not Miss Connie!" I cry.

David glares at me as Crossways continues, oblivious to my outburst.

After the ceremony has gone on for at least two hours he asks us to look into separate bottles and describe what we see. I peer for awhile and say, "I see a greenish tinge; beyond it I think there's a woman's face." I wonder if it is my own reflection. David reports seeing a male image.

Despite our insipid responses, Crossways continues his ritual. When only three candles remain lit, he announces it's time for David to drive him home. "When dese candles burn out," he instructs, "each of you mus' carry a bottle outside and trow it wid yer right hand over yer left shoulder. Leave it on de ground 'til mornin'. At daybreak, empty de bottles on de ground before de sun rays touch dem." He takes the third bottle with him.

After David returns from delivering Crossways to his yard, we finish our part and catch a couple hours of sleep before rising at dawn to empty the bottles as instructed.

When I take the children to the kitchen for breakfast, all the usual people are present. In the innocent morning light, the obeah spell of the night before has vanished. The guards, however, seem

289

restless, leaving their checkerboard frequently to stroll around the yard. After eating, I take the children to the garden and prepare soil to plant lettuce.

Looking up, I see David beside the great house, urgently beckoning. I hurry over and he says quietly, "The guards disappeared a little while ago, just as Crossways said they would. So I took their uniforms and checkerboard and carried them over beyond the graveyard." He gestures. "You see the smoke rising near the edge of the cliff? I set their things afire. Now grab the beach gear and get the kids in the car as fast as you can. We'll spend the day at Negril. I don't want to be here if they come back and see their stuff is missing."

Seeing smoke curling up beyond the family graveyard, I shudder, sensing a cloud of evil enveloping us. Within minutes we have evacuated the yard.

The day at the beach is low-key, uneventful. When we return to Carambola shortly after nightfall, all is quiet.

David parks in the customary spot beneath the naseberry and gets out of the car. Two figures wielding clubs jump out from behind the tree and knock him to the ground while shouting, "Where's our uniforms? What you did wid our uniforms?"

I spring from the car. A blow to my thigh sends me sprawling to the ground. I roll over, rise to my knees. A light comes on and I recognize the attackers as the guards who were on duty that morning, along with Headman Carter and Derek, the 17-year old grandson of Miss Connie. Three of them drag David away while clubbing him with batons. Another uses a tree limb to bash me. I struggle to stand, but am struck repeatedly until I give up and remain prostrate. David keeps insisting, "I don't know anything about your uniforms. I swear, we were in Negril all day..."

Unable to force a confession, the attackers drag David under a floodlight beneath the tree where I lie. Blood pours from a gash on his forehead. Frustrated by the futility of their efforts, one guard says, "I gonna pull dose pickney out an' give dem a goin' over."

"No," says the other guard. "It not de pickney fault. Dey didn't do nothin'. Leave dem be." They decide to wait until their boss arrives.

A tense hour passes, but no one shows up. The guards confer in a huddle; then one tells me, "Take de pickney inside and wait dere 'til mornin'." I hurry the children into the house. Someone shoves David through the door and locks it behind him. Then a guard is posted in the hallway.

Inside our bedroom David whispers, "They're in a bind. If they admit their motives for brutally assaulting us and holding the whole family captive, it will only prove their negligence in leaving the premises unguarded to start with. They've really painted themselves into a corner, and suddenly they realize their jobs are at stake."

I nod. "They might decide to kill us all and concoct a cover-up story."

He does not discount my suspicions. We resolve to use any opportunity for escape and take turns sleeping, one staying awake to guard the guard.

In the morning I am allowed a little freedom to look after the children. I tuck some money in my pocket and take Sydney's dirty linen to the laundry room. After washing it, I carry the basket to the clothesline behind the building and set it on the ground. Noticing that I'm out of sight of the guard's post, I scramble over the stone wall and dash through the bushes. Down the hillside I stumble, tripping over rocks, breaking branches, sliding on moss. Thorns scratch my face and battered legs. Panting and sweating, I don't slow down until I reach the main road. I board the first bus and alight at the Sav-la-Mar police station.

The Inspector listens impassively to my report as I show him welts and bruises on my legs and arms and he laboriously takes notes of every word I say. I leave out the parts about obeah and

291

David burning the uniforms, but wonder how much he already knows about recent bizarre events at Carambola. Finally satisfied with his composition, he assigns a detective to drive me back to the estate and sort out the predicament.

The detective confers with the guards and makes arrangements for our immediate release. However, no charges are pressed. To David's dismay, the guards remain, albeit without uniforms.

Inside the house David declares, "I'll sue their asses! Shut the whole fuckin' company down. They'll find out what happens when they screw around with me!"

Early next morning the parish bailiff serves an eviction order. His crew removes our possessions from the house and stacks them on the lawn. Then he puts a padlock on the great house door and hands the keys to the Headman.

I sit on the ground, breastfeeding Sydney, wondering where my children are going to sleep. The aura of obeah hovers. Is this the pay for trifling with the powers of evil?

David breaks my reverie. "Give me a hand with moving this stuff. Cy says we can store it in the carport for awhile. Since no one around here recognizes me for who I really am, we're moving to Negril where people appreciate me."

VI

With the remaining money from Philip we rent a furnished two-bedroom house and stock the kitchen with a month's supply of food. When we return to Carambola to retrieve our belongings, we're crushed to discover they've been ransacked and looted. Gone are leather shoes and handbags, television, toaster, blender, iron, David's photography equipment, and worst of all, my jewelry case containing not only necklaces and earrings, but all the films with Sydney's baby pictures which we hadn't gotten developed. Now without cameras, we can't take more. Anger is futile, but despair

292

engulfs me. No pictures of her as a baby! How will I ever be able to explain that?

At Negril we spend most days on the beach. The children and I collect coconuts and try to catch fish while David cozies up to tourists. He demonstrates his fountain in clubs at night, hoping to get someone interested in leasing it. One day he has an appointment with a manager of the largest hotel in Negril but doesn't take his fountain along.

Returning a few hours later, he announces, "It's all set! We're in business, starting this weekend."

"What kind of business?" I try to hide my apprehension.

"Giving massages."

"What?"

"At the Beach Hotel."

"But I don't know how to—"

"You'll learn. Read my books; then we'll practice together. A new group of guests arrives on Saturday."

"That's only two days from now!"

"I know, so get busy. I'm off to buy materials for making signs. Think of a good name for our business while I'm out."

I study the books in earnest, and we practice together until late, then again next morning. "You're doing fine," he says. "One more session tonight and you should be all set. You just gotta speed up a little so you can go over the whole body in half an hour."

He comes up with a name on his own: The Body Shop. I'm at the kitchen table carefully lettering the signs when David tells Jonathan and Angela, "Mommy and I are going to start working tomorrow, so we need you guys to stay here and look after Sydney. Next time she cries, I want you to change her nappy and fix her bottle. Gotta be sure you can do it right."

"But Daddy," Angela says, "Sydney's big now and gets into everything. We can't—"

"You'll have to." He looks sternly at Jonathan. "And you have to help your sister."

293

"But he won't, Daddy. I have to do everything." She takes a breath and adds, "He always goes off and plays and leaves me alone—"

"Well, that can't happen anymore." He seizes Jonathan's shoulders, forcing him to meet his fiery eyes. "Your mother and I have to work and it's your job to help take care of your sisters. When I get home, I don't want any reports about you not helping."

"Yes, Daddy," he answers feebly.

Aghast at the risk, I interject, "Maybe we should take the children along. They can play on the beach while we work. In between clients, I'll look after them and—"

"Don't be ridiculous!" he snaps. "Work and kids don't mix! Your problem is you don't have enough confidence in them. They'll be perfectly all right."

"Well, it'd be better if they could call us if there's any trouble. Can you write down the hotel's number and show them how to use the phone?"

"I suppose so." He looks from Angela to Jonathan. "But you're to use it *only* in emergency. And I hope there won't be any."

I add, "And we can call home between customers. So be sure to answer whenever the phone rings. Okay?"

"Yes, Mommy," Angela says. Jonathan nods.

Hearing Sydney cry, I say, "Come, let's get Sydney and you show me how well you can change her nappy. Then Daddy'll teach you to use the phone."

As we prepare to leave the next morning, I hastily review everything the children might need to know. "Be sure you close the lid on the nappy bucket, and always wash your hands with soap after you change her. I've left enough bottles in the—"

"We're late!" David yells. "Get in the car. Everything'll be fine." Backing out of the yard, he says, "Now get your mind on work. You gotta behave professionally."

I go through the motions, with one ear always alert for that dreaded call from home. The first day we have two clients and five the next. David is ecstatic. In the beginning I call the house several times, but then realize the children are better off without the interruptions. I instruct the front desk attendants to let me know immediately if they call, regardless of whether or not I'm busy.

Each evening when we arrive home and find everyone safe, I breathe a prayer of thanks. Angela's complaints that Jonathan isn't helping much worry me, but I don't want to tell David. Instead I try to encourage him. "Jonathan, I know how boring it must be to spend all your time with girls, but Daddy and I really need your help right now. If we don't earn money, we can't buy food. And it's too hard for Angie to lift Sydney. Please promise you'll give her a hand when she needs it."

"I do," he says. "Can I go and play now?"

"Sure," I sigh and watch him run outside.

The second week at the hotel we work on a team of professional basketball players from Chicago. Their enthusiastic feedback boosts my confidence. One actually says my massage is the best he's ever had. And most important, we are earning honest money, even getting tips. I maintain a strictly professional approach, but become uneasy when David starts making arrangements with certain customers to work in their rooms instead of the health club.

The next week business is slow. David gets antsy and I dread being blamed, but late in the afternoon he comes back from a recruitment walk along the beach, grinning. "I made an appointment with an ex-nun, and has she ever got problems! I'm gonna work in her room. It could take awhile, so after you close down here, just wait for me in the car."

I wait, for a *long* time, but when it's nearly dark, I give up. Leaving a note on the dashboard, I set off along the road. Then I board a bus and ride to the corner near our house. Through the moonless night I rush, my thoughts leaping ahead to the children.

At the house, all is dark. I tiptoe into the bedroom and find the children sleeping in their clothes. Covering them with sheets, I gently kiss the soft hair on their heads. Chaos awaits me in the kitchen. What a day they must have had! And they didn't even get a decent supper. Overcome by remorse, tears run down my cheeks as I angrily attack the dirty dishes, cluttered countertops, filthy floor.

Order finally reestablished, I make a cup of tea and sit to sip it, wondering how I'll make it up to them tomorrow. But he'll be furious if I stay home. Numb with weariness, I fall asleep on the sofa.

In the morning Sydney wakes up with diarrhea and won't stop crying. "She has a fever," I tell David. "I have to stay with her."

"Kids run fevers all the time. That's no reason to miss work."

"I'm not going off and leaving her, just to massage a bunch of rich tourists. Besides, you can take care of them. But I might need the car, in case she gets worse and has to go to a doctor."

"Bitch! I can't depend on you for anything but trouble! You're the one who'll need a doctor when I'm done with you tonight." He slams the door. I hear the car start.

Sydney refuses to eat, but takes some juice. I wipe her skin with alcohol swabs, give her a crushed baby aspirin, and keep pouring liquids into her.

"You okay, Mommy?" Angela comes into the room.

"Yes, Honey. But Sydney's sick, so I'm staying home to look after her. I just hope you and Jonathan don't get it, too. Meanwhile, you can have the day off." She looks puzzled. "You don't have to take care of Sydney," I smile. "You and Jonathan can play."

"Can you read us a story first?"

"Maybe later if Sydney settles down and goes back to sleep." I cradle her in my arms, rocking to and fro. "In fact, maybe we can play school. Would you like that?"

"Yes! I'll tell Jonathan to get ready!"

"Okay. Find your boxes and set everything up on the verandah."

Over the next few days David comes and goes at odd times, but says little, so I just focus on the children. We get into a routine of doing school in the mornings and going to the beach after lunch. One afternoon we come home to find David in the kitchen with wires and copper tubes and tools spread all over the table. "I'm adapting my nozzle for a new application," he says. "Want to see if it'll extract oil from ganja. If it works, I'll be able to make the purest hash in the world. Sword is interested."

"Who?" I don't dare ask about The Body Shop.

"Our landlord. I found out his main business is hash oil. He's the biggest dealer around. Buys from different sources and exports it. Has a hard time though keeping quality up, so if I can produce good oil consistently, I'll become his chief supplier. The potential is limitless!"

The kitchen progressively looks more and more like a distillery as he keeps adding tubes and bottles. Sword likes the first results and says he'll bring some buyers over for samples. David works feverishly to improve it even more. To stay out of his way, I build a fire outside to roast breadfruit and corn and toast marshmallows.

As the day for his audition with the "big guys" nears, David gets so tense I fear something will crack, but I'm not surprised that he's nervous. After all, a shower nozzle can't necessarily make hash oil, regardless of how much he wants to believe it can. No matter how good his sales pitch, the ultimate test will be the taste and the high.

The meeting is set for Monday afternoon at four o'clock. With mounting anxiety, David decides that morning to run another batch and insists I go with him to buy more ganja. Speeding along the road, he bursts out, "Why don't you say something? I never know what you're thinking, and you don't help me plan anything!"

"I'm really tired. My period started and I've run out of iron pills."

"Excuses! You women always use that!" His fist rams my jaw.

297

My hands fly to my mouth, but too late to save the crumbling molar. I grope for tissues, spit out blood, hover against the door, arm raised to fend off his attack.

"I'm so tired of your goddam bellyaching! The things I go through to earn a living for this family, and all I get from you is complaints. I'm so friggin' sick of your selfishness!" He grabs a fistful of hair, slams my head against the window. The car swerves. Tires screech. We careen across the road.

"Stop!" I cry, terrified we'll roll. He regains control, but doesn't slow down.

"What I want to know is how you're planning to fuck up this meeting I've worked so hard for." He punches my shoulder. "You don't believe in me. Never have. Always ruin everything I try, and you'll find a way to sabotage me again. It's times like this when I realize how much I need a good woman, one who believes in me and will stand beside me through thick and thin. But I never know what kind of crap you're going to pull."

He turns into a yard and halts between two dilapidated buildings. "Before I get out, I want to hear what you plan to say to the big guys to make sure this deal goes through."

"What do you want me to say?"

"That's just the problem!" he bellows like a dog with its tail caught in a door. "You take no responsibility! Don't even care enough to be thinking about how to make this deal succeed." He lights his pipe, draws on it thirstily, and continues in a voice barely audible. "This time it's on you. So you better think up something good. I've done my part with the hard work and planning. If anything goes wrong now, you're responsible. If the deal fails, I swear, I'll kill you. When I come back, just be ready to succeed...or ready to die." He takes the keys, opens the door, and disappears around the corner of a building.

VII

I tremble on the front seat, my mind blank. Minutes pass and then I realize he hasn't come *right* back. I open the door, slide out, run. Beneath coconut and breadfruit trees I race, past munching goats that look at me blankly. Reaching the narrow, bumpy road, I see two people on a porch and rush over. "Please, can I hide somewhere? My boyfriend–I'm afraid what he'll do when he comes back... to the car over there." I point.

The man grunts, glances at the woman. Then he rises and beckons. I follow him around the house and down a path shaded by towering banana plants. A hen hustles her chicks away as we step over a puddle near a water pipe. Pushing open a door at the back, he says, "Inside dere. Ya ken hide unner de bed."

I flatten myself and wriggle beneath a cot. The door closes. Nothing to see but particles of dust dancing in horizontal rays of light that reach the rough plank floor through a louver window. I huddle, barefoot and trembling, as distant shouting reaches my ears. "Jac! Where are you? Can you hear me, Jac? Come back here!"

Then his tone changes. "Where's my wife? Whoever's hiding my ras clot wife is gonna be sorry! Where the hell's my wife?" His ranting gets louder, then fainter. He must be on the road, walking back and forth. My ears ring with his last threat before leaving the car: "*If this deal fails... I'll kill you.*" Will my hosts betray me?

Finally I hear an engine roar to life and the sound of a car speeding away. Then silence, except for the spastic clucking of mother hen.

Footsteps. The man's voice: "I tink it's safe ta come out now. But ya better stay inside, case 'e come back."

He opens the door. Behind him the woman holds a steaming enamel cup. "Dis bush tea is good fe yuh nerves," she says.

I roll from beneath the bed and arrange myself in a cross-legged position. "Thanks." My hands shake as I take the cup. She nods and leaves.

The man sits on the floor near the door. From his pocket he draws a cloth pouch and a small brown paper bag. He tears a square piece from the bag and crumples it. On the wrinkled paper he carefully shakes some leaves from the pouch and rolls it into a cigar shape, twisting both ends shut. While he busies himself with lighting his spliff, I blow on the hot liquid, wondering how to get it past my throbbing jaw. The man looks to be in his late thirties, a farmer, judging by his high rubber boots and long-sleeved shirt, hot but effective protection from thorny bushes and grass lice. His short beard and close-cropped kinky hair indicate he is not a Rastafarian. "Now what goin' on?" he says. "Dat man? Yuh boyfriend or 'usband?"

"Husband." I touch the lump on my head and look ruefully at clumps of bloody brown hair that stick to my fingers. "He said he was going to kill me. I couldn't just sit there ..." my voice falters.

He inhales deeply, contemplates the exhalation. "Ya gots kids?"

"Three." My throat tightens, blocking the wave of shame and panic that wells within as I picture their worry when David arrives home alone.

"Den he's gonna come back lookin'. Ya cyan't stay 'ere."

"Right." Of course, he doesn't want to get mixed up in white people's business.

"A bus soon come down dis road. It go all da way ta Mo Bay."

"But," I look at my bare feet, "I don't have any money with me. Nothing except these old clothes." I shake my head. "If I walk away, and he drives by, it's all over."

"Just 'old on a minute." He gets up and leaves.

What will David tell the children? Will they think I've run out on them? Or that I'm dead? The tea has cooled enough that I can sip it.

When the man returns, he holds out a pair of rubber thongs. "Try dese."

"Gee, thanks!" I slip them on; only a half size too large. "They fit fine."

"Tek dis and use fe bus fare." He presses a handful of change into my palm. "It'll get ya ta Mo Bay anyway. Dis is money we bin savin', but yuh needs it, so tek it and go."

Embarrassed as I am to accept money from poor people, money I might never be able to repay, I have to. My staying endangers us all. "Thank you so much. I'll never forget your kindness. Bless you," I say, wishing I had something else to give.

He opens the door. "De bus comin'. I gonna stop it. Run out and jump on. Okay?"

I nod, struggling to my feet.

Ocho Rios

I

I keep shifting positions, but comfort eludes me in the dark cavernous bus clanking along bumpy roads. Someday I'll go back, show my appreciation... if I can find the house again. For now I have to use the couple's sacrifice as an opportunity to set myself up so I can go for the children. No idea what I'll do in Montego Bay; don't know a soul there.

In the safety of the humming bus, relentless as a tank, the twin sisters of freedom and responsibility join me on the hard vinyl seat. For the first time in eight years, I have a chance to do things my way. I must succeed. I have to be bold, but also careful. For now that means leaving the children behind...but only for a while. Perhaps it's the price of our freedom. I have to plan each move; everything's up to me. I've got to find an answer to the psychologist's second question, got to find a way that will work.

By the time we reach Mo Bay, my mind is firm. If David comes looking for me, I'll resist, regardless of how much he apologizes or says things will be different. He'll try to use the children to control me, but I will not give in, no matter what.

As the bus makes stops in the outskirts, I gaze out the window, wondering where to get off. It feels weird having no baggage, nothing but the few coins remaining from those kind farmers. At the stop near the airport I alight and walk to the terminal, hoping to find a safe place to spend the night. In the ladies room I tidy myself and spend a long time rinsing my hair and letting it dry. Then I decide to pose as someone waiting to meet a relative and stay within groups of people as I move around the terminal. After the last plane of the night has come and gone, I concoct a story about my brother missing his flight and convince a security guard to allow me to wait inside until morning. Before the last vendor closes, I buy a cup of coffee and a grater cake which I eat slowly while sitting in a dark corner of the terminal. The caffeine helps to clear my head. It's as though a shroud of marijuana fumes inhaled over past weeks starts slipping away. I wonder how David's meeting with the hash buyers went, but refuse to allow myself to worry about his schemes. Still, I realize he might get arrested. What would happen to the children then? Maybe I should go to the police, let somebody know where I am, just in case. But that would be like turning him in. And we might both lose them. Too risky.

Tomorrow will be the first day of my new life. I have to think single if I'm to make it. Every choice carries consequences that I alone will have to deal with. I remember David's advice: Think success. I have to focus on my goal. Can't be weakened by fear of failure. I will find a way to provide a home, support my family, get my children back! Exhausted, I curl up on the bench and close my eyes.

At daybreak I leave the terminal and walk into town. Mo Bay's morning bustle is underway. All modes of transportation–buses, vans, bicycles, taxis, pushcarts, cars, trucks, donkey carts, scooters–converge, chaotically exchanging passengers and goods. Jostled from every side, I make my way along streets crowded with beggars and vendors competing for attention. If only I could get to Ocho Rios! With my last coin, I buy a mango; then I turn into the driveway of a hotel. Settling on an empty bench in the shade of swaying palms, I bite into the juicy fruit and chew slowly. The children must be awake by now. What are they having for breakfast? Probably the old mainstay, peanut butter and jelly sandwiches, or honey. My nose stings at the thought of how they must be feeling. Angie's going to be so burdened. And Jonathan won't help much. He'll get bossy. They'll start fighting. Every day will get harder. I have to move fast.

A young white man comes out of the hotel. Standing at the front door, he looks left and right, as though confused. Our eyes meet. Smiling uncertainly, he approaches me. "I'm not sure where I'm going," he chuckles nervously.

"Where would you like to go?"

"I don't know. I just arrived this morning. How long have you been here?"

"Quite a while." I smile, realizing he must think me a tourist. "I live here."

"Really?" He sounds astonished, as though doubtful that white people actually *live* in Jamaica. "Well, I suppose you know your way around then."

"Pretty much. I've lived mostly in Kingston and Ocho Rios and Negril."

"Wow! Just the places I want to see. I'm not on a packaged tour. Just bought a round trip ticket, planning to explore on my own. I want to see everything, but first I need food." He rubs his belly, looks at the fruit in my hand. "What're you eating?"

"A mango. Got it from a vendor."

"Really." He clears his throat. "Would you mind showing me where?"

"No. It's not far." I rise. "By the way, I'm Jacqueline." I extend my hand.

He squeezes it. "Brian."

"Okay, Brian." I produce an obligatory half smile. "Let's go. Where are you from?"

"Chicago."

"Still pretty cold up there?" I don't hear much of his detailed answer as he follows me around a corner where we're immediately engulfed in the market crowd. I lead the way, burrowing between people, until I spot a mango vendor. His price is exorbitant, so I haggle until he comes into the range locals pay. Brian sinks his teeth into the succulent fruit and offers the bag to me.

"Thanks," I smile and take one.

"This is great," he says, "but I'm still hungry. And thirsty. Do you know a quiet place with good food where we can sit? I'll treat you to breakfast, or is it time for lunch?"

"Either. Do you want American food or Jamaican style?"

"Jamaican, of course!"

"No hotels then. Follow me." I head toward a thatch-roofed place with a chalkboard menu listing mackerel and bananas, breadfruit, callaloo, ackee and salt fish.

While we eat, I answer questions about the food, but hardly hear his description of what he does in Chicago. Like most Americans, he seems to find his job a source of pride. Having no idea how software programmers spend their days, I let him ramble, while I wonder what Sydney and Angie and Jonathan are doing. And what has David told them? At least I did all the laundry before leaving so there'll be enough diapers to keep Sydney dry for a few days. Jonathan can get things off the clothesline. Was it only yesterday I left? It feels like weeks.

I guide Brian through the clamorous marketplace and back to his hotel. He has already paid for one night, but wants to move on the next day to explore other parts of the island. I propose a deal. "How about this? I'll give you a massage in exchange for a night's lodging. Tomorrow I'll show you how to travel cheap and get you to Ocho Rios if you'll pay my bus fare."

"A massage? I'd love one! You're on."

We spend the afternoon at the beach. I tell him the local names of various shells, birds and plants we see: doctor bird, sea egg, breadfruit, conch, bougainvillea, john crow, lemon grass. It reminds me of David's litany of tropical nomenclature on my early days in Jamaica. How simple life was then. I remember the naïve girl–open, eager, full of idealism, and in love. She now seems a lost, nearly-forgotten sister.

From a beach vendor, Brian buys us each a t-shirt. Then he treats me to dinner at a seafood restaurant where we sit on a deck overlooking the dazzling Caribbean. The sinking sun paints the sky with strokes of purple, magenta, gold, green, violet, the colors continually changing, then fading, as stars singly take their places in the charcoal dome. I think of sunsets watched from the verandah at Carambola. If only... I sigh, then focus on the menu and order fish tea for him, followed by steamed snapper with rice and okra. All I can manage is a bowl of pumpkin soup with dumplings. I tell him I'm separated from my husband, glossing over details. Dare not say the children's names, or I'll lose it.

Back at the hotel, my massage puts him right to sleep. I slip into the shower and indulge myself, sampling the assortment of scented soaps, shampoo and conditioner. I wash my underwear and hang it by the window, wrap a towel around myself and crawl into the other twin bed. I give thanks for the good fortune of the day, pray the children are safe, visualize each sleeping peacefully. "Bless you, my angels," I murmur. What else can I do for them? Tears moisten my pillow.

II

Next morning Brian and I squeeze into seats on a van destined for Ocho Rios. I provide a travelogue as we munch on guava tarts and drink box juice. We bump along the narrow and pitted highway past Rose Hall, Runaway Bay, and the famous falls at Dunn's River. "If you want to climb the falls, it's best not to have all this luggage with you," I advise. "Tomorrow you can get a bus out here from Ochy."

In Ocho Rios I guide him to an inexpensive guesthouse where he gets a room. At the crafts and farmers' markets I help him haggle for two colorful beach towels and a bag of fruit. Next, the beach. We settle on the sand.

Seeing a teenager with a bundle of jelly coconuts, I ask Brian, "Ever had coconut water?"

"No. What's it like?"

"Delicious!" I wave to the boy. We agree on a price and he whacks two nuts open with a machete. After we drain the sweet water, he chops the nuts in two and gives them back with slices of husk for scooping out the jellied flesh.

"This is incredible!" Brian exclaims. "I've never tasted anything so amazing."

Savoring the sweet smugness of success, I toy with the idea of getting a job as a tour guide. Could pair up with a van driver maybe. Brian stretches on his towel and dozes off. I watch waves disappear into the sand. Brian really liked my massage. So did the tourists in Negril. Maybe I can do it here. I visualize myself walking like a vendor amongst the people on the beach, asking if they're interested. I could do the massages right here or in their rooms. Simple as it seems, I'm scared. Selling is not one of my talents. What if people ridicule me or think me a whore with an angle?

Stop it! I scold myself. Such ideas get you nowhere. David never worries about what people think. *Their problem,* he would say. I have to find a way to provide for the kids, but in this condition, I can't possibly apply for a teaching job. Don't even have an address. Gotta overcome pride and shyness and just go for it. If other tourists are as open and easygoing as Brian, maybe it won't be so hard.

When he sits up, I say, "I think I'll stay here in Ochy. Can you manage on your own now that you know about mini vans and haggling?"

"I'll be fine. You're a good teacher. But will *you* be okay?"

"I know a few people here. Might be able to find work."

308

"At least spend the night with me." He reaches over and lays his hand on mine. "Maybe I can massage *you*." He watches me expectantly.

I meet his gaze for a moment before turning my eyes to the undulating water. The room he rented has only a double bed. He probably isn't anticipating another platonic night. "Thanks, but I need to look for my friend. She lives a couple of miles from town."

"All right." He quickly covers any disappointment by releasing my hand and rising to his knees. "I wanta take a swim before the sun gets too low. Coming?"

"Sure." He dives into the surf and swims out while I stay in shallow water to keep my shorts dry.

We walk back to the guesthouse together. "Good luck with the rest of your Jamaican adventure," I say. "And thanks for everything."

"Thank *you*," he returns. "It's been great. Please take this." He presses ten dollars into my hand and gives me a hug. "Good luck yourself."

Trudging along the highway and up the steep curvy road to the estate, I wonder how Vera will receive me. She and I never talked much, but she saw David's outrageous behavior when we lived at Jericho. I suspect she didn't approve of him even though she was always polite to everyone. I have no idea what her opinion is of me. Still, I know she's kind. Probably helped the children far more than I knew. Needing her now more than ever, I abandon pride.

It's dusk when I reach the driveway; her door is open. She appears on the verandah with a broom. "Good evening, Vera!" I call.

She squints in the semi-darkness for a moment and then cries, "Lord almighty, is dat you, Miz Jac? What you doin' 'ere?"

"I left him." I walk straight into her arms. "Finally." My shoulders shake as sobs erupt.

"Come, sit. Tell me all about it." Without asking, she hastens to bring tea. Then she says, "Eat dis," and sets a plate of boiled green bananas and dasheen smothered with mackerel run-down in front of me. She sits opposite with her own cup of tea. While I eat, she listens to my story. Wagging her head, she says, "Lord knows, woman, ya sure does need help gettin' you life straight. Ya can sleep 'ere. But dose beautiful children … I jus' wonder what be happenin' ta dem."

I nod. "That's all I think about. I've got to go back for them, and soon, or it'll drive me crazy. But first I need a place for them to stay. And money."

"Stay 'ere as long as you wants. Not in da main house … Guests is arrivin' tomorrow. But you can use da extra cot I got. And if yuh needs clothes, borrow mine. We near to a size."

"You're wonderful, Vera. It's such a relief to have a safe place to sleep! I only hope I won't have to impose for long."

After she turns out the light, I lie awake. Through the open window I can see stars, hear tree frogs and owls. I picture Angie's face, Sydney's, Jonathan's. Hear their voices, smell their skin. "I love you," I whisper. "Soon we'll be together again." In the sagging cot I keep waking from dreams of them wrapped in my arms.

In the morning, I return to the beach lined by high-rise hotels and watch tourists settle themselves on the sand. Pumping up courage, I make myself walk up to people who look receptive and start talking about the weather, say anything that comes to mind. Without mentioning massage, I observe how they respond and am surprised by how friendly most are. They seem eager to speak with locals, and I sort of qualify. Gaining confidence, I tell one couple I'm a masseuse. Right away, they ask questions.

I explain, "My husband and I had a massage business at the Beach Hotel in Negril. But we're separated now, so I've come to Ochy to see about working here." It sounds plausible and accounts for my not having an office. They buy it and we agree to meet at their room later in the afternoon. Jubilant, I rush to the market and purchase a bottle of fresh coconut oil.

I massage the woman first while he watches and then do him. That way both can see nothing kinky is going on. Like everyone I've worked on, they're amazed by the power of the Shiatsu technique. Declaring it the most relaxing massage they've ever had, they even give me a tip. I can't wait to share the news with Vera, not to mention the bounty. On the way, I stop at the market to buy salt fish and yams. Tomorrow, I resolve, I'll do even better.

For a week, I walk to Ochy every day and hustle massages on the beach. I always make money, but not enough to feed the kids, much less pay rent. I have to do better. At night dreams of the children give me courage. Maybe they're dreaming of me, too.

When I investigate the resort hotels I discover that none offer massage services. Eventually I find a manager, Basil Shaw, who seems interested. He agrees to pay for a sample treatment if I come to his home near the beachfront hotel at noon the next day. Says we can have lunch first, then the massage. I suggest eleven instead, explaining, "It's not as beneficial with a full stomach. I'd rather do it right, so you can get the best effect."

"You're the expert," he smiles. "Eleven it is then, and lunch afterwards."

Arriving at his door, I knock nervously. A maid shows me to a chair in the living room. Soon Mr. Shaw greets me heartily and leads me into a luxurious, air-conditioned room with a king size bed. "Tell me what to do," he says, switching on a lamp.

"Take off everything but your briefs." I hope he's wearing some. "Then lie down and cover yourself with a sheet." I wash my hands in the adjoining bathroom and get out my coconut oil. Starting to work on his back, I begin to relax. Now I am in control. I have an hour to show him how good I am.

His satisfied moans soon tell me he likes it. Confidence growing, I apply more pressure.

311

"Ouch!"

"Sorry." I ease up. "Just relax, this is good pain. It shows me where your tension is. That's what causes pain. The more you relax, the less it hurts." Alternating thumb pressure with palm stroking and muscle tapping, I gradually coax the tension from his body. When I finish, he twists, bends, stoops, testing his back. "It doesn't hurt anymore!" He exclaims. "Your fingers are magic!"

He's not the first person to use those words, but I love hearing them again. It must be true. David thinks he's so good, but I might be better.

Over lunch, Shaw wants to know why a young white woman is on the street looking for work. Deciding not to lie, I tell him a little about David and the children, illustrating the story by pushing up my sleeve to reveal bruises on my upper arm and shoulder, remains of his last beating.

He grimaces and curses softly. "I have a studio you can work in. Come over in the morning and we'll discuss a contract. Ask for me at the front desk." He gives me a card.

"Thanks, Mr. Shaw." I put his card in my pocket, struggling to control my elation.

"And how much do I owe you for today?"

I wonder if he is expecting me to say "No charge." But I can't support the kids that way. When I say, "Fifteen dollars," respect crosses his face.

He pulls out a money clip and extracts a twenty. "I don't have the right change. This time you get a tip." He hands it over, eyes twinkling.

In the evening I take a bus and carry a bag full of groceries to Vera's. We eat heartily, celebrating my success and bright future. She offers the use of her sewing machine so I can make clothes. The children begin to feel within reach.

Mr. Shaw shows me a room in a quiet wing of the hotel with sliding glass doors opening to a beach-front patio. He says I can advertise in the lobby and use the phone for making appointments. In return, I will pay the hotel ten percent of my earnings and provide him with free massages on demand. We shake on it.

The hotel activity director, an elderly man named Richy Roberts, likes my massage, too, and begins recommending it to guests. I have business cards printed and make posters to display in the lobby.

Shaw wants his massages at home. The third time I go, he mentions that Mrs. Shaw and their two children are in England for the summer. After the treatment, he says, "Spend the night with me."

I'm speechless. His words don't come as a complete surprise, but I have no ready response. "Mind if I use the shower?" I stall.

"Go ahead. Put this on." He pulls a silk nightie from a drawer and tosses it over.

I stand under the water a long time, horrified by the thought of wearing his wife's lingerie, trying to postpone what will have to follow: a confrontation and possible loss of my job, or an assignation. If I say "no" and he doesn't fire me, it will still put a chill on our relationship which will affect how the staff treat me. Might stop getting referrals, messages, clean linen, things which now come readily. Or he could take "no" as coyness. Think I'm holding out for more favors. He's so influential. Could stop me from getting work elsewhere. And if I say "yes" … Damn it! Does it always have to come to this? But then, maybe a little sex is just what I need. Why not? He's married! That's why. But I didn't pursue him. Fidelity or not is his choice. He probably already sleeps with half the women at the hotel. Same ticket to success for everybody. What a fool I've been to think the good treatment was about respect for my profession! Now he wants me to join the oldest profession.

When I climb into the bed, he seems to be sleeping, but immediately he rolls over and puts his arms around me. "I can't stay all night," I say. "Vera will worry."

"I'll drive you over later." His hungry hand is already under the nightie.

Thereafter, I do not refuse his discreet solicitations, and I continue receiving good treatment in the hotel. When I ask about the vacant cottages on the property, he says they are being renovated, but I can rent one when they're ready. Immediately I pay a deposit before he can change his mind. At last, a place for the children!

III

As the bus sways and lurches around curves, over hills, along the coast and through villages, I wonder which stop is the one where I boarded after escaping a month before. I have new thongs for the farmers who helped me, but try as I might, I cannot identify their house. Probably this is a different bus route. I was so lost, so busy dodging David's blows that I lost track of where we were.

When I eventually spot the familiar corner near the house where we lived, I get out and set off along the track. Suddenly a car speeds around a curve, traveling straight at me. Oh, no! Not David! I step back, pressing myself into the tall grass and bushes as the car skids to a halt. At the wheel is Sword, the landlord.

"Hey, Jacqueline. What's up?"

"Hi. I've been away for a while. But now I'm back ... to see the kids."

"They don't live here anymore."

"What?" My knees buckle, the bags drop from my clutch.

"Didn't pay the rent," he says, "so I made him get out a couple weeks ago. Heard they went over to Simm's place. About a mile back toward Mo Bay. Big stone house on the right. Ya could try there."

In a daze, I thank him. He waves and raises dust as he speeds away.

I pick up the bags filled with new shoes, swimsuits, toys and snacks for the children, and turn to follow his directions, my thoughts racing. If he can't pay rent, it means the hash deal didn't work out. Do the children have enough to eat? If only I'm not too late!

After walking for awhile, I spot a place fitting Sword's description. I enter a long driveway and follow it toward an old two-story house, keeping within the shadows of tall trees. David's car is in front. Then I see Jonathan and Angela playing in the yard. "Thank God!" I swallow hard, choking back tears of relief. Noticing a man—perhaps the landlord—at the side of the house, gives me courage. At least I won't have to confront David alone. I pause by a giant banyan tree and watch the children drawing lines on the ground with sticks. But where is Sydney?

Peering around the tree, I call softly, "Jonathan! Angie!"

They look my way. Sticks fall to the ground as they speed towards me. I drop to my knees, kissing, nuzzling them, inhaling their child fragrances. Still hugging them, I ask, "Sydney, is she inside?"

"Um hum," says Jonathan.

Angela asks, "Want me to get her, Mommy?"

"Yes. No! Is Daddy home?"

She nods. "He's got Sherry staying here. They might be in bed. I'll get Sydney." She dashes to the door.

When she emerges David is behind her, holding Sydney by the hand. "Why're you hanging out there?" he calls.

"I had to see the children, but didn't want to bother you." From the corner of my eye, I see the other man raising the hood of his car. Good. He might stay around for a while.

"You shouldn't come sneaking in. If you want to see your kids, be up front. I can't stand cowards." He pulls Sydney forward. "How's your baby look?"

"Beautiful! I've missed her so much." I reach out eagerly, fighting back tears.

But he steps between us. "Same old story. You want your kids, but not me. You didn't miss me at all?" He offers his cheek for a kiss.

Disgusted, I pucker my lips and brush his face… a small price. I kneel, draw Sydney to me.

"Meet Sherry, my queen," he says.

I glance up at a plump young woman with long dark hair wearing a flowered muumuu. "Hi," I say and turn back to Sydney, intent on finding out if she remembers me. Pulling bananas from my bag, I hand a bunch to Angie, and peel one for Sydney. We take turns biting off chunks.

David is explaining how Sherry was sick when he found her on the beach, and he saved her life. Through pouty lips she says something about David being her savior. I notice bruises on her arms, and her left eye is puffy.

He boasts that Sherry is going to finance the development of his invention. "Only problem, she has to go to Boston personally to get access to her investments. But when you ran off and abandoned your children, you left me with all the burden, so I can't travel or concentrate on my work." His voice has grown strident. "Amazing how one way or another, you always manage to hold me back. I've finally found a woman who believes in me and wants to put her money behind me, but because of *you*, we can't get it."

"Hold on a minute." I extend my palm vertically to block the onslaught. "Isn't it obvious why I showed up today? I've come to take care of the children while you and Sherry go to Massachusetts."

Momentarily speechless, he quickly recovers. "You can't look after them alone."

"They'll be fine. I have my own place now."

"You want to take them away?"

"I wasn't planning to stay here."

"Sounds like a good idea," Sherry puts in. "Mr. Simms says we can't stay much longer anyway."

"That's beside the point," he snaps. "I'm not having her take my kids without knowing where."

Quickly reviewing my options, I say, "We'll be staying at Jericho." I'll warn Vera.

"That's where we used to live," he explains to Sherry, "near Ochy."

She puts her arm around his waist, smiling adoringly while pressing her buxom body to his side.

"Really think you can manage until we get back?" He eyes me skeptically.

"Yes," I struggle to keep my voice steady, "but they have to come with me today."

"Well, I suppose the sooner we get up there, the better." He looks at Sherry. "What do you think? Shall we take her up on it?"

"Sounds perfect," she says and kisses his cheek. I can imagine she must be dying for some time alone with him. Undoubtedly I am the answer to her prayers. And she, mine.

I get busy packing clothes and toys. We can't carry much so I must be selective. Anyway, I have to make it look like just a visit.

David soon interrupts my work. "Before you leave, come into my room. Remember, you're still my woman."

I cringe, but focus on my goal: leaving before nightfall with the children. Mustn't let anything jeopardize that.

He tells Sherry to fix lunch and then summons me to the bedroom. He drops his trousers, kicks them aside, pulls off his shirt. His muscles look harder, leaner than ever. "Take those clothes off," he says. As I disrobe, his penis rises. He lowers me onto the bed, smelling as if he hasn't showered or brushed his teeth.

Ramming his organ into me, he twists, gyrates his hips. "I don't care who you've been with," he pants, "nobody is as good as me. I know it, even if *you* never want to admit it."

I close my eyes as his pumping grows intense and emit a low groan of mock ecstasy. Then I let my body go limp, hoping the "big orgasm" will satisfy his ego.

It's after midnight when we reach Jericho.

"Lord almighty! You did it!" Vera cries as she opens her door and sees the children. "I been prayin' fe ya all day. Dere *is* a god." She hugs each child and moves quickly to make everyone comfortable in her cramped quarters. All the while she hums softly, "He got de whole world in his hands ..."

IV

Our cottage by the sea is cramped. It has one bedroom, a sitting room, bathroom and veranda. Not even a kitchen, but at least there's a small refrigerator. From a pawnshop I get an electric skillet, perfect for one-dish meals. For the first time ever we can talk honestly, laugh freely. I can hold Sydney on my lap without fear, and I don't have to mete out punishment every time someone spills a cup of juice.

I hate to leave the children alone while I'm working but have no alternative. At least hotel workers are always nearby and Angela quickly makes friends with everybody. I phone between clients to check on them and they can call me whenever they want. I always keep food in the cottage, and I give precise instructions about what they can and cannot do in my absence. One of them must stay with Sydney at all times. It is far too much responsibility, but at least Negril was a training ground.

We live close to the edge in every sense, and each day is different. I never know who might walk through the door of my studio. One day it's the Prime Minister's wife. She likes the massage so much that she comes back the next day and brings her husband. Security guards stroll back and forth on the beach outside while I work. At first they distract me, but soon I'm able to focus on locating and releasing his tension, just as I do for anyone. When he leaves, he looks too relaxed for a politician; I'm glad he has those bodyguards.

While waiting for a client to arrive one afternoon I look at a calendar and notice my mother's birthday is next week. It suddenly hits: I can talk to her again! After years of thinking her daughter might be dead, it will be quite a gift to know I'm alive. Perhaps the best present any mother can receive. Later in the lobby I buy a large card with a picture of the hotel surrounded by resplendent hibiscus and bougainvillea shrubs. On it I write:

> Dear Mother,
> I send this to wish you a happy birthday and to let you know I'm alive and well. I'm truly sorry for the pain I've put you through these past years, and I hope you can find it in your heart to forgive me. I can't undo the hurt, but I want you to know things are different now. I sent you that terrible letter from Australia because I was so afraid of David. I have finally left him, and the children are with me. Your youngest granddaughter, Sydney Lynne, is over a year old. I'm working and living at the beautiful hotel pictured here. I'll write more later, but for now I just want to say I hope you and Dad are well, and I love you.
>
> Jacqueline

Forgiveness might not come easily, given that harsh letter. It could be a long road back, but at least I'm on it. I just hope that she's still alive.

Richy Roberts is always giving me things for the children: toys, candy, leftover food from the luncheon buffet. One evening he invites us to join him on the hotel terrace. We sit with the tourists watching crab races and limbo dancing, and he buys "Shirley Temples" for the kids to drink. I think it's the most fun they've ever had.

Business ebbs and flows. Between appointments I spend as much time as possible at the cottage, giving Jonathan and Angela a chance to play with other children. Jonathan likes to fish with neighborhood boys along the banks of White River that empties into the sea a short distance from our cottage. Angela keeps finding new playmates on the beach. When I'm working they are both supposed to stay at the cottage with Sydney, but Angela says Jonathan doesn't always do that.

One day after a session runs late I hurry back and come upon a crowd of people milling around in front of the cottage. "Oh, my God!" I gasp, sprinting forward. "What's wrong? Where are my children?" Running past everyone, I burst through the door. Two hotel staff stand inside. With them, three wet children wrapped in towels. At once, everybody starts talking and I piece together what happened. Jonathan went fishing with the boys, and when he didn't come back, Angela and Sydney walked along the riverbank looking for him. It was slippery and Sydney slid in. As she disappeared beneath the water Angela screamed for help. Jonathan came running, dove in and managed to grab her arm before the current swept her away. He towed her to the edge and held on to her while Angela pulled her up the muddy bank to safety.

I'm overwhelmed by competing emotions of anger and joy. Holding Sydney on my lap, I check her over carefully. She's breathing all right, not even coughing. Apparently she hasn't swallowed much water. I look at Angela and Jonathan, "Come over here, my heroes." I give them big hugs. "You two are so brave. I'll never forget this for the rest of my life, and neither will you. Now, we've got to get you into dry clothes before you catch cold."

I thank everybody and then go to the door, lift Sydney for the crowd to see, and assure them everyone is fine. With shouts of "Praise the Lord!" and "Hallelujah!" they disperse, muttering to one another and casting gazes my way.

Quickly I bathe the children, get them into warm clothes, and prepare chicken noodle soup. Before I finish reading "Jack and the Beanstalk" they are asleep, so I kiss them goodnight and slip outside. Sitting on the dark veranda, I try to calm my mind by reciting what I can recall of the first Psalm. The word "ungodly" repeatedly brings up images of David: "The way of the ungodly shall perish." Surely this day's events confirm that God is with us, protecting the children like "trees planted by the river" which will bring forth fruit in their season and whose leaves will not wither. But how close we came to tragedy! I must heed the warning, must make other arrangements. But first, we need a break. I'll declare tomorrow a holiday, reschedule appointments, and we'll go out. My first day off since the children's arrival. But then what? School, daycare, sitter? With no car and little money, options are limited, but I'll have to figure something out.

"Hooray!" Angela and Jonathan shout next morning when I tell them. Excitedly they put on their best clothes as I pack a bag with towels and swimsuits. With Sydney on my shoulders, we walk into town and go into a restaurant for lunch. Then we buy snacks and a beach ball and head to the fishermen's beach—away from tourists—where I arrange our towels on the sand. All afternoon we toss the ball around, swim, race, play leapfrog and build sandcastles. Weary, I finally collapse on my towel but keep my eyes on the children in the shallow water.

A dull worry is growing sharper, cutting into my consciousness whenever I'm not busy: My period is overdue. Almost time for the next one. I've been hoping my body just skipped a cycle, perhaps from all the stress and poor nutrition. But if it doesn't come soon, I have to face facts: This is serious. We're so on the edge; how will I ever manage with a baby? Not possible. "Please, God," my lips move as I fold my legs into a lotus posture and gaze at the expanse of sparkling water before me. "Please take this cup from me. It's more than I–we–can bear. My mission is to make a better life for the children. Don't let me fail. I can't take them back to him. Ever. But if I'm pregnant, I don't know how..." Then a weird thing happens–I start to bargain with God, try to make a deal. Much as I'd hoped to have another son some day–two boys and two girls– I'm ready to sacrifice that dream for our survival. "Please, don't let me be pregnant now. I'll give up the chance to ever have another baby. That's how important this is. I release it to you. Let it be so." I chant "Om" three times and bow my head.

V

"Hi," a soft bass greeting comes from behind me. I turn and see a short, husky black man, wearing dark glasses and a tam. "Mind if I stop to talk for a minute?" His broad grin exposes perfect gleaming teeth.

"No." I raise one eyebrow quizzically.

He crouches nearby in the sparse shade of a dwarf coconut tree.

"I sees you don't want to tek ya eyes off dose children. Is dey all yours?"

I nod.

"You is a lucky woman. Must be proud o' dem."

"I am."

"I saw you all racing in da water. Dose pickney ken swim good. Most Jamaican pickney cyan't swim at all. Even da little one behave sensibly. You is one good mudder."

"Thank you," I smile. If this is a come-on, he surely knows the way to my heart.

"I got pickney, but none of dem is dat sensible, or even strong. Look at yuh boy. Back straight, limbs solid like a tree. What's dat ting he throwin'?"

"A boomerang. We brought it back from Australia. They're hard to throw, but he keeps trying to get the hang of it. Never learned myself, so I can't teach him."

"Australia? Is dat where ya from?"

"No. We just lived there for a couple of years."

"Hmmm. Ya looks familiar. I is tryin' ta figure out where I knows ya from. Married?"

"Separated."

"What yuh husband's name?"

I hesitate, then mumble, "David."

"David. Hey! Bet I knows 'im." He laughs. "Is 'e dat dude, goes 'round preachin' all da time and talkin' about 'is great inventions? Used to live up by da golf course. Right?"

"How did you know?"

"David used ta come down ta da beach and talk all sorta ting 'bout 'is inventions 'nd 'is wonderful family 'nd dat dere is no god. Dat guy 'e loved ta smoke de bong.

"Sounds like the same David. What's your name again?"

"Dey calls me Magic."

"I'm Jacqueline."

"Dat's it, Jacqueline. David calls ya Jac. Now I remembers." He extends his hand. As we shake, he says, "What da kids' names?"

I tell him, and he speaks to each individually as they come to investigate Mommy's visitor. I open box drinks and dole out snacks as Magic explains that he's a farmer. Plants bananas, plantain and yams and also raises pigs and goats.

"So where did you get the name Magic?" Angela wants to know.

"Oh dat goes way back. Started when folks used to say I move so fast dat nobody could keep track of where I was goin'. Before anybody could catch me, I disappears. So people took to callin' me Magic."

"Oh," she says. "Mommy, can we go back in the water?"

I nod. "Just for a little while."

They all run off as we watch. Then Magic asks, "Where's David now? I 'aven't seen him dis long time."

"He went to the States."

"When 'e comin' back?"

I shrug. "Never, I hope."

"Don't believe it. Wid beautiful pickney like dese," he nods knowingly, "'e soon come back from foreign. Mark my word. Crazy maybe, but 'e no fool."

"I'm not so sure," I say. "He went up there with an American girlfriend. Maybe they'll stay."

Noticing the sun is getting low, I call the children and start packing our things.

Magic says, "I bet dey likes bananas."

"It's their favorite."

"I got a bunch of ripe ones almost ready fe eat. I'll bring dem by. Where ya live?"

"You're very kind. Know the White River Hotel?" He nods. "We're staying in the old gatekeeper's cottage near the back gate. No one uses that entrance anymore, so it's always locked. If you come by and holler, I can let you in."

"Okay. I'll bring dem over. See dat big Suzuki parked over dere?" He gestures with his chin at a shiny blue motorcycle. "Dat's mine. Don't be surprised when you hear it roarin' up to da gate."

"Thanks for the warning!" I smile.

The holiday does us all good, but I still have no solution to how I'm going to look after the children, pregnant or not. I decide to schedule my appointments farther apart so I'll have time to return to the cottage between each client. We get through the next day with no mishaps, and in the evening I open a letter from my mother. After glancing through, I read most of it to the children, skipping the sermonettes. She suggests we move to Iowa. Over dinner we talk about Grandma and Grandpa and the possibility of going there for a visit. They like the idea, and Jonathan suggests we start saving for it. Just what they need—something to look forward to.

After they're asleep, I take a shower and discover blood. "Oh, thank you, God!" I shout in a whisper. "Thank you! Thank you!" Whether it came from God or from the day of relaxation, I don't know. Am I now infertile? Only years will tell if God accepted my deal. Maybe he *can* be bargained with. I'm certainly not the first to try. The important thing is the freedom from at least one worry.

I dress and walk to the hotel lounge to meet a travel agent who wants to know more about my massage service. Over drinks we discuss promotional possibilities and then dance to a reggae tune. As he escorts me back to the cottage, I see lights on and hear adult voices within. Panicked, I race to the door, push it open, gaze in horror.

VI

Boxes and luggage litter the place. Three people are laughing and talking loudly. There in my house stands David. At his feet sit Sherry and a sallow complexioned chunky woman wearing an orange and green tie-dye dress and beads. Sherry's knotted purple wraparound accentuates her voluptuous cleavage. David is hyped, oozing conceit.

How could I be so stupid as to think he'd never return! Why oh why didn't I go someplace where he couldn't find us? Why didn't I heed Magic's warning? Grasping the doorknob, I shrink back and turn to my companion. "Thanks for everything. Maybe I'll see you tomorrow before you leave." I squeeze his hand, go inside and shut the door.

With the women gazing at him adoringly, David's inflated ego makes him appear twice his usual size, triple his normal strength. Angie sits on the floor, while Jonathan clings to the slightly open bedroom door. It appears that only Sydney hasn't been roused. I feel energy seeping from my body, as though a valve has opened at the base of my spine. Security? Shall I go to the lobby for help?

"So, you've been out partying," David says sarcastically. "It's about time you stopped letting the kids hold you back. Just what I like to see–my woman enjoying herself with other men!"

Judging by the fumes, I can tell they've been smoking. And a bottle of Chianti is making the rounds. "Angela," I move toward her. "Time to get back to bed."

"No!" David says. "Forget your rules. Let her see Daddy. It's been a long while."

I turn on him. "Take your traveling circus and get out!"

"Fuck you!" He lunges, presses his thumbs into my throat and knocks me to the floor.

Angela screams, "Stop, Daddy! Stop!"

The next thing I remember is David's voice: "Stop gawking and get yourselves to bed. She's faking it." I open my eyes in time to make contact with Jonathan's just before David slams the bedroom door. Then he's standing over me saying, "Just what I expected, a rousing welcome." He looks at the two women. Now you see for yourselves what I've been telling you about this bitch. I ask you, is that any way to greet a man?"

"No!" they chorus.

"Now you understand why I need you... people who appreciate me. But she's not totally worthless." He eyes me thoughtfully, as a horse-trader in the process of selling a mare would peruse his possession. "She's a great cook and knows how to run a house. Good at the mundane stuff, but I need more. With you, I've got my team. We can make a fantastic difference!" His foot nudges me. "Up now; help us get settled. We have work to do tomorrow."

Next morning I hear a motorcycle and dart outside. David is already at the gate. On the other side stands Magic carrying a huge stem of bananas. David guides him to an opening between two posts where he can enter. That must be how he got in last night. But how did he find out where we are? Vera maybe?

"I guess word gets around fast when the savior returns," David is saying. "Bring your gifts inside. I have some people for you to meet." As they pass, Magic shoots me a questioning look. I can only imagine what he must be thinking.

David introduces Sherry as his number two wife and identifies the other called Holly as the lady in waiting. "Magic is the first of my disciples," he tells them. "Many more will come. You'll see. Now, Holly, I want you to play your flute and walk along the beach naked. It's your job to announce my arrival. Bring the people to me." She undoes the knot on her tie-dye, lets it drop to the floor, and sets off, flute pressed to her lips.

Sherry cuddles up to David on the veranda settee while he proceeds to tell Magic about their adventuresome month in America. "You wouldn't believe how gullible people over there are. They've no idea what's going on in the world. It's like they were all given sedatives at birth, or lobotomies. I can't understand how people who can figure out how to send a man to the moon can be stupid enough to believe the lies and idiotic propaganda the media keeps dishing out. But you know, sometimes I wonder if they really did send anybody to the moon. Have you ever thought about it? Hollywood could have staged the whole thing."

I close the door and call the hotel switchboard to find out if I have any appointments. The only one scheduled is at noon. While the children attack the fresh bananas, I peel and crush enough to make a huge batch of fritters. Jonathan helps turn them over in the skillet. Angie makes the topping by squeezing limes and stirring sugar into the juice. As the children feast, Holly returns with a follower who joins the circle on the veranda.

I put toys out for Sydney, and give Jonathan and Angie crayons and coloring books. Then I rush to my studio and hurry through the massage, too preoccupied to do a good job. As I walk back toward the cottage, I hear a flute. Holly, naked, is moving along the edge of the water, displaying her flabby chalky flesh while playing as though in a trance. My first thought is that if Basil hears about this, I'm finished. I don't want to be seen nearby, but if anyone detains her, she's bound to say she is staying with me. Summoning the most authoritative voice I can muster, I go up to her and say, "Come with me." Hardly missing a note, she follows slowly. A few steps ahead of her, I move toward the river. Once we have crossed the hotel boundary, I stop and face her. "If you want to walk around here naked, go that way." I point to the beach across the river.

"But there aren't any people over there." She's looking at me, but her eyes aren't focused. "David said to bring people back to him."

"This is a family hotel. If you follow what he says, you'll wind up in jail. Then who do you think is going to bail you?"

"David says you work for Babylon. You're not free. If you were free, you'd take off your clothes and dance with me."

"He's right. I'm not free. For years he imprisoned me, and now he's captured you and Sherry. But I am free *not* to take my clothes off and *not* to dance with you. And, by the way, if you come back to my house, get dressed!" Turning, I hurry toward the cottage. Thank God, Basil is off island.

VII

It doesn't take long for David to decide the hotel is a perfect setting for his musical fountain. He tells me to arrange a deal with the manager. Thinking quickly, I say, "I think Sherry can do a better job of it. I've heard Mr. Shaw has a thing for long dark hair. You know, he's an Englishman. Probably got fixated as a child with

Bess, the landlord's black-eyed daughter, or something. I bet if Sherry plaits a red ribbon in her hair, he'll do anything for her."

"You really think so?"

I shrug. "It can't do any harm. He's not here now, but he'll soon be back."

I know my days at the hotel are numbered. Basil went to England to get his family, so may not have heard about David yet. Once he does... If only I could think of a way to forewarn him, and to distance myself. I decide to confide in Richy, but am told he is out sick. I just hope he comes back tomorrow. Somehow I have to prevent the explosion that is bound to happen if David and Basil come face to face.

Next day I give two massages. Returning to the cottage I find out that Basil is back and Sherry has already made her pitch. David will be demonstrating his fountain that very evening. He's working feverishly to get everything ready. I only hope Basil hasn't connected Sherry and David with me.

I pack a picnic supper and walk with the children to the far end of the beach. We gather driftwood, build a fire, and watch the full moon rising while we eat. Jonathan skips a stone across the water that ripples the reflection of the ascending moon. Angie wants to learn how to do it, too, so he patiently shows her. Whenever one of hers bounces, she shouts, "Mommy, Mommy! Look!"

Sydney keeps shrieking and running to me every time she sees a soldier crab skitter across the sand. "They won't hurt you," I assure her over and over, but she remains dubious.

As the fire dies down to embers, we roast marshmallows for dessert. When the mosquitoes attack, we pour water on the charred wood, stuff remnants of food into bags, and hurry homeward. The children have no idea how much I dread going back.

We pass Holly on the verandah, playing her flute. I get the children ready for bed and tuck them in saying, "Too late for a story tonight." I tell myself that the longer David and Sherry stay away, the more likely things are going well.

When the flute music stops, I hear Magic's voice, talking softly with Holly. A commotion follows and the door bursts open. In comes Sherry, the others behind. She's crying, and one eye is swollen almost shut. "He's gone!" she wails. "They took him!"

"Who? Where?" Magic demands.

"What happened?" Holly thrusts tissues at her.

I go for ice. Sherry blows her nose, dabs at her eyes. Sniffling and shaking her head, she holds the ice to her eye, struggling for composure. Her halting story comes out in snippets. David was still making adjustments to the fountain controls when Shaw arrived. After watching for all of two minutes, he extended his hand and said something like "Thank you very much, but this isn't really the sort of thing that would appeal to our kind of guests." He suggested that David try the Hilton, looked at his watch, announced he was late for a dinner engagement, and hurried away. David then turned on Sherry, berating her for not using her wiles to charm Shaw into staying while he made final adjustments. All her fault for letting the man get away. That's when he hit her.

She sips on the water I give her, sniffles, takes a deep breath, and continues. "After I helped David haul the fountain apparatus out of the pool and back to the cottage, he told me I had one more chance to do my job right and dragged me back to the dining room. I didn't know what I was supposed to do. Seduce him, I guess." Chin trembling, she bursts into tears again.

Eventually she manages to tell how they found Shaw at a table with an elegantly coifed blonde wearing an evening gown and pearls. He was joking with the waiter busily opening a bottle of champagne when David strode up and told the waiter to get two more glasses. The waiter scurried off, and David planted himself in front of Shaw, saying he'd been insulted outside and was there to teach him some manners. When David called him a "ras clot, pussy sucking bastard," Shaw blanched and gestured almost imperceptibly to the maitre d'. Instantly three men surrounded and grabbed

David. One had a gun. He was ushered into the kitchen so swiftly that hardly any guests noticed.

I don't know where he is!" she wails. "I don't know if they shot him, or beat him up, arrested him, or what. What are we going to do?" She looks imploringly at Magic.

"I'll check 'round and see what I ken find out," he offers. "What dey looks like?"

"Big guys, but ordinary looking. They weren't wearing uniforms. Just regular dark pants and light shirts, probably white. No, wait! The one with the gun, he had on a jacket. May have been wearing a tie, too. I'm not sure. It all happened so fast."

"Did David resist?"

She shakes her head. "Once he felt that barrel in his back, he quieted right down. It was so awful!" She bursts into tears again.

Magic rises. At the door he pauses and turns. "Dey not gonna kill 'im. Dey's just gonna rough 'im up. I'll let you know if I finds out anyting."

David shows up around noon, walking stiffly, head bandaged. "This isn't the place for us," he announces. "These capitalists aren't who I've come to save. We're getting out. I've found a house a few miles down the coast. I want everybody to pack right away." He looks at me. "You can come if you want, or stay here and jerk off your sugar daddy, but the children are coming with me. It's time for you to choose once and for all which side you're on... theirs or mine. Just remember, if you choose the enemy's side, you'll never see your children again. We've got to get serious. Time is running out. I can't have people around me I don't trust. You're either for me or against me. Which side is it?"

My children's side, I think, but dare not say it. His muscles look taut like a snake ready to strike at the slightest provocation.

As Holly and Sherry start packing, I slip out the back door, head for the beach. With every step I curse myself for letting it come to this. I should have gotten to Basil before he did, but now

I'm too ashamed. After last night, he's sure to evict us anyway. I can't face him again. Kicking up water, I splash along the shore, searching for an answer. Nothing comes except the image of David driving off with the children while I remain alone in the cottage. I turn back, dragging my feet through the heavy sand.

Angie sees me and comes running. "Mommy! Hurry! You gotta come with us!" She grabs my hand, pulls me to the cottage. I kiss her forehead and silently begin stuffing clothes into bags.

VIII

At Villa Lenore somebody always has a black eye. David seems to need to hit as often as he needs sex.

After finishing the stack of banana pancakes I serve for breakfast one morning, he surveys the three children and three women at the table. "Well, now that your bellies are full, what are you going to do to justify your existence?"

Silence answers him. I pick up a damp cloth to clean Sydney's fingers and face. Catching Angela's eye, I nod almost imperceptibly. "Excuse us, Daddy?" she says. He glances at her and grunts. She and Jonathan scoot back their chairs and carry their dishes to the sink. I lift Sydney from the highchair. Angela takes her hand and they disappear out the back door.

Sherry is saying, "... drive into town and get some money from the bank. If anybody needs something, I can stop at the store."

Holly says, "I was planning to do laundry—"

David slams his fist on the table. "That's just the problem! Nobody around here ever does anything creative! Nobody gives a thought to tomorrow, or to improving yourselves, or to making the world a better place. Just a bunch of parasites, sucking blood outa my veins! Hanging around waiting for me to come up with all the ideas. Nobody ever has one worthwhile plan for how to find a manufacturer for my invention. No one ever volunteers to go out and talk to people about me. What's the matter? Don't you believe in me anymore?"

Sherry, having moved to the sofa, is twining her hair into a plait. "I do, David," she purrs. "You know that's why I brought my car and money and why *I'm* here."

"Yeah, yeah, I know. But we've got to move quicker. While we're sitting around basking in the sunshine, oil is being sucked from the bowels of the earth at the rate of millions of gallons per day. Millions! The hole in the ozone is growing with every air conditioner and refrigerator and can of aerosol sold. More and more pesticides are poisoning our food. How can you be so damn complacent!"

He paces around the living room, pipe in hand, arms waving. I hastily clean up the kitchen while Holly clears the dining table. All ears are tuned to his soliloquy.

"Look out there." He pauses before the glass doors and slides them open. "All that water, the beautiful Caribbean. Dying. When I went out snorkeling the other day, I could count the fish I saw on one hand. And they were all tiny. Would you believe that when I was a kid, you couldn't swim in this water without bumping into fish? Big ones!"

I say, "Do you think Jonathan is ready to use the mask and snorkel?"

He looks at me blankly. "What?"

I take a breath, wet my lips. "I don't mean in the sea yet. But maybe he could practice in the pool. He's a good swimmer now. Would you let him use your mask?"

"It won't fit. And no, we can't afford to buy one for him. He'll just have to wait."

I want to argue, tell him Jonathan deserves some reward, some recognition for rescuing Sydney from the river, but I let it go, afraid he'll find a way to twist and sully the whole thing or steal the credit.

Sherry hands him the bong she filled and holds a match while he puffs to light it. He takes a long draw and stands at the open doors, gazing out as though lost in space. Finally turning around, he says to me, "Get Basil on the phone."

"Shaw?"

"You heard me. I wanta talk to him."

I hesitate, but see no point in arguing. I dial the private number to Basil's office. When it starts ringing, I pass the phone to David.

"Hey, Basil," he says, "David here. How're you doing? ... Good. Look here, I'm really sorry if I embarrassed you in front of Mrs. Shaw the other night. I just went off a little because I really had my hopes up that you'd like my fountain. But you know what? The display was lousy. You were right to turn it down. I was so nervous that I couldn't fine-tune all the adjustments. And the music stank too. The signals from that pathetic portable sound system didn't do it justice." He nods and grins while listening to Basil's response.

"You got it, Man. So the reason I'm calling you is to let you know I've been working on calibrating the system, and now I think I've got it to the point where you'll really like it. I want to invite you over to take a look. No obligation, of course. Just a social evening where we can sit and have a couple drinks, get to know each other, and watch the fountain. Whadayasay, Old Man? Willing to give me another chance? I want you to get to know Holly and Sherry better, too. I think you could appreciate them, if you know what I mean..."

I open my mouth, but nothing comes out. He's chuckling. "Any night is fine. We're not too booked up right now. Okay, Thursday's good. You name the time... Eight it is. We're at Villa Lenore. About five miles up the road toward Tower Isle, on the left ... You got it. See you then."

I make a point of being in the kitchen so I won't have to greet Basil when he arrives. David ushers him out to the pool and turns on the fountain. While adjusting the controls, he hollers at me to serve drinks. I do so inconspicuously, trying not to interrupt his monologue on the invention's merits. After the performance he brings Shaw into the living room and flatters him by talking about his achievements and influence in the community. Then he takes Sherry's hand, draws her to Shaw's chair, and says, "Here she is, Basil. All yours for an hour."

Shaw gapes, his head inclining slightly as though doubting what he just heard.

"Go ahead; take her into the bedroom. Have a good time," David assures him. "I want you to see the good life we have here, where everybody is free, without hypocritical morals about what we can and can't do. Freedom is what we live for. Freedom and truth. To show my goodwill and friendship, I give you my queen." He places Sherry's hand in Shaw's whose perplexed expression gives way to awakening appetite as she leads him away.

David puts a record on the turntable, turns up the volume, and presses his harmonica to his lips. Around the room he whirls in a dance of jubilation to the strains of "What a Lady, What a Night." I go into the kitchen to put away dishes and heat water for tea.

As I return to the living room, Magic arrives. "Hey," I say, "just in time for bush tea."

"Irey. Dats what I need."

Holly moves the bong and bag of herb to make room on the cocktail table. David puts on a quieter record, and the melody of "Turn Your Lights Down Low" fills the room. I pour tea and pass honey around. We've almost finished drinking it when Shaw emerges from the hallway.

David rises. "So, did you enjoy my queen? Good stuff, huh?"

"Yes," Shaw nods, flashes a smile. Then he looks at his watch and says, "Rats! It's late. Gotta get going." He glances around the room, sweeps his hand in an inclusive arc and calls out, "Good night now, everybody."

"Not so fast!" David steps between Shaw and the door. "You've forgotten something."

"What do you mean?"

"Your manners. You haven't even told me thanks. What gives you the right to come in here and screw my woman without saying thank-you? You think we're your slaves?"

"Oh, I beg your pardon." He reaches in his pocket. "Here..." He thrusts a wad of bills at David.

"You miserable asshole!" David knocks his hand aside. "I don't want your fuckin' money! I only want some respect. A *proper* show of courtesy would be to offer me your wife in return. If you're not prepared for give-and-take, you shouldn't have accepted my offer. You got the manners of a shark! Then you add injury to insult by offering money for what money can't buy!"

Shaw draws back, but not in time to avoid David's fist. He tumbles to the floor.

I rush over, drop to his side. He's dazed but still conscious.

David glares. "It's all right. I wouldn't want your wife anyway. Don't think my cock would stand up for a chrome-plated icicle." He leaves the room.

IX

I help Basil up, mumbling apologies, and lead him outside. His face is ashen, one eye already puffy. Wordlessly he climbs into his Mercedes and speeds away.

I return to the house in time to hear David say, "... sure put that sonovabitch in his place! How do you think he'll explain the black eye to his wife?"

"Ha, ha, ha!" Holly and Sherry chorus.

Magic comes through the back door. "Soon as I see what goin' on, I ducked out," he says. "Didn't want Shaw ta connect me wid what you was doin'. Maybe you don't know, but he be one powerful dude. Shouldn't mess around wid him. Big mistek."

"Go on; sneak around hiding from your own shadow if that's how you want to live. Not me! Don't care how much money a man has, I make sure he treats me and my women with respect!" David

336

pulls a record from the stereo cabinet. "Let's play music and smoke some herb. Build a wall of protection around us." He places a disc on the turntable, picks up his harmonica, begins playing along with Peter Tosh's "Legalize It."

"Gonna need more dan music ta protect him," Magic mutters as he moves to the front door. Loudly he announces, "I'm outta here now. Later."

Holly gets up to lock the door behind him. Returning, she takes out her flute and attempts to harmonize with David. Sherry fills the bong. I check on the children and then go to bed.

An insistent knocking on the door jerks us awake. David jumps up to investigate, and I follow him to the living room. At every window are uniformed policemen. "Damn it! The place is surrounded!" He goes to the door and opens it to an officer holding a search warrant. Forces sweep in and confiscate the bag of marijuana on the cocktail table.

They ransack the house, turning every room inside out, but find nothing else illegal. The commander places us under arrest. "But Officer," David pleads, "you can't take everybody to jail and leave the children here alone." Getting no reaction, he continues, "Come on, you gotta let one of us stay to look after da pickney dem."

The officer hesitates. At that moment, Magic enters through the back door. He looks around. "Hey, what goin' on?"

"You know these people?" the officer asks.

"Yeah. Dey buys bananas and food from me. I come by ta see if dey needs anyting today."

"Magic, they're going to lock us all up!" I cry. "The children will be alone. Can you stay with them? Please?"

"Sure, Jac. Doan worry. Jonathan and me is good buddies. And Angie and Sydney, too. Doan you fret. I'll see to it dat da kids dem is fine."

With that, the police hustle us outside. I kneel to hug the children and try to reassure them. Then I climb into the van that carries us to the Port Maria jail.

David is put in a male lockup. We women are confined in a dank cell with stone walls that feels like a dungeon from slave days. The tiny window above eye level provides enough light to reveal roaches scurrying across the floor as we enter their territory. Around dusk we are served hard bread and a spoonful of beans on tin plates. To rest, we huddle together on a stone slab, sharing body heat. My dashiki has never felt so thin, but at least it covers my ankles and elbows. I curl into a ball, back pressed against Holly, but sleep eludes me.

I can't stop fretting. Jonathan and Angela understand what is going on, but Sydney–she'll feel abandoned again. At least Magic will see that they're fed well. Thank God for him. When younger I had imagined being thrown in jail for a cause: protesting nuclear arms, war, racial discrimination, destruction of rain forest... but this is so pointless.

I replay the agony of recent weeks, reliving how David's communal experiment became what the Bible calls a "den of iniquity" as we frittered away our days hanging out in the living room, applauding David's discourses, defending ourselves from his attacks. By night we watched and praised the fountain display in the pool until our eyes grew weary. He had continually demanded Sherry's attention and mine. Though he railed against jealousy, I sensed he was expecting us to compete for his favors. My refusal to do so probably infuriated him, but he couldn't admit it. Much as he liked the attention of multiple women, the task of keeping a harem had worn on his nerves. I'd even given up having school with the children because every time I started, he'd have some urgent thing for me to do, like writing down one of his brilliant new ideas or composing a letter. Usually the children stayed out of his way by playing on the swings or in the pool under Magic's supervision. Magic had been spending more time with them than anyone else.

Sherry mumbles something. Probably talking in her sleep. If only we could confide in one another! But even now I dare not let them know how I really feel. Anything I say, they'll carry back to him for gold stars. And I'll be punished.

Maybe it's good that the police came. "God, help us," I pray softly. "Help me use this to end our nightmare. Help me free my children from any more of this craziness."

In front of a magistrate the next morning we are charged with possession of marijuana. Bail is set for David and me only. The others could too easily escape prosecution by leaving the island.

With my one phone call I reach the hotel and ask for Richy Roberts. Swallowing my shame, I briefly explain the predicament. He agrees to come over.

As he signs papers, the conditions of bail are explained: I'll have to report to the station every twenty-four hours and show up for trial in ten days. I'm determined not to violate Richy's trust.

Pulling up to the villa, Richy says, "Promise me you'll call if you need any help ... like with getting to the station every day."

"I promise." I kiss his cheek. "You're a saint. I won't disappoint you."

Magic is inside with the children. They dash toward me. "Mommy! Mommy!" I embrace them and sink into a chair, overcome with relief. Magic hands me a glass of soursop juice. "Drink dis," he says. "Calm yuh nerves."

He prepares lunch while I answer a barrage of questions: "Yes, the jail's a horrible place, and the food is terrible...I have to report back every day, so I'll take clean clothes and food to them...You can help pack the bags... No, you can't go. Children aren't allowed inside...I'm sure Daddy would love to have his harmonica, but I can't take it; somebody will just steal it. But we can bring magazines..."

That night after the children are in bed, Magic and I open beers and sit outside. Under the half moon we consider the days ahead.

He offers to take me to the station on his motorcycle. As we discuss recent events, I start to unwind for the first time in weeks.

"You remember what I told David after he hit Mr. Shaw?" Magic says.

"Wait! Basil sent the police?"

"Could be. Lots of folks round here doesn't like David. Everywhere he tries ta upset people. Doan get me wrong—some change is good. Some a dese people needs ta be shook up. But David gots ta be more intelligent 'bout who he offends."

"You're right."

"Dere's lots about David dat's good. He really gets people ta look at tings in a different way. At first I tought he was brilliant. But now I see dat sometimes he act like a damn fool. It tek more dan brains. A man also need ta have sense."

"I used to think he was brilliant, too. And I loved how he was always thinking of ways to make the world better. He has so much energy and enthusiasm, but he's inconsistent. He preaches love and freedom, but tries to control everything we do. And don't buy his rap that discipline is the purest form of love."

"I know. I hates da way he treats Jonathan. I love dat lickle bwai, and I feels like I just gots ta be around ta mek sure David doan hurt him."

I purse my lips, fight back tears.

"I doan worry 'bout Angie. He doan get on her case much. But Jonathan an' Sydney, dem's da ones I watch out fer. An' you."

I nod, swallow grimly.

"Why do you tink I bin comin' round here? Remember when we met down at da fisherman beach, and I did tell ya I would bring a stem o' bananas over fe da pickney?"

"Yes. And when you came David was there and I thought you'd come to see him."

"Well, it was you I come ta see. I tought David had gone foreign. Dat's what you told me. Ken you imagine my surprise when I shows up wid da bananas, and David walks out! Dere I stands wid a gift fe da man's wife. I dint know wat he might do."

I smile wryly remembering the scene and my own confusion.

"I just let him believe I was dere ta see him. Den he wanted some herb so I gets it fe him, and he keeps askin' me fe more..."

"So that's why you've been coming."

"No. I've been comin' ta see you and ta find out da truth of what's goin' on around here. Dat first day when David invited me into da cottage and I sees dose two white women widout a speck of clothes on, I didn't know what ta tink! But since I could see dat he and dose women just arrived, I figured ya wasn't lyin' ta me 'bout bein' separated."

"I wish you had asked me."

"What confused me was how you puts up wid him havin' all dese women. I hears before 'bout white people doin' weird tings, so I hung around and watched. Dat and da pickney. I really loves dem. But I swears, dere was times I wanted ta kill him. I just had ta jump on my bike and get away cuz I gots no right ta interfere wid what a man do in his own yard." Magic reaches over and squeezes my hand.

That does it; I break down, sobs explode from my chest. His arm goes around me.

"Dat's all right," he says, pulling me close. "Just let it out."

And I do, as if I've never wept before. Months of humiliation, beatings, the children's lost years... I can't stop. Patiently Magic embraces me, providing one napkin after another. When my tears finally subside, I keep blowing my nose and gasping, too weak to talk. We sit quietly, numbed by the enormity of my outburst.

He breaks the silence. "Whatever David gettin' in jail tonight, it not as bad as he deserves!"

"You really feel that way?"

"I swears on da moon shinin' above dat every word I speak is God's troot, right from mi heart."

"You believe in God?"

"Of course."

"Sometimes David says there isn't any, and other times he talks as if he is God."

"Dat's blasphemy! God will punish him."

"I don't know what the word 'god' really means. I don't think any person can define the higher power. That's the problem with religion... always trying to control people's minds by telling us what we should think about this or that brand of God."

"Religion, dat just a social ting. People goes ta churches ta impress dere neighbors. It don't impress God none."

I like his reasoning. "Tell me about yourself. I don't know anything about you really, except that you're always here when we need you."

"Well, I lives out by Dunn's River Falls. I gots t'ree pickney dat stay wid me. Da rest lives wid dere mudders in Kingston."

"So you're from Kingston."

"No. I was born in St. Mary, but I lived in Kingston for a time when I was a rude bwai. Den I started seein' me buddies get shot down, and I knew dat if I was goin' ta survive I had ta leave town. I bin in St. Ann ever since, growin' food and sellin' a lickle 'erb ta tourists 'n ting."

"But how do you look after your children when you spend so much time here?"

"I got a woman dat cooks and washes dere clothes and sees dey gets ta school."

"Why don't you ever bring them over?"

He shakes his head. "David wouldn't like dat. Don't have time fe other folks unless dey have some use ta him. He's only interested in his own ideas 'n inventions."

He is so right. As I gaze at the moon, a feeling of peace fills me. I have a friend. When Magic suggests that we have another drink, I decline but accept his offer to stay the night and show him to Holly and Sherry's room.

The next day the children help pack two bags with food, clothes, and magazines, and we carry them to the police station. I insist on being escorted to each cell so I can deliver the things personally, not convinced that anything will reach them otherwise.

"Thanks," David says, "but I gotta get out. Wasted my call on Fairweather; bastard wouldn't even talk to me. You have to find someone to bail me. If Philip won't, call Uncle Sid."

Back at the villa I make the calls. Both refuse. I can think of no one else with money whom David has not already alienated.

After dinner Magic returns from his yard, and again we sit under the moon, making plans for the next day. I dread telling David that nobody will bail him.

"Ya done yer best," Magic assures me. "Dat man got too many enemies. Nobody will help him now. He just be lucky dat you is bringin' food."

"You're right," I say, but can't stop worrying. If only I could find a way to use this brief window of freedom to...

"Stop frettin' and get yuh rest." He rises, takes my hand, leads me toward the door. "I'd stay, but I don't trust meself." He leans against the doorjamb, looks at me intently. "Just give me one kiss before I leaves." His lips, smooth and soft like plush velvet, send shivers through me. He draws away. "Gots to go now, or I ken never leave."

When I report the news of no bail to David, he says, "Figures. When the chips are down, you find out who your real friends are. Mine are sufferers; they don't have money to bail me. Just another way the system is stacked to keep poor people poor." He grips the bars between us. "All right, I accept this cup. I'm not the first man that Babylon has put in chains. Remember Samson. Remember Jesus, Gandhi. Think of Mandela. That's what they do to people they're afraid of. I can take it. I'll come out stronger than ever. Here's the plan. Pay attention." He glances around and lowers his voice.

He most fears that Sherry and Holly will get deported, a certainty should they be found guilty. If he is convicted, he'll probably get a sentence. That worries him too since no one will bail him pending an appeal. "But you're the baby mother," he says. "They'll let you off with no more than a slap on the hand. You plead guilty."

"What!"

"It's the only way. Don't fuck around."

"Time's up," the guard announces, tapping David's shoulder. "Back inside."

I stumble out into the sunshine. Plead guilty? Get a record! How will I ever find another teaching job? The herb wasn't even mine. I'd be lying under oath. I can't! But if I don't? Regardless of the outcome, he won't stay in jail forever. If I refuse to follow his plan, he'll kill me whenever he does get out.

I have a week to decide. I can't skip out on the bail bond Richy signed for me. Besides, if I don't show up, I'll automatically be considered guilty. Can I somehow get the kids away, but still appear in court? Shall I tell David that I'm going to plead guilty, and then not do it? But if he's convicted and the judge gives him time to pay, he'll walk out, and I won't have a chance to get the kids away. I must do something before the trial. But what?

X

Later that night when Magic and I are again sitting by the pool, I hint at my intentions, wanting to check his loyalty, for I remember David's misgivings about him hanging around the yard. He alluded to possible connections with the C.I.A., but he says that about everybody, me included. Nevertheless, I have to be certain.

Even though Magic supports the idea of taking the children away, I still hesitate, wondering why. How does this reconcile with his friendship with David? I keep probing, checking his

344

motivations, but am unable to come up with anything other than sincere concern for the children and me. Finally I decide to take him into my confidence. With his knowledge of local ways and people, he could be invaluable with planning a successful strategy.

"One of the problems," I confide, "is bail. I mustn't let Richy down. And if I don't show up in court, I'll be a fugitive. So I have to find a way to get the children out of here without breaking bail. The other problem is money. Who am I kidding?" I hold out my hands, empty palms up. "I haven't worked since leaving the hotel. We've all been living off Sherry's savings. I don't have money for plane tickets, and where on this island can we hide? Look how David found us at the hotel! There's no way," I shake my head.

"Course dere is. We just gotta reason and figure dis ting out, tek it step by step. Dere's four tings. Finding a safe place for da kids dem. Gettin' you off dis ganja charge widout a record. Keepin' yous safe from David. And money. Money is always da problem dat meks it hard fe poor folks ta do tings. If you had a bank account like Sherry, it would all be different. You could pay for expert advice da way rich folks always buys da knowledge dat lawyers got."

"Wait," I say. "You've hit on something. If I had a lawyer to represent me, I might not have to show up in court. Maybe Richy can suggest a lawyer who won't mind doing a personal favor. Like one who works for the hotel."

"Now you're tinkin' smart. Use da people ya knows. Dat's what friends is for."

"Besides, Richy said to let him know if there was anything else he could do. I'll call him tomorrow. Then at the station, I'll just report in and leave the food."

"I'll mek lunch and look after da kids so you can get yuh business done," he says. "Together we goan work dis out." He reaches for my hand. "Come, sit beside Magic."

I shift to the lounge where he's sitting. He puts his arm around me and gently strokes my hair, sending tingles through my body. I lean against his warm chest.

"Dat feel good," he says, "but yuh sweetness is killin' me. I gots ta mek love ta ya."

I stiffen, pull away, my head spinning. "But, we're just… I mean, we're friends."

"Yes, but dat doan mean we cyan't be more. Much more," he says huskily.

"I, I don't think I'm ready. I mean, I'm so confused by all this mess with David. It wouldn't be fair to either of us. Do you understand?"

"If ya cyan't tell de difference between David an' me—"

"That's not what I mean! Of course, I can tell the difference. But I'm too confused about my own future to know what's right for me, for us, right now. For years my life has revolved around David, whether it was working with him, loving him, placating him, running from him, or what. It's all been about David. When you and I met on the beach, I was just beginning a new life. Then he came back and ruined it, and I have to start all over with getting free of him. How can I know what I truly feel for you until I've cleared my head of his stuff?"

He looks crestfallen. "So ya still loves him."

I shake my head. "That's not what I said or meant. Don't pressure me."

"Okay. Just remember dat I loves yuh kids dem, and I wants ta love you, if you'll let me."

I follow him to the door. "Thanks for understanding. I don't want you to take this personally. It's just my own confusion."

"Ya fret too much." He touches my face. "See ya in de mornin'."

After the door closes, I wonder if I've made a mistake. Physically I long for him. But I'm truly not ready. If he can't understand and wait, then it isn't meant to be. Still, I hope I haven't alienated him.

XI

Richy orders tea for us on the hotel terrace. Sailboats dot the glimmering water. Surf with frothy meringue peaks gently rolls ashore, collapsing at the feet of sun worshippers sprawled along the beach on towels and recliners. Waiters stand in the shade of palms, ready to rescue any guest's empty glass. Before getting into my issues, I want to bask in the memories of how good I felt while working here...

He breaks into my reverie. "So how are you and the children getting along?"

"We're holding up, thanks, but I need your advice." I explain my dilemma. "It's so complicated. I think I need a lawyer. Is there anyone you can recommend? Somebody who won't charge much?"

"Sure, I'll put you in touch with the firm that does all our work. They have a couple of sharp apprentices who might do it just for the experience."

"But I need someone knowledgeable..."

"Don't worry. They have access to the best minds in the firm. They know when to ask for advice and who to ask. Trust me."

I smile. "Reminds me of a saying I've heard, something about if you need a favor, ask someone who has helped you already. They don't want to lose their investment."

"A lot of truth in that," he says gesturing to a waiter. "What do you want for lunch?"

Having ordered, Richy excuses himself to make a call. Returning, he says, "You're all set for this afternoon at four." He writes the lawyer's name and address on a card.

"Great!" I reach for it. "Thank you so much."

While we butter crusty rolls and dribble dressing on our garden salads, Richy says, "I don't mean to probe, but I'm wondering if you've considered a divorce?"

347

"That would be logical, but there's not really money for such niceties."

"Maybe you should mention it to the lawyer."

"Okay. My primary concern right now is the drug charge. But I'll try to get two for the price of one." I chuckle.

Ignoring my feeble attempt at humor, he leans forward. "That was an awful mistake David made, hitting Basil. The man's a lunatic! Only in Jamaica can he be loose on the streets. You can't stay on this island. But you need money to get the children away safely. Didn't you tell me once that you come from the Midwest? Is there someone in your family who can help?"

Holding back tears, I take a deep breath. "My parents and brother live in Iowa where I was born. I haven't spoken to them in years, but we write sometimes. I suppose I could call them." A pang of guilt stabs me, remembering the horrible letter I sent from Australia. I hate to ask for anything. But Mother's recent letter did urge me to bring the children to Iowa. Then things got so crazy, I haven't even answered yet.

"Listen, Jacqueline, you have more here than you can handle by yourself. This is definitely a time to call. Would it help if I talked to them to explain the seriousness?"

"Thanks, but that's not necessary. Besides, I don't remember the number. I'll have to look it up in my address book."

"The court date is less than a week away. That's not much time to make arrangements to get the children off the island. You better call right away."

"I'll talk to the lawyer first, then decide."

The earnest young lawyer, in a black suit and crisp, white, cuff-linked shirt set off by a pale yellow tie, sits behind a sturdy mahogany desk in his air-conditioned office and takes notes as I sum up the situation. "The first thing to do," he says, "is draw up separation papers and a petition to file for legal custody of the children. Then you'll be free to take them anywhere. Do you want me to do that?"

"Yes, please."

"As for the court case, you must keep reporting to the station. Meanwhile, I'll arrange to take a deposition from you with regard to the charges. I'll also find out from my superior if we can file for a writ to have you excused from the court hearing. Are you willing to testify under oath that your life will be endangered–that is, that your husband, David Wellington, has threatened to harm you–if you refuse to plead guilty to charges for which you are innocent?"

"Well, he, he said ... Yes, I am."

"Okay," he nods, puts the cap on his pen, and slips it into his breast pocket. "We should have a case. If it is allowed, you may be able to report to the station the day before the trial, then leave the island that afternoon, and let us represent you in court. That way your husband will have no forewarning of your plans, and you'll be out of the country before he knows what's happened. It shouldn't be hard to convict him, but that doesn't really matter. Except, you may be interested to know, the U.S. has become very strict. With a drug conviction on his record, he won't be able to travel there again. Our main concern though is keeping your record clean, and getting the children and yourself out of harm's way."

"Your plan sounds good. Thanks a lot." It feels strange to have the law behind me now after spending so many years with David on the other side of the divide.

"I'm sorry we can't get the deposition done today," he glances at his watch, "but the stenographer has left already. Can you be here at nine a.m. tomorrow?"

"All right," I nod and rise.

In the center of Ocho Rios I load up on bread, milk and patties. Laden with bags, I catch a bus to Port Maria where I check into the station and asked a guard to deliver patties to David, Sherry and Holly. Then I rush home.

"Yippee!" Jonathan and Angela shout when they spot the patties. I warm them in the oven and the children carry drinks and plates to the table by the pool. While we eat I tell them I'm going to write to Grandma and Grandpa and ask if they want to help.

Angela's eyes light up. "I'll draw a picture of the sun rising over the sea with lots of fluffy clouds and I'll put a red boat on the water."

"I can't draw," Jonathan says.

"But you can write," I encourage.

"I don't know what to say."

"How about starting with 'Dear Grandpa and Grandma'? I'll tell you how to spell it. If you think of anything else to say, I'll show you how to write that, too."

"What's Grandpa's name?"

"Donald," I say. "But everybody calls him Don. That's easy to spell—d, o, n."

After we clean up the dishes, I get out paper and settle them around the table. Sydney scribbles with a blue crayon on a big piece of paper. Angela presses her lips firmly as she boldly executes her picture. Jonathan asks for the spelling of each word. As they work, I start my letter. "Shall I tell Grandpa and Grandma we want to visit them?" I ask.

Jonathan says, "Do you have enough money?"

"Well, no, but I might be able to get some. That is, if we really want to go." At least he can't follow us, according to the lawyer. We won't have to stay in Iowa forever, but it'll be a refuge for now.

"Look, Mommy!" Angela squeals. "I'm done. Do you like it?"

"It's wonderful, Honey! Grandma and Grandpa will *love* it! I bet Grandpa will make a special frame and hang it on the wall. I'll get a big envelope at the post office so we don't have to fold it. Be sure to write your name at the bottom."

"I'm done, too," Jonathan says. "Can you read it?"

"Let me see. 'Dear Grandma and Grandpa Don.' That's very nice. 'How are you? I hope to see you sometime. My name is Jonathan. Goodbye.' It's perfect! They'll love reading your letter!"

"And see Sydney's picture, Mommy." Angela holds it up. "You know what it is?"

"Of course, it's the river by the hotel. And those are the coconut trees." I point to brown vertical lines intersecting a mass of blue. "You've all done a wonderful job. Let's put the crayons and paper away now and get ready for bed."

"Can you read a story?" asks Jonathan.

"All right. Just one. But you have to brush your teeth first."

Soon after turning out the light in their room, I hear the soft putt of Magic's motorcycle. He kisses my cheek and hands me a bag of ripe plantain and green bananas.

"You're so good to us." I head for the kitchen to put them away. He follows, and I fill him in on my meetings with Richy and the lawyer.

"Just what I tought. Dose lawyers know all da tricks."

"You're right. If I hadn't gone to him, I wouldn't know any of this. I fix gin and tonics and carry them outside where we sit in the light of the nearly full moon.

"Everything's falling into place," I sigh. "Much as I've tried to raise my children in Jamaica, with David carrying on so, we can't have any decent life here. So we still have to leave. His being in jail is like the parting of the Red Sea; I just need the faith to walk through."

"Ya gots ta get dem away from David. He's a no good fadder. But I sure is gonna miss you and dose pickney."

"I'll miss you, too." I squeeze his hand, let my fingers linger on his. "A couple pieces of the plan I still haven't figured out."

"Where you're going."

"That's one. The other is, how to pay for it. Richy suggested I call my father. The kids seem to like the idea of visiting their grandparents. I hate to ask for favors, but I think I owe it to the children to swallow my pride and beg. Do whatever it takes."

"Yes. Give dose pickney a chance ta live some good life. I'd like ta do dat fe dem right in Jamaica. But I is poor and times is hard. You is better tekin' dem Stateside. But I sure will miss ya." He looks at me somberly. Have ya decided? Is you ready fe Magic's luv? Or ya want me ta leave?"

"Don't leave." I return his gaze, heart quickening.

"Dis is a private ting," he says huskily. "Just between us. Nobody's business but ours. I is gonna tek a shower first, den mek love ta yuh properly."

I freshen up in the other bathroom and then light a candle in the bedroom. He comes in with a towel tied around his slim waist. Muscles ripple on his chest and arms. His raven skin glistens in the flickering light. The fresh scent of Dove soap fills my nostrils. He loosens the towel, and his erection, curving upward, greets me. "Let's tek it slow," he says softly. "I wants ta enjoy yuh real good. Just relax and let Magic tek yuh on da sweetest trip o' yuh life."

He lowers me onto the bed, kissing me reverently. His tender fingers caress my skin as though it's fine silk. Passion welling, I force myself to relax, determined to let him control our flight. Finally, he abandons restraint, and we go into freefall together, dissolving into one another. Our fury abated, we sprawl on the bed, limbs intertwined.

When his breathing returns to normal, he touches my brow. "I waited fe yuh so long, but was 'fraid we'd never get together. I tank da Almighty fe givin' us dis time."

"Just when I'm making plans for leaving," I sigh.

"All because of dat wicked dude David, I might never see my sweet Jac again. But I want yuh ta remember dat I is always yuh best friend in Jamaica. I loves you, and I loves yuh kids dem." We kiss and hold each other close, eventually drifting off to sleep but keenly aware of one another through the night.

XII

Having no international phone service at the villa, I go into town early to use a pay phone. Luckily I catch Dad in the house having breakfast. After recovering from the shock of hearing my voice, he becomes excited, wants to know how we are. "The children wrote letters and drew pictures for you and Mother last night," I say. "I'm mailing them today."

"Great! Your mother misses you terribly. Any plans to come up here?"

"Maybe. I can't talk long because I'm at a phone booth and don't have much change. David found us again and moved in. But now he's in jail, so I've decided to use this chance to get the kids away for good. A lawyer is helping me. I'd like to bring them up to Iowa. David may get out next week, so I have to move fast. The problem is, I don't have any money."

"We'll send some. How much do you need?"

"I'm not sure. I'll have to check with the airlines. Can you really afford this?"

"Yes. Just get those kids out of there."

"Your time is up," says a recorded voice. "Deposit four dollars and fifty cents..."

"Call me back with the details," I hear him shouting.

"Okay," I say, and the line goes dead.

I try to answer the lawyer's questions truthfully, but when the stenographer reads back my statement for verification, I nearly lose my nerve. I can picture David's rage and disappointment when the deposition is read in court. He'll call it a betrayal. I'll never be able to set foot in Jamaica again. After all these years of trying... I steel myself and sign.

At the post office I mail the pictures and letters and find out how to have money wired from the States. Then I update Richy.

353

He introduces me to a travel agent who finds out the prices of available flights. She gives me two choices: one-way tickets directly to Chicago on American Airlines, or Air Jamaica to Miami, continuing to Chicago on Braniff. On the Air Jamaica segment, round-trip fare is nearly the same as one-way. That flight is available the morning of the court hearing, four days away. I choose it. Suddenly I realize that I haven't reported to the police station.

I trudge to the market to buy bananas and patties. On the bus to Port Maria I eat a banana, my first food of the day. Much as I dread seeing David, I have to keep him from getting suspicious. As I slide food through his tiny opening, he says, "You look tired, Jac."

"I am. This is wiping me out, traipsing back and forth every day, doing laundry, looking after the kids, carrying groceries on the bus." I sigh. "Can't wait till it's over."

"How are they? Do they ask about me?"

"Of course. Is there anything you want me to tell them?"

"Just tell them Daddy loves them and will soon be home."

A guard clangs on the bars. "Time's up."

"And I love you, too," David calls as the guard tugs him away.

I wait until I have the tickets in hand before telling the children, which leaves only one day for packing. "We might be staying for quite a while," I tell them, "so put in everything you want."

"Daddy says America is a bad place," Jonathan balks. "We shouldn't go there."

I force a light tone. "There are lots of bad things about America. Daddy's right about that. But there are good things, too. Grandma and Grandpa, your uncle and aunt, and your cousins are there. And Grandpa has horses, sheep, chickens, cats, a dog. You'll have fun." Angela starts putting her things in a bag. Jonathan stands firm.

Magic has remained in the background as I try to rally everyone, but now he squats by Jonathan and looks into his eyes. "You and me is buddies, right?"

Jonathan nods.

"Buddies always tell each other da truth, don't dey?"

He nods again.

"Well den, you gots ta believe Magic on dis. Yuh see..." I leave them alone. When I return a few minutes later, Jonathan is gathering his things.

"Is Daddy coming, too?" Angela wants to know.

"No. He's staying here with Sherry and Holly."

"You're afraid of what he'll do when he comes out of jail, aren't you, Mommy?"

I look at her sharply, startled by her insight. "Yes."

"He blames you for everything, so he'll hit you because you didn't get him out sooner."

I nod grimly. "That's only part of it. Someday I hope you'll understand."

"Just don't go away and leave us ever again, Mommy."

I kneel and hug her tightly. "Okay, Sweetie. I promise."

Dad sends enough money to spend the night before our departure in Kingston. We check into a guesthouse, and Magic goes out for a pizza. He also gets a toy for each child to entertain them on the long flight. After calling my parents to confirm our arrival time, I report back, "Hey, Guys, it's snowing in Iowa! Grandma's bringing coats and boots for everybody to the airport. You'll get to see snow for the first time!"

After they go to sleep, I make arrangements for a taxi to pick us up early. Magic sits in the lobby as though keeping guard. "Get youself settled," he says. "I'll be in later."

When I feel him slip into bed, I roll over to hug him. Quietly we make love. Sweet but melancholic, an elegy to our separation. As we lay in the darkness, tears dampen my pillow.

At dawn, he embraces me again, but a knock on the door interrupts our coupling. I leap up. It's the taxi driver. Returning to the bed, I kneel and whisper, "Sorry, Magic, we have to go. I'll write to you though."

He sits up and reaches for his trousers while I fumble in my purse for pen and paper to write down his mailing address.

Only a few minutes behind schedule, we get the children and bags into the taxi. "This is far as I ken go," Magic says. He pokes his head inside the window. "Bye now, Angie. Bye, Sydney. Bye, Jonathan. Tek good care a yuh mudder."

We wave as the vehicle moves away. My eyes lock with Magic's, holding the connection until he vanishes.

Iowa, 1977
I

As new snow falls on the cold, dark plains Jonathan and Angela run barefoot across icy tarmac from the small aircraft to the terminal. I follow in flip-flops, struggling to carry Sydney and two heavy bags. Inside the door I find Mother and Dad busily putting boots on the children and enveloping them in coats. Blanket in hand, Dad reaches for Sydney. Mother gives me a perfunctory hug and asks, "Where on earth are the children's shoes?"

"In Jamaica they didn't need any. Every time I bought some, they'd kick them off and lose them, or else the shoes would sit in the closet and get too small..." my voice trails off. Our arrival feels like a replay of seven years before when I landed with Jonathan in my arms, only now I have more children, fewer teeth, and no cash.

In the following days, I focus on softening the transition for the children. Gratefully I accept donations of clothing from relatives and neighbors and keep explaining household rules in an effort to prevent them from getting on Grandma's nerves by disrupting her forty-year routines.

"Why do we have to get up so early?" Jonathan whines when I wake him at quarter to seven.

"It's time for breakfast."

"I'm not hungry. Why do I have to eat?" Angela asks.

"Because if you don't eat now, you'll be hungry later, but then you can't eat."

"Why not?"

"Because when Grandma puts the breakfast things away, she starts to get dinner ready, so she doesn't want us getting in her way. Come on. Just wash your face and brush your teeth. You don't have to dress."

In pajamas they stumble to the table. "For life and health and daily food, we praise thy name, O Lord," Dad recites and promptly switches on the seven o'clock news. Accompanied by reports of hog, corn and beef prices, car accidents, and the weather forecast, I pour juice, spread jam on toast, spoon scrambled eggs into Sydney's mouth, and strengthen the watery coffee with a scoop of instant.

After breakfast, I get Sydney dressed and return to the kitchen to wash dishes. I want to get to them before Mother so as not to become more of a burden than necessary.

The kids like to watch television, but it isn't allowed during the daytime. Going outside is a big production with the donning, fastening and adjusting of warm pants, boots, jackets, mittens, scarves and hats. Nevertheless, Jonathan braves the snow banks to play with Whitey, the dog. He also helps Grandpa exercise and groom the horses in the barn. I admire his pluck. Angela wants to play with the cats, but no animals are allowed in the house, so she has to go outside. I help her get dressed and put a snowsuit on Sydney. The two wild cats we find in the barn don't want to be held, so just petting them isn't enough fun to get the girls outside every day.

Dad finds an old sled in the garage which the children take turns sitting on while I pull them around the yard. Then Jonathan decides to hitch up the dog the way he saw on television. Dad helps him rig a harness and they get Whitey to pull the sled, but he refuses to budge if any weight is put on it.

In a corner of my bedroom we set up a school cubby, but it's hard to arrange productive lessons since I always feel I should be in the kitchen helping Mother prepare the next meal or clean up from the last one. At dinner everyone has to be seated prior to twelve so Dad can say the blessing before the news starts. Then we have to whisper lest he miss a word of the broadcast. When dishes are done, Mother always rests, so it's a good time for the children to take their naps. Supper is on the table at six-thirty. Thus the ritual around food structures our lives.

The only variation comes on Sundays when breakfast is a little later, followed by a mad dash to get ready for Sunday school and church. We can't be late because Mother teaches a class, and Dad is a deacon. Not going is out of the question, so I go to avoid any argument, even though I hate the thought of my children getting the same indoctrination I endured. They are traumatized enough by David without now being taught that virtually everything natural is sinful, even their birth. I try to put the Bible stories they bring home in the context of religious history: "Christians believe Jesus was a great prophet. Every religion has its own prophets. Muslims believe in Allah and the teachings of Mohammed. Some of the Jews' prophets are the same as the Christians'. For example, Moses," and so on.

Mother arranges for Angela to visit distant girl cousins who are a couple of years older. She is excited, never having known cousins before, but afterwards confides that they seem kind of boring. "They're so babyish. Most things I say, they don't understand or care about. But they sure have lots of toys and clothes—so much stuff they don't know where to put it all. You should see their closets!"

Fortunately they let her bring home things for everyone: watercolors and paintbrush for herself, two school bus children for Sydney, and a plastic motorcycle for Jonathan.

Sydney, nearly two, observes everything somberly with wide eyes. Her single syllable utterances express basic requirements.

When I'm not present Angela responds or translates for Grandma. If anyone else picks her up, she wriggles away to seek refuge on my lap. A soiled stuffed rabbit, dragged along from Jamaica, lives in her arms.

One Sunday afternoon we pull out old albums and look at photos from my childhood. The pictures bring back the boring years attending the one-room country school in Iowa, but before then, those idyllic four years in the Colorado Rockies. Photos of my sheep dog, motley collection of cats, and the old bay mare I rode everywhere. Best of all are the shots of my brother and me climbing the gigantic boulders on our property. Endless hours we spent playing cowboys and Indians and exploring caves in our beloved rocks. "Look!" I point. "There's the log barn I helped Grandpa build."

"You built it?" Jonathan looks dubious.

"I helped him strip bark off the logs, and handed him nails and tools, and helped stuff insulation between the logs, and..."

"I remember," Mother chimes in. "That was the year before you started school and I didn't know what I was going to do with you in the house. But every day you followed your dad outside, even when it got really cold. And the only thing you'd wear was blue jeans. Except on Sundays. Then I made you put on a dress and bonnet."

"I know." I shake my head, smiling at the memory. "That was torture."

Dad speaks up. "You remember Ed Akrey? How he used to tease you about being such a tomboy?"

"What's a tomboy?" asks Angela.

"It's what people around here call girls who like to climb trees, play ball, wear jeans... you know, the kinds of things boys do all the time. For some reason they think girls shouldn't, but I liked to be outside and do things with Dad."

Mother takes the album from my lap and returns it to the shelf.

The call I've been dreading finally comes. David is furious. He calls me traitor, coward, deceiver, and other epithets I refuse to register. The court let him off with just a fine and even gave him time to pay. Sherry and Holly are still there, but it doesn't sound like things are going well. After cooling down a bit, he inquires about the children. Then he tells me to use my time during "this little holiday with the kids" to find a sponsor for his invention. His persistent drive to make a difference in the world still touches me, but I say, "I'm way out in the boonies. Nobody would have any idea what I'm talking about. Believe me, there's nothing I can do here."

"Well, I want to speak to my kids. Put Angie on the phone."

"Too late. They're all in bed."

"Then call me tomorrow when they're awake so I can talk to them."

I write down his number. Days slip by but I don't get around to making the call.

II

I think of Magic a lot, dream of him at night. I try to write, wanting to thank him and let him know how I feel, but hesitate. Much as I miss him, I don't want to build false hopes for either of us. For all I know, he might still be spending time with David's group. Finally, I send a carefully edited letter:

Dear Magic,
I hope this finds you in good health and spirit. I think of you often and wonder how you are. Life is very different here; I won't even try to describe it. The children are keeping healthy. Jonathan goes outside with his grandpa most every day, but it's too cold for the girls. I haven't found a job because even if Jonathan and Angie go to school, I can't leave Sydney with Mother. Her nerves

361

couldn't handle it. I need a plan but haven't put one together yet.

Have you talked to David lately? You helped me to see him for what he really is, and I'm grateful. You gave me the support I needed to get the children away. I don't know how I would have managed without you. It's impossible to tell you how much I appreciate all you've done for us.

When I look at the moon at night, I think of you. Even though we are thousands of miles apart, we still see the same moon, in the same phase. Its very same light shines on both of us. I hope you're getting the good vibes I send on those moonbeams. I shall always remember you and be grateful.

Your friend, Jac

I also mail a note to the lawyer inquiring about the progress of the divorce petition.

Hating to be a burden on my parents, I face up to the prospect of applying for welfare. At least it will enable us to get food stamps and guarantee medical treatment if, God forbid, the children need it. When the caseworker comes to verify the facts of my application, she is not impressed by our home schooling. Though Mother confirms that we do lessons nearly every day, she still insists the children be enrolled in public school before any payments can be authorized. I'm livid. All my struggles, and still they'll grow up indoctrinated by the system's racism, hypocrisy, materialism, and "in God we trust" ideology! Besides, kids here can be vicious to anyone who's different, be it poor, fat or wearing the wrong style of shoes. Angela is skillful at adapting, but not Jonathan. The thought of his being further abused by peers fills me with rage. Children as sacrificial lambs, for the sake of a lousy welfare check! I hate it! Feel the same powerlessness as I did with David.

In the evening Sydney falls asleep with her head on my lap as I read aloud a chapter of *Robinson Crusoe,* one of my old books which Jonathan found. I tuck the kids into bed and kiss them goodnight. Then I go to my room and crawl under the covers, knees bent to prop up my journal. My fingers get stiff from the cold as I write, trying to sort out the morass of welfare, schools, work, money. Mother's nerves are near the breaking point. I can tell because her hands now tremble even worse than when we arrived. She's too old to have to deal with children for more than short visits. I must come up with a plan. A soft rap on the door interrupts my thoughts.

"Yes?" I call, expecting Jonathan. The door creaks open and there's Dad. Startled, I close my journal, straighten my legs as he slips in and shuts the door softly. "What's up?"

He hesitates, then lowers himself gingerly on the end of my bed and clears his throat. "You know," he begins in a husky voice, "your mother never got over your leaving Iowa. She hasn't really been a partner to me since you went away. It's been awful hard. Still is. I'm so glad you're back."

"Well, I sure appreciate your and Mother's hospitality. I hate to be a burden, but for the sake of the kids..."

He reaches out, lays his hand on my leg.

I fight the impulse to jerk away. He isn't hurting me, but I'm glad for the blanket.

"I was hoping that maybe we could... be close again." His heel taps, making his knee bounce. "I know... well, I suppose that after living in Jamaica for so long, it must be really hard for you now. I mean, without a man and all."

My stomach tightens as I tug at the blanket to draw it close around my throat.

"An old guy like me isn't going to be anything like a young Jamaican, but I might be able to do a little something for you. Especially with this." He reaches inside his half-unbuttoned blue plaid flannel shirt and pulls out a long round cylinder resembling a

363

flashlight. Then I notice the end is somewhat pointed and it doesn't have a lens.

"I even have batteries for it," he goes on quickly. "Let's try it?" He shoves it in my direction while his knee jiggles furiously. "I'll help you with it and then you can…"

"I don't need that kind of help!" I hiss, glaring as my heart races, unable to believe what I just heard.

"Oh. So now you're getting fussy. You sure needed my help a couple weeks ago. Look, I've been good to you. And you gotta understand, this is just between you and me." He touches my knee. "You and me, we're a lot alike," his voice quavers. "You have no idea how hard it's been without you all these years—"

"Get out of here!" I jerk my leg away and clutch the blanket, poised to scream if he touches me again.

"So that's the thanks I get!" he says huffily while rising.

"And take your weird toy along!" I turn my face, refuse to meet his gaze.

"Think about it. Can always change your mind." He backs out, closes the door.

I jump from the bed, shove a chair under the doorknob. Bile burns my throat. Just in time, I grab a plastic wastebasket and catch the eruption of putrid liquid. I sink to my knees, head bent until the retching stops. I crouch, trembling, don't know how long, but then the stench overcomes me. Carefully opening the door, I listen. Then hearing nothing, I carry the basket down to the bathroom, flush the contents, wash it out, gargle with mouthwash.

Back in my room, I sit on the bed, my head swirling with disgust, shame, confusion. Eventually I remember having similar feelings before. Long ago. *Dad walking around upstairs that sweltering July night when Mother was away, complaining about no breeze. From the doorway he says, "It feels a little better in here. Maybe I can finally get some sleep." The bed creaks as he sprawls beside me. I pretend to be asleep. Then I feel his body press against me. His fingers touch my nipples, they stiffen. His groin prods my behind. Strange sensations ripple through my body. I want to get away, but am afraid to move. Maybe he's asleep, dreaming he's in bed with Mother...*

I spring to my feet in an effort to escape the memory. Were there other times? My God! What if he goes after Angie? With him on the prowl, we can't stay here.

I inhale deeply, try to focus on breathing, but a lump wells in my throat. Why did he have to spoil everything? My eyes blur as tears brim over, and the vault of pain gives way to uncontrollable sobbing. I cry in mourning for the other father, the one I had loved so much, followed around as a child. Why did he leave me? Where did he go?!!! When the sobs subside, I'm drained; only the ache remains.

I pull blankets from my bed and carry them to the children's room where I arrange a makeshift pallet to block the door from inside. I lie down, cover up and close my eyes, but sleep doesn't come. All my senses are tuned to noises in the old house. For the first time, I'm grateful for the creaky wooden staircase.

I've always been able to fall asleep virtually anywhere—on park benches, lawns, beaches, in planes, busses and automobiles, even while floating in the sea—but that night sleep never comes.

III

Both letters from Jamaica arrive the same day. Saving the best for last, I open the lawyer's first. Briefly he explains the outcome of the trial: I've been totally exonerated! The date set for the divorce hearing is only a month away, and he needs to confirm David's address so a summons can be delivered. Does this mean I'll have to appear too? Next I tear open the envelope with Magic's return address.

My sweet Jac,
I pray to God dis letter find you in good health and with a smile on your face. And I hope dose precious children is

365

happy and enjoying some good living. The letter you sent brung tears to my eyes. So happy you remembers your friend Magic. When you left Jamaica, I never expected you to look back or think of me again. I stopped by David's yard a couple days back and found out he in big trouble. He was driving Sherry's car to Kingston when he hit a chile on da roadside and she dead. Police searched da car and found erb. So he in jail again. Might be more charges, maybe manslaughter. If Sherry and Holly is smart, dey soon leave Jamaica. Kiss dose kids for me and tell Jonathan and Angie and little Sydney dat Magic loves dem.

Yours always, Magic

Not a single word about his own sadness or missing us. Other people might ask for money or gifts in exchange for helping, but not him.

So David's in jail again. Will he be able to appear in court for the divorce hearing? And another problem—what if I don't? Will the divorce be abandoned? Gotta call the lawyer.

After putting the children to bed that evening I approach Mother and Dad in the living room. "Got some interesting letters from Jamaica today."

They look at me with guarded expectancy.

"The lawyer sent notice of the date for the divorce hearing. And our friend Magic wrote and said that David is in jail again."

"What!"

"He was in a car accident and a child was killed—"

"Oh, no!" Mother's hand flies to her mouth.

"—so he may be charged with manslaughter. The police are still investigating."

Mother looks dumfounded, unable to comprehend the tempo of life in Jamaica. Dad says, "So when's the divorce?"

"The hearing is scheduled for the middle of next month, but I'm wondering if it will be affected by David's being in jail. I need to call. May I use the phone tomorrow?"

They exchange glances; he nods.

The lawyer confirms that if I don't appear at the divorce hearing to verify my residency in Jamaica, there will be no jurisdiction and the whole effort will become null and void. I explain what I know of David's latest predicament, concluding, "So it looks as if you may have to deliver his summons in jail. What if he can't appear?"

"If he has been duly served and does not appear, he forfeits all rights. A *decree nisi* will be issued, and it will automatically become final in six months."

"But if he doesn't appear because he's in jail? Is that an extenuating circumstance that might cause the hearing to be postponed? I need to be sure, because I can't afford to keep traveling back and forth–"

"I'll check for you. Call me same time tomorrow."

I can't believe the good luck of having those round-trip tickets. All I have to do is get to Miami. When I tell my parents, Mother starts trembling. "Don't worry," I pat her hand. "You won't have to look after the children. They're coming with me."

"That just proves what I suspected all along! You're not fit..." She bursts into tears.

"Your mother's right," Dad takes over. "How can you even consider–"

"Wait," I hold up my hand. "Remember, David's in jail. He's no threat to us. And this way I can get a virtually free divorce. If I don't do it now, who knows how or when I'll ever be able to afford it. I don't want that standing in my way forever."

Mother laments that, despite all her prayers, something must have happened to my brain.

367

"It's the hypnotism," Dad says. "You're probably still under his spell."

"If you really think so, let's ask a professional. You pick the psychologist. I'll take any test he wants to give, and I'll tell him *everything* there is to know." I cast a pointed glance at Dad. "*Absolutely everything*. We'll let him decide."

"Oh, it's probably not necessary." Dad shakes his head and then looks at Mother. "What she says makes sense. Good idea to have it over and done with. Frankly, I don't like her taking the kids, but if she doesn't, who'll look after them?"

"I really appreciate all you've done. I know how much you love the children, and I promise, no harm will come to them."

All that remains is getting money for bus tickets to Miami. I wonder how much it's worth to my father to keep my mouth shut, but decide not to be greedy.

"How long do you intend to stay?" Dad asks.

"I'm not sure. My main concern is getting this divorce over with."

After Mother goes to bed, I approach Dad in the kitchen, where he's performing his nightly ritual of peeling and eating an apple. "I'm glad you agree that we shouldn't put more stress on Mother. Her nerves can't handle the kids much longer."

"Yeah, her blood pressure's high again. The medicine doesn't help much." He offers me a quarter of his apple, just as he did throughout my childhood years. "I'll miss you. More than you'll ever know."

I feel sorry for him but am too conflicted to respond.

"So if you just let me know when you'll be back," he continues, "I'll try to rent a place for you, and we can help out with furniture. Got extra stuff in the attic. And you might be able to work at the nursing home or maybe get on at the meatpacking plant—"

I interrupt. "If you're offering money to help us get set up, it would go a lot further in Jamaica. And I'd rather have the children grow up there. The problem has been David, but now with him in jail, I don't have to worry."

"You never know when he might get out."

"True. But the children have a right to live in the country where they were born. And I don't want to spend my life running and living in fear."

After a moment he says, "Well, corn prices are pretty good right now, and I was planning to sell a few loads to pay a note at the bank, so I could sell some extra. Probably let you have a couple thousand. Would that be enough?"

"It would sure help."

"Don't say anything to your mother. She wouldn't like this."

"Just between you and me, Dad."

Like always.

Jamaica, 1978

I

Speeding along the coastal road from Montego Bay to Ocho Rios, I keep looking out the window of the minivan, my eyes feasting on graceful palms, resplendent hibiscus and bougainvillea, blossoming mangos, the relentless surf crashing against the shoreline. Gone for only six weeks, but it feels like years. Nearing Ochy, I ask the driver to stop at Magic's. He's not home, so I leave a message with a neighbor and jump back in the van. We check into the Porpoise Point Hotel, and I take the children to the pool. They let loose—running, diving, splashing, giggling. The exercise is just what we need after all those hours on the bus and plane. Sunshine, clear air, azure sky, fruit punch, Calypso music wafting from the poolside bar—it's marvelous to be home!

I have pizza delivered to our room. We eat on the balcony overlooking the glistening Caribbean as darkness descends and stars appear on cue for their nightly performance. After the children are bathed and brushed, I tuck them in bed and dim the lights.

Hearing a tap on the door, I look through the peephole. It's Magic! I open the door, and we stand staring at one another as a smile spreads over his face. "Jac! It's really you! I couldn't believe my ears when dey told me you was back, but now I see wid me own eyes!" His arms open. We hug and he spins me around. Gesturing with his chin toward the room, he says, "Is Jonathan an' da girls dem inside?"

I nod. "They're sleeping. Exhausted after our long trip. You want to come in?"

"I is too excited to sit. Let's walk. Gots to get my head straight."

We wander along the beach, arm-in-arm, intermittently pausing to kiss as we luxuriate in the joy of being together and the freedom of knowing David is nowhere around. Fragments of what has transpired since the day of our hasty departure tumble out. David is still in jail awaiting trial. Holly and Sherry moved to Saint Ann's Bay. He knows nothing about their plans or David's prospects.

"Dat guy's dangerous, an' foolish. Always bringin' trouble down on hisself. I is just glad I wasn't wid him dat day. He wanted me ta go along ta Kingston, but I didn't get good vibes. So I sed I cyan't mek it. God was protectin' me. But David, he doan believe, so God cyan't protect 'im."

I shake my head, chilled at the thought that David might be beyond help even from the Almighty. Magic's comforting arm tightens around my shoulder.

We return to the room and slip into bed. I can hardly believe we're together, actually continuing the union that was interrupted by that knock on the door six weeks before. Lying in his arms, I feel happier, safer than I have in years.

Magic leaves early in the morning and returns with a basket of fruit just as the children are getting up. He hugs them and hands out bananas. Then he passes around tangerines and slices of succulent mangoes. Holding Sydney on his lap, he feeds her from his plate. Jonathan tells him about helping Grandpa with the horses.

"Dat's good, Jonathan. Ya ken learn lots from yuh granddaddy. Sounds like 'e knows 'bout lots a tings."

I excuse myself and call the lawyer to let him know I'm in Ochy and to confirm the date for the divorce hearing. "Oh! I, I'm surprised," he stammers at the sound of my voice. "I just mailed a letter to you yesterday. I thought you were still in Iowa."

"What was the letter about?"

"Well, David's petition to have the hearing postponed was granted. Now we're awaiting a new date."

"Why didn't you call and tell me?" I cry. "You knew I was planning to come down for the hearing and you know how slow the mail is—"

"I'm sorry. I had no idea you would be coming already."

What's the use of arguing? Guess we get what we pay for. "Never mind," I say. "The important thing is I'm here. What next?"

"I'll request that a hearing be scheduled for immediately after his trial which is set a month from now. That's all I can do."

"Okay. Go ahead. I don't have an address here yet, so I'll call you next week."

Magic is at my side, helping with everything as I undertake the task of resettling. He advises, "Don't spend all da money yuh daddy gave you on living high like David done. You gots ta use dat money ta set yuh self up so dat you an' yuh kids ken stay here."

I soon discover that an affordable place is not easy to come by. When I find a three-bedroom furnished house that is available for three months, Magic says, "Dat's da kind of place David always goes for. If ya rent dat, yuh daddy's money will soon finish. Den what? Ya gots to be smart. Mek dat money work fe ya."

Desperate to get out of the hotel, I settle for a dilapidated house in a tenement yard on the outskirts of Ochy. I scrounge a few pieces of furniture from yard sales, and we move into five small rooms with a primitive flush toilet and cold shower. At least Jonathan has his own room again, and we have a gas stove and small, albeit noisy, refrigerator. The worst part is the lack of a washing machine. I have to do laundry in backyard tubs using cold water and a scrub brush. With nearby neighbors watching our every move, I feel rather like a prisoner in my own house. The constant scrutiny soon gets on Magic's nerves, too. "Dis is just wat da Rasta man was singin' about," he says. "'Too much watchy, watchy,

watchy; too much soucey, soucey, soucey.' Dat's why I-Man cyan't live in no tenement yard. But at least ya got some conveniences here."

Magic advises against sending Jonathan and Angela to the public school that his children attend because they will be the only fair-complexioned students. Instead he recommends a private preparatory school a few miles from Ochy which I visit and find satisfactory. Dad will be pleased that his money is being used for their tuition and uniforms. Seven-year-old Jonathan is placed in the second grade, and Angela starts in first grade but is moved to kindergarten because she doesn't read well enough. Despite the strict discipline, Jonathan manages to stay out of trouble, but Angela gets sent to the headmistress's office and receives three whacks with a ruler on her palm. I'm outraged, but Magic says I shouldn't interfere, that such discipline is normal.

Too embarrassed about the trouble David caused at the White River Hotel to approach Mr. Shaw about working there again, I decide to look for a teaching job. Wearing my most respectable attire, I fill out applications at every school district within twenty-five miles despite knowing that a position is unlikely in the middle of the school year. Some days I go with Magic to help take care of his crops planted on captured land in the midst of a virtual jungle. Sydney comes along and plays in the shade while we cut weeds, plant seeds, and trim dead leaves from plantain and banana plants.

In the evenings Magic and I usually prepare dinner together—he contributes food from his field and sometimes goat meat. Then we help the children with homework and play games. After they go to bed, we sit in the dark on the verandah or in my room, talking and pampering one another. He makes medicine tea for me from bush he gathers. "You got battered blood from all dose beatings," he explains. "Dis tea can clean yuh blood. Otherwise, in years to come, yuh skin will get baggy, an' you is gonna get cancer or someting." He rubs coconut oil into my skin to renew its resilience and restore the flesh that David pummeled.

374

While I massage his feet he fills me with lore about medicinal properties of the plants that surround us and tells me of his life growing up in the hills of Saint Mary. His mother bore him at the age of fourteen after her parents kicked her out. His brother and two sisters all have different last names. Since quitting school at twelve he's been mostly on his own. He loves his mother fiercely and proudly describes the small home and shop that he and Dylan, ten years his junior, built for her. "Soon I gonna tek yuh der ta meet 'er," he says.

II

Magic hears through the bush telegraph that David was acquitted of the manslaughter charge. "Ya gots ta be careful," he warns. "He's probably in Saint Ann's Bay now wid Sherry an' Holly. So watch yuhself. Somebody's bound ta tell him you is back in Jamaica. An' da pickney—we cyan't tek no chances. One of us always gots to tek dem ta de bus stop an' be dere to meet dem comin' 'ome."

"You're right. The good thing is that now I can get on with the divorce. I'll call the lawyer tomorrow about setting another date. I don't think David will do anything foolish that can be held against him in the custody hearing. Do you?"

"Lissen, Baby, good sense don't be one a David's strong points. Yuh cyan't count on him not ta do someting just 'cause it doan mek sense. How long yuh knows him?"

I sigh. "Sometimes I forget how much he's changed. There was a time when he was rational, at least usually. But now after another stint in jail, he'll be madder than ever."

Magic and I take turns escorting the children. One bright morning after they board the bus, I head downtown to buy salt fish. The sun quickly evaporates puddles from an early shower as birds frolic and chirp in the hedges and trees. A car speeds around the curve behind me, goes past, and then screeches to a halt. Oh, no! A Blue Volvo! Panic surges through my veins.

David springs from the car and hurries toward me. "How long have you been here?"

My heart pounds as I stammer, "A, a few weeks."

"And where are my children?"

"They, they're with me."

"You brought them back and didn't even tell me?" His voice rises accusingly.

"They don't need your permission to live here. It's their country too."

"I want to see them NOW! Where are they?"

"I'm not telling you."

"Oh yes, you are!" He advances, arms poised for attack. "I'm their father! You can't keep them from me!"

I draw strength from the cars speeding past–He won't beat me out in public–and stand straighter, chin high. "Hit me, and you'll never see them again."

He stops, eyes me with unveiled hatred. "I've got a right to see my children!"

"If you want to give me your number, I'll call after I've spoken to my lawyer."

"What? A lawyer decides when I can see my own children! I can't believe it's come to this!" He sinks to his knees, beats the ground. Then he gazes up imploringly. "Look at me, Woman! Can't cha see how desperate I am? I'll do *anything* to see my children. I'll eat dirt for them!" He leans forward, scoops handfuls of earth into his mouth. Tears stream down his face as he cries, "Haven't I suffered enough? I beg you; let me see my children!" His voice gives way to sobs.

Cars slow as occupants peer at the man with the muddy face weeping on the roadside. Then they speed away.

"Please, Jac! Bring them to my place in Saint Ann's Bay and we can all live together." When I don't respond, he adds, "At least bring them for a visit. Just let them see their father. Please! Let's try to work things out."

I shake my head. "I'll never move back again."

"Don't forget this is your children's father you're talking to." He rises to his knees, his tone suddenly less contrite. "What gives you the right to keep them away from me?"

"It's up to the court. I'll talk to my lawyer."

Glaring, he reaches for a scrap of paper on the ground. "Well, take my number." He writes on the paper and hands it to me. "When are you going to call?"

"Soon." I turn and walk away.

"Hey! I bet you could use a ride." He rushes ahead of me and opens his passenger door. "Hop in. I'll take you wherever you're going."

"I prefer to walk," I say as I make my way around him.

No sooner does the Volvo disappear over a hill than I begin to shake violently. At the first shop I buy a box drink and collapse on a bench in the shade. Staring at my dusty feet in yellow flip flops, I slowly sip the cool lemonade. My head starts to clear as the shock wears off and suddenly I know: he is *never* going to hit me again! Finally I've stopped him, without Magic's help or anyone else's. I'm free at last!

When I tell the lawyer what happened, he says, "Well, for the moment, you have temporary sole custody of the children, so you're not required by law to let him see them. You'll have to decide what's in their best interest. Generally, except in the most extreme circumstances, the judge requires the non-custodial parent to have visitation rights. If you demonstrate you're capable of being reasonable about such arrangements, it might be easier in the long run—"

"Okay, thanks a lot," I say. Clearly he's not going to be of any help.

I tell Magic about the roadside encounter and we discuss possible responses. Not wanting to give the judge grounds for thinking me unreasonable, I finally call and tell David he can see them for an hour on Saturday.

"Oh, come on," he says. "Must you really set limits on how long I can see my own children?"

"Yes," I reply. "We'll see how this goes."

Magic is sitting on the front porch with the children when David arrives. He brushes past me and without even greeting the children, addresses Magic. "Now I see why you don't come to my yard anymore. Just what I suspected. You're fucking my wife. After all I've done for you! You fucking traitor!"

Magic rises and looks him in the eye, "Doan bodder wid any a dat rubbish. You come ta see yuh pickney dem, so doan waste no time on me. I is just sittin' here. Go on 'n try ta be da father dat you always say you is."

Rebuffed, David turns his attention to Jonathan, Angela, and Sydney who are easing their way down the steps. Awkwardly they follow him to the far corner of the yard where he hunches down and talks to them. After awhile he goes to his car, takes out a soccer ball and kicks it toward Jonathan. Everyone chases after it as Magic and I watch from the porch. Before an hour elapses, he puts the ball back in his car and leaves. Couldn't even leave it for them to play with, I think, fighting back tears.

The next week he plays with the children briefly and then complains about the arrangement being too restrictive. He wants them to spend a week with him. I refuse. He rants and raves, but I don't relent. "If you don't like it, tell the judge," I finally say.

David does not show up for the divorce hearing. I am given custody with instructions to make reasonable accommodation for the children to see their father. The *decree nisi* will become final in six months.

When Magic checks around Saint Ann's Bay, he discovers that Sherry and Holly have been deported. No one knows where David is. The landlord says he left some things in storage so is expected to return. Other people think he may have followed the women stateside. I wonder how he managed to get a visa. So much for laws.

III

"Thievin' white woman! You is a man stealer!" a woman shouts my way as I stand in the long line at the supermarket hoping to obtain rationed laundry soap and cooking oil. I look around, wondering whom she's talking to. No other fair-skinned people are in line.

"If ya doan leave my man alone, I's gonna rip ya apart wid me bare hands!" she screeches.

Then I recognize her: Magic's housekeeper. I saw her once before, but it was at a distance and we didn't speak. Without taking a backward step, I coolly look her in the eyes and declare, "I didn't steal anything from you. And it doesn't matter what you say, I don't live in fear."

I turn, make my purchase and march off without glancing her way though my heart is pounding and my palms sweating. It's not the woman who frightens me so much as her claim that Magic is her man.

Back home, I report the incident to Magic, trying to keep my voice steady as I observe his reaction closely like a lizard stalking a fly.

His failure to deny anything only stokes my anxiety. Eventually he admits to having sex with Daisy but insists it was never love. He provides her with room and board in exchange for housekeeping duties. "But since you an' me got together, I only kept her on ta tek care of da pickney dem. Nuttin' more goin' on. I know she dint like it, but I didn't want ta kick her out."

"That's not the way she sees it," I retort, fuming within.

"Well, she got it wrong. I is yuh man only. I's sorry, Baby. Never expected dat she would trouble ya. I'll go out in da mornin' an' set her straight, see dat she doan bodder ya again."

"That's not the issue. I can take care of myself. I just hope that *you* can."

"Doan fret! And doan be jealous. Jealousy is poison. It kill love. Our love has the sweetness dat come only from perfect trust. I will never do anyting ta spoil dat." He dips me back and deposits a tender, long and very persuasive kiss.

Next morning Magic leaves early to take his kids to school. When he returns about noon, his motorcycle is laden with bags and boxes. "Help me, Jac," he calls. "I gots terrible trouble!"

"What happened?"

"Dat wicked woman!" he seethes. "I could kill her!"

I help him carry the bags inside. He slumps onto a kitchen chair, removes his cap, rubs his head in agitation. As I fix tea, his story pours out. After delivering the children to school, he checked on his herds, did errands, and then returned to the yard. Daisy was nowhere around. Instead, he found a ransacked house: furniture chopped in pieces, dishes shattered, windows broken, everything upturned. Hastily he gathered as much clothing as he could and headed for my place. "I doan know what ta do," he says. "I cyan't let da kids go dere after school and see dat mess. Ken I bring dem here?"

"Of course." He rescued my children; I can do no less for his.

Richard, twelve, and Clayton, nine, move in with Jonathan. Seven-year-old Pearl shares with Angela and Sydney. Suddenly we are eight.

Magic is on edge, afraid his kids will make mistakes. They never sat at a dining table before and have no idea how to handle cutlery. But outside the youngsters have fun together skipping rope, playing hopscotch, cricket, soccer and handclapping games. They each have duties, but keeping track of who is supposed to do what and concocting punishment for various degrees of slackness gets to be harder than doing the work myself. Life becomes a constant struggle to forestall chaos as I toil to wash and iron school uniforms for five, in addition to cleaning, cooking and doing the shopping. To help pay for groceries Magic says he will slaughter a pig every week. Gone are the hours of relaxation and romance. I try to be upbeat but feel overwhelmed as my fragile control over home and family becomes increasingly tenuous.

Finally a letter comes asking me to interview for a teaching position in a high school some twenty miles away. When they offer me an appointment as head of the English department, I take it despite the hour-long bus ride in each direction. Magic finds a maid to stay with Sydney and do the laundry. That plus bus fare consumes half of my salary, but from every paycheck, I put money in the bank for Jonathan and Angela's tuition. What bothers me about the job is being away from Sydney so much. I get the impression that she spends most of her time creating her own imaginary world with two Barbie dolls she brought from Iowa. For hours she dresses them up, fixes their hair, and engages them in conversations that I can't understand. She changes her own clothes several times a day, too, each different mood or activity requiring a new costume.

One evening as I wearily climb the steps to our house, Magic greets me at the door with a kiss and a glass of limeade. "Guess wat happened today!" he exclaims.

"What?"

"Sydney called me 'Papa.'"

"Really!"

"I loves dat lickle girl, an' she know it. When I come by today ta eat me lunch, I gave her a couple pieces o' chicken and she sed 'Ta, Papa.'" She call *me* 'Papa!' Tink wat dat stupid David is missin'!"

381

"I know," I sigh. "I'm so glad you're here to give her some love. And me, too." I hug him.

IV

To avoid national bankruptcy, the government ransoms the population of Jamaica to the International Monetary Fund. Without warning, a four hundred percent increase in petroleum prices hits overnight, followed by commensurate hikes in all consumer items but not in salaries. Now the bus fare to and from work alone costs half my pay. The de facto devaluation creates even worse shortages of imported and manufactured goods. Store shelves stand empty. Occasionally word spreads that a shipment has arrived, and people line up for hours, just to get a bar of soap, bag of flour, or pound of salt fish. Our refrigerator doesn't keep food cold anymore so I tell the landlord, but he just laughs at my suggestion he replace it. "I got a better idea," he says. "Buy a block of ice."

When the cylinder of propane gas for our kitchen stove runs out, I order a new one, but none is available. Thereafter we have to cook on a wood fire in the back yard, a particularly daunting task on rainy days with Jonathan and Richard holding a sheet of corrugated iron over the flame. Some mornings we leave without even a cup of porridge. Magic then gives the kids change to buy a bun and box of juice at school.

Life becomes an unrelenting struggle to put sufficient food on the table to satisfy six growing children. Squabbles over who gets to lick the pot depress me. Protein is the problem. Nobody gets enough. Chicken for Sunday dinner becomes a big deal; the rest of the week we get by with bits of salt fish, small portions of dried beans, and chicken-foot stew. Wanting to make sure the children have enough, I deprive myself. My clothes get looser, my hair thinner. When a neighbor gives me a photo he snapped of us all standing in the yard, I can't believe how haggard I look. My once-shapely buttocks and breasts have disappeared, my face is gaunt, my straggly hair looks lifeless.

Magic peers at the picture and back to me. "Dis life ain't no good fe you, Jac," he says. "You works too hard and doan eat enough. Nobody does. And it only gonna get worse from what I hear. Even da government goin' broke. Might not be able ta pay teachers much longer."

"What! You actually heard that?" I cry.

He nods. "We gots to have a plan so's we can survive widout goin' to store and ridin' in van 'n ting."

I shrug, turn palms up. "But how…"

"Gots ta get our own place where we can grow food and not have ta pay no rent. Dat's what I was tryin' ta set up before, but dat ignorant Daisy go and mash everyting up. But dat was on captured land. We's got ta get our own place. Land is cheap now since so many people runnin' off ta foreign. I wants ta tek yuh up to St. Mary to meet me mudder and ta look at some places for sale."

On Saturday Magic's son Richard is left in charge of the children while Magic and I ride his motorcycle to St. Mary. His Mother is surprised to see him but shows no shock by my appearance. Probably news of me has reached her already. She has a small country shop with a bedroom in the back and a piece of land on which grow abundant bananas, yams, breadfruit, ackee and mango trees. A pot simmers over the fire pit, and she hastily peels some green bananas and throws them in to cook while she gets a can of Vienna sausages from her store and opens it. All the food is served on one plate and given to Magic. He crouches on the ground while I sit on a pile of banana leaves. His mother refuses any food, saying she already ate, but he shares his portion with me. I suspect she has only one plate and fork. The dialect they speak is so hard for me to understand that I give up trying. Eventually Magic tells me we are going to see some land she told him about in a nearby district called Grove.

Turns out that Magic worked there when he was a boy. Since the owner died five years before, the property has been so neglected that even the "for sale" sign is hidden behind weeds. Holding my hand, Magic leads me through the banana walk and up the hillside, pulling weeds and identifying coffee, chocolate, gungo pea and cassava plants as we climb. Then we descend to the other side of the hill where a stream of sparkling water forms a pool. While I rest Magic picks tangerines and soursop and peels them for us. "Dis is da perfect place," he says. "We can build a house right here on the riverbank and always have plenty of clean water and fresh food. Dis will be our paradise. How much money ya gots left from wat yuh daddy give ya?

"About nine hundred."

"Come." He gets up and pulls me to my feet. "Let's go look for Miz Brown. Her shop is a few miles down the road. She's bound to want more than dat, but maybe we ken mek a deal. Ya see how much food growin' on dis place? If we ken get her to let us have a couple of years to finish paying her, we'll be able to start harvesting bananas and selling dem right away. Money for her and money and food for us. Can't do any better dan dat!"

"Well, this could be a good place for a last stand," I say, "but I don't think we should rush into it. I couldn't get a teaching job here or do massage. Too far from the coast. And where would the children go to school? I hate to move them again!"

V

Magic comes home one evening with news of David: He followed Sherry and Holly to the States and beat one of them so badly that they had him arrested and deported. Now he's in a Jamaican jail awaiting trial for raping an American tourist.

"What!" I gasp. "Doesn't he ever learn! I guess that explains why he didn't show up at the divorce hearing and why he hasn't been asking for the kids."

"Dey could put him away a long time fe dis. Yuh know how da government is about publicity dat might damage tourism. Much worse dan if he raped a Jamaican woman."

"For sure. He probably picked up a rich stoned hippy on the beach. When she woke up the next morning and said something he didn't like, he hit her. I'm *so* glad not to be living in that den of madness anymore."

"David's finally gettin' 'is pay. Everyting 'e brought on 'isself."

"Right. Still, I can't help remembering what he was like before all this craziness–charming, hard working, brimming over with enthusiasm and new ideas. When I think of what could have been..." I shake my head in despair.

We agree not to tell the children about their father's latest debasement, hoping they won't hear from anyone else either.

When I stop at the General Delivery window of the post office to get my mail I'm handed a letter with a U.S.V.I. postmark. To my astonishment, it's from Marcus, David's old buddy. Eagerly tearing it open, I discover that he decided to write after his brother Desmond reported hearing I was separated from David and living in Ochy. Marcus and Liz have two children now and are living in the Virgin Islands. He got a good job there, sold the boat and bought a house. Knowing how difficult life has gotten in Jamaica, Marcus is concerned how we're making out. He suggests the Virgin Islands as a good alternative with tropical climate, ample work, and stable politics beneath the umbrella of the U.S. flag.

I read the letter to Magic. "Who is dis dude?" he says. "Tell me more about 'im."

I relate the history of David's friendship with Marcus, including how David alienated him by being rude to his wife. "I'm touched that he made this effort to reach me. It shows he still cares about us, despite all David's nonsense. I'll write and tell him what's going on. I don't know anything about the Virgin Islands, except something I read a few months ago about a massacre... I think a bunch of tourists were murdered there. Guess they have problems, too."

"Maybe we should consider goin' somewhere else," Magic says. "But if I goes ta America wid you, Baby, I wants ta go as yuh husband. Will you be my wife, Jac?"

"I, I can't marry you," I stammer. "My divorce from David isn't final."

"Den ya can check dis place out on yuh own an' let me know. If ya wants me ta come, den we ken get married. But if ya doan like it, ya ken bring da kids back ta Jamaica. I is yuh rock and refuge here."

"How are you going to manage without me?" An image of Daisy lurks in my mind.

"I doan know." He shakes his head, eyes downcast. "Won't be easy."

I write to Marcus, thank him for his concern, and confirm our dire circumstances. I also ask about racial problems on his island, and tell him about Magic.

A few days later Magic surprises me when he brings an American about my age to our yard. "I want ya ta meet Greg," he says. "From New Yawk."

We say "Hi" and shake hands.

"Me and Greg is old friends," Magic continues. "Him comes ta Jamaica every year fe do bidness. Last year he carried back some herb dat my brudder Dylan packaged. Everyting went real smooth, so now he wants Dylan ta fix up some more. He gets nuttin' but da best from us. We was just tinkin' maybe he could also get a batch next month when he's gonna be in Puerto Rico. Dis might work in wid you goin' ta da Virgin Islands."

"How so?"

"Didn't ya say dat ya cyan't fly direct from Jamaica ta dere? Ya gots ta go ta Miami or Puerto Rico first, right?"

"Yes."

"Okay. Maybe we're in bidness. Lissen, dis is da way it go..."
He and Greg lay out the framework for a drug exchange in Puerto
Rico that involves me carrying a disguised package of marijuana
through U.S. customs in San Juan. As they see it, the children
traveling with me will be great camouflage. Acknowledging he
knows little about airports, Magic expresses complete confidence in
my ability to handle the intricacies of customs and security.

"I suppose you're also planning to stuff herb inside Sydney's
dollies!" I quip, not wanting to take him seriously. "Well, if you'll
excuse me, I got to cook dinner." I rise. "Could you get Richard to
start the fire so I can put on the pot?"

In the kitchen while grating a coconut I can hear them
discussing plans, like guys planning how they'll spend the money if
they win the lottery.

After Greg leaves, Magic confronts me. "Why you act so
ignorant in front of dat American dude? Dis is serious bidness we
talkin'. He a good guy. I know 'cause Dylan's deal wid 'im last year
went real smooth. No funny stuff like dose American crooks go on
wid. Dey just looks ta rip off poor folks. If ya don't get serious
'bout dis, Jac, dere's no way we is gonna be able ta lift ourselves
outta dis hole we in. It hard ta find somebody ya ken trust. All
season I didn't talk wid no tourists girls 'cause I didn't want ta give
ya no reason ta fret. Now I finally gets a chance ta do bidness.
Don't mek me miss out on it."

First David wants me to take the rap for his drugs. Now Magic
wants me to smuggle them! "And who's going to raise my kids if I
get thrown in jail?"

"Lissen, Jac, yuh not gonna get busted. Believe me. I'd never
let ya do dis if der was any danger. I loves ya. But ya gotta get yuh
head straight. Ya gots tree beautiful kids ta look after, but dose few
dollars from teaching cyan't do it. We gots ta help ourselves. We
cyan't even afford ta get out o' dis country unless we does a deal.
How ya tink other people manage? Doan ya know dey all gots

someting goin' on da side? How many times ya gonna call Daddy fe help?"

The spectre of prison dances in my mind amidst a collage of children fighting to lick the pot, David adjusting his musical fountain, Dad leering at me, Jonathan and Richard struggling in the rain to hold a piece of tin over the sizzling fire, Angela bouncing a ball and scooping up jacks, Sydney vocalizing her dollies' intrigues, barbwire atop prison walls, the moon glowing from behind stormy clouds...

Magic relates other tales of past successes, insisting there's virtually no risk. "I beg you ta open yuh mind. Dylan can come over ta show ya how he packs it. An' I'll bring Greg by again, so ya ken get ta know him better. Just hear us out, Babe, and trust me."

"I have been trusting you all along, but this is ridiculous! I never thought I would say it, but it reminds me of what David wanted me to do... risk my reputation, my freedom, my children! All for ganja."

"Nonsense. Dis not da same ting. David never made no money from ganja. All he did was smoke it an' talk foolishness. I is offering ya part in a bidness dat will make good money fe yuh kids dem. I is showing you how ta live in da real Jamaica, not in da upper-class make-believe world dat fucked up David's mind. I tought ya was serious. I tought ya really loved me an' wanted ta make it here wid me. I tought you was da woman I did vision in my dream."

"What dream?"

"Back when I was just a lickle bwai. I was sittin' on da roadside up in da mountains near ta where me mudder lives. I was waitin' fe a bus, an' dis vision comes where I sees myself as a big man drivin' along da road in a big shiny car wid a white woman beside me, an' she be my wife. I never told nobody 'bout da vision before, 'cause nobody would believe me. All of dem would laugh at Magic's foolishness for dreamin' of ever marryin' a white woman. It seemed impossible den, but now I knows it ain't. You an' me ken have a good life together. It doan be about black and white; it be about lovin' each other and workin' together."

"I'm sorry to disappoint you, but not everybody white is rich. At least not where I come from. I might never be able to buy you a big car. If that's what you're expecting, maybe this is all a mistake. Do the deal with Greg if you want, but count me out." I hurry from the room, head spinning. What exactly does he love—me or my whiteness?

Early next morning Magic leaves. Says he has to help his mother and will be staying with her a few days. The honeymoon over, and we aren't even married.

VI

Marcus's next letter encourages us to come, offering a room in his house and help with finding a job and a place to live. I lay awake at night, considering his proposal and fretting over Magic's vision. I can't get over the thought that to him I represent the ticket to a good life. But admittedly, he means something other than pure love to me, too. He provided strength and security when I needed it. I couldn't have stood up to David without his support. Now with David no longer a threat, and poverty assaulting us every day, how long will love suffice? So many differences divide us. He has hardly attended school, has never been outside Jamaica, never held a job. I learn from books; he learns from observing people and nature. He lavishes my children with love; I find his hard to tolerate. We definitely prove the old saying: opposites attract. But can our relationship withstand the opposing forces?

Magic shows up Sunday afternoon in time for chicken dinner. Weary of being solely responsible for the kids all week, I greet him with a litany of problems. "Richard and Clayton leave here in the morning wearing uniforms, but I'm not sure if they go to school. Clayton says he lost his book bag, and Richard says he left his at school. They come in late, expecting I'll have food for them, but if they're not here for dinner, the other children finish everything–"

"Ya leaves my kids hungry?"

"If they're hungry, it's because they don't come in time for dinner. Maybe you should find out what they're doing on the street."

Pearl enters. "Papa!" she cries, running over for his kiss.

He hoists her onto his knee. "Give Papa a hug." She does, mumbling something I can't hear. He says, "We'll talk 'bout dat later. Tell everybody ta come fe dinner now."

"Yes, Papa." She slides from his knee and scoots outside.

He looks at me, eyes flaring. "Did ya send my precious girl pickney ta school dat way?"

"Of course not. She always wears a uniform."

"I'm talkin' 'bout her knotted hair. Ya cyan't send a black pickney out on da streets lookin' like dat!"

"I don't have time to plait her hair every day. Do you forget that I have to catch a bus at seven? Besides, this is the weekend. I was planning to comb her hair after dinner."

"Doan bodder. I'll pay Miz Fern ta do Pearl's hair."

"You're going to ask a neighbor to fix her hair? That'll send the message to everybody in the yard that I can't manage! You know what they're going to say?"

"Tcha. Everybody knows dat white folks doan understand black people hair. I cyan't have my chile go to school lookin' dat way, but doan fret youself. I know ya got lots ta do. Maybe she should just stay wid her mudder in Kingston. She'd get better care dere."

Is this a threat or a promise? Suddenly the children pour through the door, all greeting long lost Papa.

Later I read him the letter from Marcus, and we agree it's time to make plans for a move. I offer to help him with getting a passport and visa, but don't ask how his ganja deal is going. We make love hungrily as though desperate to reaffirm our bond.

Jamaica Farewell

I

Next Saturday Magic puts Pearl on a bus to Kingston presumably to spend the school vacation with her mother. Then he and I walk into Ochy for weekly supplies. We separate and stand in lines at different shops to get meager portions of rationed items—soap, rice, sardines, oil, salt fish, condensed milk, flour. It's late when we return, arms laden with provisions. Exhausted, I drag around the kitchen, unpacking and putting things away, at the same time lining up the makings for a cold supper. Magic, complaining of aching feet, goes to lie down in the bedroom.

Angela comes in and offers to help me. Carefully folding empty bags for reuse next week, she says, "Mommy, I got something to tell you."

"What is it, Honey?"

"Richard. When you and Papa was gone today, he did things he wasn't s'posed to."

"What kind of things?" I abandon the can of sardines I'm opening and crouch to her eye level.

"He chased me, and then he held me down and kissed me. And he kept grabbing me. It felt nasty..."

"Grabbing you where?"

She points to her crotch.

"My God! Papa has to hear this. Come!" I grasp her arm and pull her to the bedroom.

"Sit up and pay attention, Magic. Angie has something to tell us."

He hoists himself to a sitting position. "What's dat, Angie? What you want to tell Papa? Sit here." He pats the bed beside him.

She sits gingerly. Face ashen and lips pursed, her eyes dart to the open doorway.

I close the door. "Go ahead, Sweetheart," I prompt. "Tell Papa what you just said."

She begins, "It's Richard. When you and Mommy was gone today, he was chasing me around and grabbing and kissing me."

"Where? On de mout'?"

She nods.

"An' what else?"

"He... he pulled my panties down."

"Oh, no!" My hand flies to my mouth. I kneel and put my arms around her.

"Where is dat bwai?" Magic seethes, jumping to his feet. "I'm gonna murder him!"

"Wait!" I say. "You can murder him later. Right now, listen to what she's saying. Go on, Angie. Tell us exactly what happened."

Lips quivering, she gropes for words. "Well, he kept bothering me, and so I decided to stay in the bedroom with Sydney. We was playing with our dolls. Then he came in and told Sydney to go outside and get some candy from Jonathan and Clayton. When I tried to go, he stopped me."

"How?" I ask.

"He pushed me down on the bed like he was playing. Then he, he closed the door and said, 'Take down your panties.' I said 'No!' so he grabbed my shorts and pulled. I tried to get away and screamed, but he jumped on top of me and put his hand over my mouth so I couldn't..." Her voice breaks as tears brim over and slide down her cheeks.

"My poor baby." I wipe her face with a tissue while hugging her.

Magic and I exchange looks of shock, bewilderment, rage as she blows her nose and catches her breath. Sniffling, she resumes. "He sat on top of me and said I must shut my mouth or he'd break my finger. He was twisting it back and it really hurt. I was scared, Mommy, so I tried not to cry so loud." She's trembling all over.

"I'm goin' after dat bwai!" Magic storms out.

"Don't kill him, Papa! Please don't kill him!" Angela cries.

The commotion draws everyone as Magic drags his son into the living room and grills him. Richard insists he's done nothing more than tickle and kiss her.

"What business you got kissin' a lickle chile like she anyway?" Magic draws his belt from its loops.

"I dint mean no 'arm, Papa. I dint!" Richard cowers on the sofa.

"You is lyin'! I told ya not ta turn big man before time. But ya wouldn't lissen!" Magic raises the belt and brings it down across Richard's shoulders. He turns, shielding his head with his arm. Magic continues strapping him and shouting. "Doan turn big man on me! Dere is room fe only one man in dis yard. When ya decide ta tek woman, ya ken leave me yard!"

"Please, Papa! ... Don't Papa! ... No Papa!" The cracking belt punctuates Richard's screams as it slashes his body, again and again.

A horrible dread comes over me: Maybe this isn't the first time he's molested her. Most likely it's not! All these months when I've been out working, shopping... so many opportunities. Just what we left Iowa to avoid. I've totally let my daughter down.

"Enough!" I finally say, realizing Magic's righteous anger will make no difference.

He relents so quickly that I wonder whether the performance has been primarily for my benefit.

"Get to your room!" Magic commands, and the sniveling boy hobbles away. Then he assures Angela that Richard will not trouble her again.

How does he know? They maintain a facade of respect around home, but he knows nothing about their street lives, the company they keep, the habits they're developing. Angela was very brave to tell, but what might the recriminations be?

Magic finishes fixing the food while I help Angie shower and massage the tension from her delicate body, soothing her tensed muscles. Then I get Sydney and carry a plateful of sandwiches to the bedroom. When we've finished eating, I read them Dr. Seuss's Foot Book and a story about Babar, the Little Elephant. By the last page, they are both asleep. I cover them with a sheet and sit watching them for a long while, my mind in turmoil.

II

On Monday Magic rises before the sun and dresses quickly, in a rush to get to his fields. He has hired helpers for the day to cut and carry bananas to the boxing plant.

"How can you just go off and leave your sons for me to deal with?" I ask.

"What do ya mean?"

"It's school vacation. How am I supposed to keep my eyes on everybody?"

"Would it help if I tek Richard wid me?"

"I suppose," I shrug and listlessly get out of bed, discouraged that he still doesn't get it. I can only hope Clayton won't be too much of a problem.

Since I have a bunch of errands planned for the day, including going to the library, shoe store and bank, I decide to take the girls with me. While they get ready I assign Clayton and Jonathan the task of gathering a supply of wood for our cooking fire and stacking it in the lean-to. "After I get home, you can chop it up," I say, "but no messing around with machetes while I'm gone. Wait until after lunch, okay?"

"Okay," Jonathan says.

Clayton grunts something unintelligible and with a pouty face disappears out the back door. Jonathan casts a quizzical look my way. "Don't mind him," I say. "He's always grumping about something. You don't have to work together. Just gather all the dry branches and sticks in the field and throw them over the fence. If Clayton doesn't do his share, I'll tell Papa. It'll be his problem, not yours. Now tell me, what books do you want me to bring from the library?"

Without hesitation he answers, "*Black Beauty* and *Robin Hood.*"

"I don't know if they have them, but I'll try. And I'll bring some patties for lunch."

The sun is already hot by the time the girls and I leave the yard. They look adorable in matching flowered chintz sundresses I made. Angela's straight cinnamon-colored hair is swept into a ponytail. Blonde ringlets cover Sydney's head, reminding me of Silas Marner's golden-haired child. We walk to the town center, frequently stopping in shade along the way. First, we go to the library. Their only copy of *Black Beauty* is missing, but I'm able to borrow *Robin Hood* and two books for each of the girls. Then I cash my check at the bank and withdraw all the money I've been saving for school tuition except for one dollar to keep the account open. We spend over an hour trying on shoes and finally decide on a pair of black school shoes for Angie and jelly sandals for Sydney. She wants to wear them so I put her old rubber flip-flops into my bag. I buy a box of patties and hail a van.

Back at our yard, we are trudging up the steps to the house when a terrifying shriek splits the air. Panicked, I drop my bags, scoop up Sydney and run, Angela right behind. No one's inside, but the back door is open. I put Sydney down and dash out. Jonathan is lying on the ground, blood on his shirt; Clayton stands nearby— grasping a knife!

397

"Drop that this instant!" I command, striding toward him. Clayton's weapon tumbles to the ground as I advance. "Now back up! Go on. Turn around and walk to the gate. Go tend Papa's goats and don't come back until sundown!"

I watch him disappear down the hill; then I turn to Jonathan. Angela is crouched at his side. His eyes are open, but he's not moving. Blood mixed with dirt has stained his tattered clothes. I lift his head out of the dust. Cradling it on my lap, I say, "Where does it hurt? Tell me what happened." Tears roll from his eyes. "Angela, run inside and get some water. Put red syrup in it. Hurry!"

Sobbing, Jonathan moans, "I hate him, I hate him, I hate him…"

"He's gone now, can't hurt you anymore. I'm here to take care of you."

"Ooow, everything hurts … my leg, my head, my arm, my thumb…" he cries.

"Try to relax, Big Boy. You're going to be all right. Here, drink this." I take the cup from Angie and tilt it to his lips. After a few sips, he relaxes a bit.

"Me and Clayton was sword fighting…with sticks. Then he threw a rock at me. It hit my head and…"

"I gotta get you inside. You can tell me more while I clean you up."

I carry him to his bed; then I race outside, pick up the knife and hide it in my bedroom. Armed with soap, water, towels and rag, I carefully remove his torn clothes and clean the cuts and scrapes. He has a huge bump on his head, a deep gash on one arm probably needs stitches, and his swollen thumb may be broken.

"Angela," I say, "Get me a big piece of aloe. Then you and Sydney go ahead and eat your patties."

As I dress his wounds, Jonathan tells me more. While they were gathering fire wood Clayton started jabbing him with a stick. Jonathan jabbed back and soon they were in a full-fledged sword fight. Clayton's stick broke, so he turned and ran, Jonathan in pursuit. Clayton then hurled a rock that struck Jonathan's head. The next thing he remembers is being on the ground and seeing Clayton coming at him with the knife. That's when he screamed, hoping the neighbors would hear.

Something breaks inside me at the thought of what might have happened if I'd arrived even one minute later. Trembling, I place my hands in healing positions alongside Jonathan's head and try to calm myself. Then I close my eyes and take deep breaths, sending him strength and peace. When I open my eyes, our course is clear.

I check the clock. Magic won't be back for four or five hours. "Angie, Sydney," I call. "Come here. We need to talk."

They enter with solemn faces and sit on the floor. "Listen carefully," I say. "I need your help. We have to take Jonathan to Dr. Grey in Kingston. Put on your best clothes; then pack as much of your stuff as you can. I'll get out the suitcases and then go to the road to find a taxi van going to Kingston. I don't know how long it'll take, but just make sure you're ready when I come back. Can you do that?"

"Yes, Mommy!" Angela beams. "I know what you're thinking. We're going far away and not coming back, aren't we?"

"You're a bright little girl." I kiss her forehead. "Now let's get busy."

I bandage the gash on Jonathan's arm, fashion a makeshift splint for his inflamed thumb and fix a sling around his neck. He doesn't have any appetite, but I insist he eat a pattie, take an aspirin, and drink a full glass of water.

Then I pack our clothing and a few keepsakes still remaining after the years of ruin with David. At the foot of Magic's bookcase bed I hesitate. Inside it we have been hiding what money we can accumulate for our escape from the island. I reach inside, find two bags of ganja. I dig deeper and pull out a coffee tin. Inside it is our savings: the money from Magic's deal with Greg and the tuition money left from my father. Shall I take it? It's not all mine, but he'll have the furniture and house. I wrap half of the bills in a couple of towels and pack them with my clothes. Then I put the money I got from the bank into a drawstring bag and pin it inside my blouse.

At the roadside I hail each passing van. Finally one driver says he can take us to Kingston for twenty-five dollars, but will stop for other passengers along the way. "Fine!" I say. "Just pull into the driveway across the road. We have things to load."

Hastily I stuff drinks and fruit into a bag while debating about leaving a note for Magic. I hate to make him worry. Still, I don't want to leave clues in case he might try to follow. Undoubtedly Clayton will fill his head with lies, and peering neighbors will offer their own versions of events. I decide to get in touch later and shepherd the children out of the house and into the van.

III

"Please drop us at the All Seasons Hotel," I tell the driver as we approach Kingston. It's a small establishment near the flat where David and I lived years before. Even though they have no vacancies, I tell the driver to unload our things. After he leaves, I call the Sandman guesthouse and reserve a room, using an alias. Another taxi transfers us. The switch will make it harder for Magic to find us...if he tries. Undoubtedly, he'll be angry, but beyond that I have no idea how he will react. Try to follow us? Contact the police? Fall apart? Anything is possible. I consider sending a telegram to spare him the agony of not knowing, but if our escape is to be successful, I can't give in to worrying about his feelings.

In the morning I find a phone booth and place a call to Marcus. "Hey!" he says. "It's great to hear your voice! How're the kids?"

"They're fine, but a lot has changed since my last letter. We're no longer with Magic, and I'm making plans to leave Jamaica. So I'm thinking of taking you up on your offer. Is it still all right?"

"Absolutely. We have plenty of room. You can stay here as long as you need. What happened with Magic anyway?"

"It's a long story. I'll fill in the details when I see you."

"I'm glad you're getting the kids out of there. Thousands of people are leaving every week, going to the States and other places where they have a chance to live decent lives. Your kids are American citizens. It's their birthright."

"I know. If I keep them here, they'll look back in ten or twenty years and never forgive me for the opportunities they missed."

"You're absolutely right. You've got to take them away! Just call collect and let us know when to meet you."

"Shouldn't you clear this with Liz?"

"I already have. Everything's fine. She's right here, nodding as we speak."

"Okay. Tell her Hi from me. And thanks a lot, Marcus. See you soon."

"But just a word of caution. Be careful at the airport when you're leaving. You can't take more than $100 U.S. with you. Currency police are checking now."

"Okay, thanks for the tip."

When I call the airlines I discover we'll have to wait three days for the next available flight to Puerto Rico, whence we can get a shuttle to St. Croix. I make reservations and return to wake the children and tell them.

Angela throws her arms around me. "Hurray! Thank you, Mommy! I guessed it yesterday when you told us to pack. That's why I got Sydney and me all dressed up."

I hug her. "I knew you suspected, but I couldn't tell you because I didn't want you kids to say anything to the taxi driver or anybody else. So I let everyone think we were just going to the doctor."

Jonathan says, "I guessed, too, but pretended I didn't know anything."

"You guys are great! I'm so relieved you're okay with this. Just think, we'll get to see Uncle Marcus again! And his family—he's got two boys now. Mikey is your age, Sydney, and their baby Nat has just started to walk. Now, let's get ready for breakfast." I look at Jonathan. "How's your thumb?"

He shrugs. "Not too bad."

I touch it gently and notice the swelling has subsided. "Let me see you move it."

He does.

"Good. Now bend it here."

He tries but winces.

"Probably just a sprain. There's nothing a doctor can do except immobilize it and tell you to take aspirin. I can do that, too. So I don't think there's any need to see him. How do you feel about it?"

"Okay, I guess."

"My brave boy." I hug him. "But you have to be careful. I'm going to the desk clerk to get a new bandage for your cut and some tape to make a proper splint. Then we can eat." I rise. "Come on, everybody."

We spend the rest of the day at the guesthouse pool. The girls splash in the water, while Jonathan and I sit at an umbrella table playing checkers and dominoes. He gets tired of that so I show him how to play chess and am amazed how quickly he catches on. When the girls take a break to have a snack their lips are blue and their fingers shriveled. "Let the sun warm you before you go back in," I tell them.

After they eat, I re-inflate Sydney's armbands and the girls jump back in the pool. Jonathan has found a stack of comic books and is reading *Batman*.

Reclining on a chaise lounge, I adjust my straw hat and dark glasses, open a magazine and stare at the page, but can't focus on the words. I'm doing it again, running away. It's been ten years since I left Alex. Then I fled to Iowa with baby Jonathan, but before I knew it, I was escaping from my parents. And no sooner had I freed myself from David than I had to flee from my father again. Now, Magic's kids. Will it never end? Am I incapable of taking a stand, of protecting myself and children, of being faithful through good times and bad? Am I hopelessly flawed, destined to one ill-fated relationship after another? Somehow I've got to stop depending on others, even if it means living without love. Have my children; don't need anyone else. Still, this isn't just about need and freedom and love. It's about dignity, defending my mind and body and my children's. It's about not being victims. How does one know where to set limits? Where to draw the line between love and abuse? If only I could learn… and set a better example for them.

Angie peers down from the diving board, pinches her nose and leaps, landing with a huge splash. When her face breaks the surface, I clap and cheer, "Great! Did it hurt?"

"Nope!" She shakes her head, swims to the ladder and climbs back on the board.

I have to get over the old assumption that men are wiser than women and we can't get along without them. Now it's up to me, and only me, to make sure things go right. I, and no one else, am responsible for my actions, my welfare, and my children. Mother always talks about praying for us. I wonder if it has helped. There's something provident about how all this trouble surfaced before Magic and I moved to the States. What a mess if I'd sponsored his delinquents over there! I shiver.

Standing, I stretch my arms upward, then bend and touch the ground. Yes, I am running again. But this time feels different. It doesn't matter whether I love Magic. For the children's sakes, we have to leave. Maybe they can have a decent future in the States. The Vietnam fiasco is over, and from what I hear, Carter seems to be a decent president. At least he's keeping the country out of war. I'll try to think of this as going back rather than running. Going back to deal with my own issues, to find out who I really am.

IV

When shadows fall across the pool I tell the girls to get out, and they shower while I order pizza. After we eat, I turn on the television. The news features several stories about "currency criminals," people arrested for illegally exchanging or exporting U.S. money. It appears to be the crime which most concerns the police, or at least the media. The repeatedly devalued Jamaican currency is worthless abroad. Undercover agents called the Financial Intelligence Unit have become an elite and feared branch of the constabulary. Conviction of currency crime involves both prison sentence and large fine. The news reminds me of the restrictions on how much money people can carry abroad. Jamaicans can get only fifty U.S. dollars from the banks, but as an American, I am allowed to carry more. The problem is how to get it. I need to find a safe underground source to exchange any money remaining after I've paid the hotel bill and our airfares. It involves two risks: getting arrested and getting robbed. I'll have to be careful and smart if I want to find someone who can exchange the money but won't rob me. If the wrong people know I want to do a deal, they could break into our room or take the money and kill me. Such things happen all the time, especially in Kingston.

After turning off the T.V. and tucking the children in, I remember how Magic exchanged currency with a Chinese shopkeeper in Ochy, but here I have no idea who might be an informer. I'll have to rely on my own judgment in finding strangers to do business with. In the dark, I pray for guidance. Then I clear my mind and sit quietly.

Opening my eyes, I get up, carefully lock the room door, and walk to the lobby. I pick up a newspaper and sit in an armchair. Pretending to read, I keep my ears tuned to conversations around me. One taxi driver wearing a large knitted tam comes and goes several times. I wonder if he's a hotel employee. When he sits down nearby, I seize the opportunity.

Uncrossing my legs and folding the newspaper, I lean forward to make eye contact. "Looks like business is good tonight." I try to sound casual.

"Not so bad, but could be better."

"You work for the Sandman?"

"Not exactly. I 'as me own cab, but does lotsa drivin' for da guests here. Gots a special arrangement wid dese people. Ya unnerstan'?"

I nod. All of Jamaica now seems to operate through various special arrangements. Without private contacts and compacts, people wouldn't survive. "I'll be needing transportation to the airport," I say. "How much do you charge?"

He asks how many passengers, and we haggle over price until agreeing on a figure that seems reasonable. "How can I find you when I know the exact time we'll be going?"

"Just ask at da desk. Everybody here know how ta find Joshua."

"Nice meeting you, Joshua," I smile. "I'm Jacqueline."

"My pleasure." His head inclines slightly.

"I see you're wearing a tam," I say. "Dreadlocks under there?"

"Yes, I," he grins fleetingly and chants, "Hail Selassie I."

My comfort level increases, for I've always found the Rastas to be reasonable and kind. They're gentle, spiritual people, dedicated to pure living, with a strict code of conduct. Usually the only crimes they're arrested for involve the herb used in their religious ceremonies. They shun politics.

Joshua rises and salutes me as his passenger enters the lobby. I order a rum and ginger at the bar and carry it to my chair. I'm still sipping my drink and glancing through magazines when Joshua returns. He sits down and we resume our conversation. Eventually I take the plunge and say in a hushed voice, "You know anyone who might be willing to sell some U.S. dollars?"

Without hesitation, he replies, "How much?"

"Just a little. Three hundred or so."

"Dat'll cost ya more dan a tousand Jamaican."

"I wasn't expecting to pay so much."

"Dis business is risky. People doan tek chances fe nuttin'. I and I ken check around an' see what I comes up wid. When ya wants it?"

"The sooner the better."

"Where ya gonna be later?"

Unwilling to divulge the location of our room, I suggest, "I can meet you back here. How about two hours from now? Is that enough time?"

"I an' I ken be back in one."

"Okay, I'll see you here then."

I return to the room and check that the children are sleeping soundly. With paper and pencil I do some figuring of the amounts involved so I will be prepared to negotiate. Nearly an hour has elapsed when I return to the bar, order another drink and carry it to the lobby. Joshua shows up punctually and sits near me. The desk clerk has retired to an inner room, so we are alone.

He speaks softly. "You ken get tree hundred tonight, but it'll cost a tousand Jamaican."

Things are moving fast. I decide to get blunt. "How much U.S. can I get for eight hundred Jamaican?"

"Fe dat, you'll be lucky ta get two fifty. Even den I an' I is not mekin' a ting."

"How should we handle the exchange?"

"Sight. I ken be back in an hour. Which room yuh is in?"

His quiet directness feels reassuring. "Number six," I say.

"Watch fe I an' I ta drive up an' park. Den come ta da car. Ya ken tek da package inside ta count and den bring da Jamaican money out."

"Okay. I'll see you in an hour."

I return to the room and sit in darkness, everything as still as the reputed eye of a hurricane.

He arrives on the dot, alone, and passes me a wrinkled brown paper bag. I retreat inside to count the money and examine the crumpled bills closely for marks; then I stash it away. Hurriedly I dole out eight hundred Jamaican dollars. When I step outside, he is waiting near a croton hedge in the shadow cast by moonlight. I hand him the bag and whisper, "Thank you."

"I-rey," he says and disappears.

I slip inside and turn the lock. Moments later an engine starts. I blockade the door with furniture. If anyone tries to enter, it won't be easy. Tucking the money beneath my pillow, I whisper, "Thank you, Lord." It isn't much, but with this, plus the two hundred I can get at the airport exchange, we won't be arriving on Marcus's doorstep penniless.

Sitting by the pool the next day, I keep thinking about Magic, still feeling guilty for running off without explaining anything. This, coupled with my rage at his sons, leaves me in a quandary. Finally, I decide to write. He deserves to know the truth. I tell him what happened and why we had to leave, and end the letter:

> You saved us from destruction at David's hands, and you've helped me to get my head straight. I shall always be grateful. But I cannot stand by and allow my children to be abused. I hope you understand why I had to take them away before more damage was done. I took some cash, but the furniture and house are now yours. Much as I miss you, I can't turn back. Since I can never trust your children with mine, you and I can't be together. This isn't about you and me. But I pray for you every day, and wish you only the best.
>
> Jac

I struggle against the temptation to write "I'll always love you" at the end. Why torture him? Quickly I seal the envelope and tuck it away to mail from the airport. Next I compose a letter of resignation. I regret giving such short notice before the next school term begins, but I can do no better.

V

We get an early start, but when we arrive at the airport, queues of travelers snake out of the terminal. I line the children up with our boxes and suitcases, and we inch forward. Upon reaching the ticket agent, I learn of an equipment problem. A smaller plane is being used, so sixty passengers, including us, have been rescheduled to leave the next day. We will be put up overnight at the Kingston Intercontinental Hotel. I sigh but don't argue as he gives me taxi and hotel vouchers. Spying a mailbox, I drop in my letters.

We load our luggage into another taxi and head back to Kingston. On the way to the hotel, we pass an old three-story red brick structure which stretches on for what seems like several blocks. Pointing, Jonathan asks, "What's that long building?"

"Dat's da General Penitentiary," our driver volunteers.

"Really," I say. "I've heard of the place but never seen it." I lean over to get a better look as we halt at a traffic light. "Hey Guys," I whisper, "that might be where your dad is."

Wide-eyed, they press their noses to the window.

The driver elaborates, "Dat's a maximum security place. Nobody ever get out of dere before time. And if dey survive, dey comes baaad, real bad. Dat place tough. Tek a long look, and den mek sure ya never reach any such place! Dat's wat I always tells me own pickney dem."

Still digesting his words, we arrive at the Intercontinental and are shown to a suite on the fifteenth floor. After a quick look around, we head to the rooftop pool. I watch the children swim while enjoying the panoramic view of the city, harbor and surrounding hills. The airport is visible and what looks like the roof of the penitentiary. The unexpected sight of the place plagues my thoughts.

After lunch, I take the children inside to shower and dress. "Just think," I say, "here we are staying in the nicest hotel in Kingston, enjoying air-conditioning, pool, all we want to eat, and not paying a cent. Out on the streets heat is stifling the city, and a few blocks away your father is locked up behind bars. He probably doesn't have a bed to sleep on and hardly anything to eat. Could that be why we didn't get to fly out this morning—because we were leaving Jamaica without checking on him? You think we should go see him? Take him something?"

Jonathan and Angela shake their heads.

"Maybe we should pass on some of our good fortune," I continue, "by showing mercy to him even as God has to us."

To my surprise, Sydney nods and says "Yes." Ever since she started to talk, she has maintained that David is not her daddy. Still, she is the one who now votes for kindness. The others eventually agree about the mercy thing, but don't want to see him.

I call the penitentiary and confirm they indeed have an inmate named David Wellington. The spokesman tells me the visiting hours and rattles off a list of approved items for prisoners.

While the children rest, I call Marcus to explain our delay and new arrival time. Then we set off to buy things on the list. Being Sunday, most shops are closed. We walk for blocks as gusty winds propel us along nearly deserted streets in an area where graffiti adorns walls and sidewalks. Gradually we fill two bags: peanut butter, magazines, newspaper, condensed milk, jelly, a can of Milo, boxes of crackers, coconut candy, soap, paper and pens, toothbrush and toothpaste.

At the prison gates, I explain, "I'm David Wellington's ex-wife. We brought a few things for him and I'm wondering if his children can come in to visit."

"No, Ma'am," the officer says. He takes a deep breath, denoting great patience, and speaks slowly, as though it takes enormous effort. "Children are not allowed inside the prison, and inmates cannot see their children. They can wait there." He points to a wooden bench against the dungeon-like walls. Briefly he talks on the phone, then addresses me. "This way," he beckons and heads toward a door.

Carrying the bags, I follow, thinking I'm going somewhere to get the contents inspected. We pass through a long stone corridor and across a courtyard. I feel stares, endure whistles and shrieks from hundreds of men clutching bars and gaping like primates in zoo cages. Looking straight ahead, I glimpse David inside the building before me. His sudden appearance catches me off-guard, and I clumsily try to avoid his sight by stepping behind a column. I hand my bags to another guard who takes them inside and removes the contents, showing them to David. Then I hear his voice: "Whatsa matter, Jac? Why don't you come in? You ashamed?"

I step into view and gaze at him from a distance. His voice is the same strong, clear bass I have always known; his posture is erect and confident; but his countenance is a study of horror. Emaciated, his face looks inches longer than I remember; he has no cheeks, only bones; no front teeth, only streaks of redness on his gums. Shirt and pants, sizes too large, hang loosely on his skeleton frame.

Limply I stand in his presence. Tears roll down my cheeks.

Reading the horror in my eyes, he says, "I warned you this would happen, but you didn't believe me."

I hold my breath, stifling sobs.

"Thanks for bringing this stuff," he continues. "How are the children? ... My mother came to see me ... There's a war coming ... You still live in Ochy?"

I manage monosyllabic responses, trying not to stare at the gaping hole in his mouth where he used to have straight, white teeth.

He notices. "Yeah, I got into a fight and they knocked out my teeth. Broke some ribs, too. And see this." He flashes open his shirt, revealing a jagged scar across his abdomen. "They tried to kill me, but can't. Nobody can. We've got a movement going inside that's gonna change this island. Mark my word! When my group gets out of this shit hole, things will be different in Jamaica. We're making big changes! Everything will be I-rey." His eyes glisten.

"Great," I say. The gap between his vision and his reality has never been so wide.

"I was framed, you know. Didn't rape anybody. All this because of a lying, spoiled American bitch. Needed to learn some discipline, like all of you, but she didn't appreciate what I did for her."

His pathetic figure stirs such compassion in me that I can't say, Just think of it as punishment for the years of abuse you inflicted on your family. Instead I mumble, "I've got to go now. Can't make the children wait any longer."

"Tell them Daddy loves them and thanks for coming. By the way, just so you know: There is no God."

That may be true, I think, but karma cannot be denied. You're living proof.

I hesitate, struggling to accept the fact there is nothing I can do about his predicament or about mistakes we made. David is David. The failed prophet, the one who knows the path up the mountain but alienates everybody who would climb it with him. "Believe what you will," I finally say and turn. My job is to ensure the children's safety, and hopefully somewhere down the road, their happiness. Theological mysteries will have to wait.

I follow the guard toward the gate, tears blearing my sight. When I spot my little family, huddled on a bench, Sydney squeezed between Angela and Jonathan, my heart leaps with love and resolve as I fall to my knees and embrace them. "Daddy thanks you for the gifts," I say. "Now let's go. There's nothing more we can do here."

VI

We clasp hands and walk toward the hotel. For the first time I feel free, free of the commitment I once made not to take the children away from Jamaica. Times and circumstances are very different now. But a part of my soul will always remain here, always be connected to David, despite the pain and craziness. He is my children's father. They were conceived in love and with the highest hopes. But both of us failed in more ways than I can count. Hopefully I will one day glean the meaning of it all. For now the children are entirely my responsibility, my reason to live.

Next morning I reconfirm our reservations and secure the cash from Joshua inside my bra. At the airport I exchange the last of my Jamaican currency and put it in my wallet. Our plane lifts off on schedule and makes the customary dipping curve over Kingston Harbor. Peering down I whisper softly, "Farewell, beautiful island." Tears blur the view as a lump fills my throat. I won't be returning. So much of my past is here, but not my future. And justice has finally been done: David has received his pay for all the years of torture he inflicted on us without me having any hand in the retribution. For that I am thankful. Beneath the roar of engines I pledge, "The future belongs to my children. Jamaican or American, now they can choose."

AUTHOR'S END NOTE

Writing this book is in part an act of contrition for failing to protect my own children adequately from their abusive father. It is also an effort to raise consciousness about family violence and to urge anyone who suspects that a child is being physically, emotionally or sexually abused to do everything in their power to separate and protect that child from the perpetrator. Often children are too intimidated, confused or ashamed to tell anyone, but the child must come first, so responsible adults need to make an effort to find out.

Proceeds from this book will be donated to Rosie's Place in Boston, as well as other battered women's shelters, and to the Child Development Agency which administers foster care placement in Jamaica.

ABOUT THE AUTHOR

Born in the Midwest, Rebecca has lived on the east and west coasts, as well as in Canada, Australia, Jamaica and the Virgin Islands. She taught English in several countries and did graduate study at Boston University where she worked for many years while her three children completed school in Cambridge and all graduated from B.U. Then she taught writing at several colleges in the Boston area until moving to Cape Cod with her husband, William. They now reside in California where she continues writing in between tennis matches.

In her writing, Rebecca draws on personal experiences, talents and research. Her first book was a how-to guide for massaging children called *Loving Touch for Your Child* written in response to popular demand from clients when she was an acupressure therapist. While teaching writing she collaborated with another professor on *Teaching Without Textbooks* and contributed two bonus sections to *The Revision Process* by Robin Stratton. After taking classes in screenplay writing at UCLA, she wrote *The Bee Preacher* which is set largely in early 20th century Jamaica and California. She is now working on a sequel to *The Flaws That Bind*. Poems and excerpts of her prose can be read at rebeccaleo.com.

A Message from Rebecca Leo

Dear Reader,

I hope that reading this book has been a good experience for you. If it has, I expect that you can think of other people who would appreciate it. Here's how you could help them and me. Many books are competing for readers' attention, and the most important way for a book to get more notice is for readers to write favorable reviews and post them on the Amazon web site (www.amazon.com).

The more positive reviews or comments a book gets, the more it moves up the ranking for exposure when people search on Amazon. When a book has ten reviews it becomes eligible to be included in the "also bought" and "you might like" recommendations. These listings add to the number of books likely to be purchased and read.

But if you don't want to write a review, please take a few minutes to read and rate reviews posted by other readers. Just the act of "liking" a review moves it up the queue in which they appear.

Thanks in advance for your effort to boost the distribution and exposure of this book, and look for the sequel to *The Flaws That Bind* due out in 2015.

Made in the USA
Charleston, SC
14 December 2013